# Rating & Raising Indoor Plants

# CONSUMER GUIDE®

# Rating & Raising Indoor Plants

Library of Congress Cataloging in Publication Data

Beatty, Virginia
     Consumer guide rating and raising indoor plants.

     Includes index.
        1. House plants. I. Consumer guide. II. Title.
III. Title: Rating and raising indoor plants.
SB419.B28        635.9'65        75-14219
ISBN 0-671-22050-0 lib. bdg.
ISBN 0-671-22051-9 pbk.

Compiled by the Editors of CONSUMER GUIDE Magazine and published
in this edition by New American Library, New York, NY.

**About the Author**

Virginia L. Beatty is a consultant in environmental education and urban horticulture, a Fellow of the Royal Horticultural Society, a member of the American Horticultural Society, American Society of Horticultural Science, and a number of single plant societies. She has conducted many workshops and seminars in environmental education, urban horticulture, and horticultural therapy in this country and abroad. Mrs. Beatty has her own radio program, "Plant Talk," and regularly appears on a variety of television and radio programs.

**Lawrence Teeman**
**Editor and Publisher**

**Louis Weber**
**President**

**Staff:** Jerold L. Kellman, senior managing editor; Peter Du Pre, Arthur Hammerstrom, A. K. Turley, editors; Jill A. Boldt, Kay Conlon, Joan A. Lepp, Linda Muterspaugh, Helen C. Parker, assistant editors; Linda Bishop, Gloria Goldberg, Sylvia Greenberg, Sanna Hans, Marian Mirsky, editorial assistants; Frank E. Peiler, art director; Janet Clingerman, Janice Saltz, art assistants; Jack Lynn, production consultant.

Estelle Weber, assistant to president; Jack Lowell, business manager; Steven Feinberg, public information director.

Cover design: Frank E. Peiler        Illustrations by Gregory Thornton.

# CONTENTS

# INTRODUCTION

There is no such thing as a house plant — only plants indoors. Depending on how flexible they are and how accommodating you can be, plants can be grown in any room of the house or apartment. Some plants are easy, some are fun, and some can be exasperatingly difficult. Plants can improve the environment, hide cracks in walls, brighten up places and people, and can provide salads, sachets, and conversation starters. Plants can introduce you to a broader knowledge (if you want it) of geography, history, and people.

Some people feel that they can meet more interesting people in a plant shop or a flower shop than at a singles' bar. Plant people are special; they have a love of life and a feeling of adventure. They come in all ages, colors, sexes and national origins. Communication between them is never restricted by language.

### How to Use This Book

No picture or word can describe a plant or the growth of plants, but like a road map they can indicate a direction or a relationship. A map that shows everything — mountains, rivers, railroad tracks, and points of historic interest — is often harder to comprehend than one that sticks to one or two things. This book is a map that sticks to the basics: how to choose plants, how to care for them, how to grow them, and how to have fun with them.

There are no photographs of plants in this book, but there are drawings that will give a suggestion of their "bones" — their shape, and their size. If you really want to know what a plant looks like, there is no substitute for meeting the real thing. Look at plants in other people's homes, in shops, and in conservatories. Many times seeing an old plant in a conservatory will give you an idea how your plant is going to grow.

The plants covered in this book were selected by plant people who grow plants inside. The descriptions were written in terms of what the plant looks like and needs when growing inside a house or apartment under today's living conditions. But the best way to learn about plants is

# Time and Attention

**O**ne of the most important facts to remember when you are about to launch yourself as a plant lover is that plants will take up some of your time because they need a certain amount of attention. How much time and attention they need depends on the plant. So you should choose one whose demands match the time and attention you can spare.

If you don't have much time, invest in large, mature, well-established plants. Generally they need less care than young plants that are just getting started. Mature plants are slower growers, their larger pots dry out more slowly, and they are usually used to people. You should also look for a plant that is tolerant of varying light intensity and day length, is not too particular as to watering, air circulation, temperature, or humidity, and doesn't need different kinds of treatment at different seasons of the year. Any of the Five-Star plants listed in "Rating the Plants" would make good plants for busy people. A plant such as a large philodendron, rubber plant, or pony tail can always entertain itself although it is happy to visit when you have the time.

If you're short on time, concentrate on plants that are compatible with each other, plants that have the same requirements and preferences. If you're really well-organized, have them all in the same kind and size pot and potted in exactly the same potting mix. That way, the only thing you'll have to concern yourself with is making sure they all get exactly the same amount of light and water. If you have plants with all kinds of requirements, not all of them will need the same amount of water or need to be watered on the same day. And if they are planted in different sizes and kinds of pots, you will soon discover that plants in small pots dry out more quickly than plants in large pots, and that plants in clay pots dry out more quickly than plants in plastic pots. Plants in the sun dry out

---

more quickly than plants in a shady location. And some plants are just thirstier than others.

Generally, people in their middle years tend to underwater while younger and older people tend toward overwatering. If you are forgetful or an underwaterer get larger plants in larger pots (preferably plastic). If you are a compulsive overwaterer make larger holes in the bottoms of your pots, increase the amount of sand in your soil mix, and use clay pots.

Plants need more than just watering though. Sometimes they need turning, pruning, or some other special care. For example, tall plants and large bush plants should be turned regularly to keep the growth even all around. (If you like the oriental look — with branches shooting out into space — you may have to put some heavy rocks in the pot to keep the plant from falling over.) If you haven't time to prune and train plants, pick a plant that is a compact slow grower. And if you are short on patience, don't get involved with plants that have dormant periods or require special care just before, during, or after blooming.

**Vacation Care**

If you have concentrated on well-trained, self-reliant plants, you can usually leave home for a couple of weeks without having to do much except give them a good watering and pull them back from the bright light. However, if you're a worrier, or if you're not quite sure what they will do while you're gone, here are some alternatives:

• Board your plants at some accommodating greenhouse. Sometimes this is the best solution if you're going to be away on a long trip, but it can be expensive and sometimes a little chancy. If all your plants are kept together, they will be exposed to the same cultural conditions — light, watering, temperature, etc. — even if they have different needs. But if they are separated, some of them may be sold by "accident" to plant buffs who scour greenhouses and know a good thing when they see one. There is also the chance that they may come home with bad habits or bugs.

• Hire a plant sitter. This is a good solution, but it can sometimes be expensive and complicated. And if you aren't sure of your sitter's competence, it can occasionally be a traumatic experience, for example if you get back from a trip and find that your African violets have been given cold showers or that the little brown stubs on your wax plant (that the flowers come from) have been pruned off.

• Have a relative or friend come in and do the same for free. You often have the same problems as above, but in addition you have the frustration of not being able to demand, "Why did you give the African violet a cold shower?" or "Why did you take the little brown stubs off the wax plant?"

If none of the above solutions appeal to you, there are often things you can do to encourage plants to still be there when you come back home.

• Since the plants in small pots are the ones that will generally miss

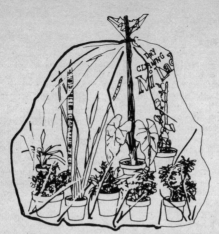

*Use a clear plastic cleaning bag to make a terrarium tent.*

you most, gather them all together and group them by their water preference. All the succulents can be watered well and pulled out of the direct light. The ones that like to be evenly moist can be watered well and then put on a tray of wet gravel inside of a large, clear plastic cleaner bag (a terrarium tent). If you put them where it's cooler and out of the bright light, they will do quite well for a couple of weeks.

• For larger plants, you can put water in your tub and set the plants on top of bricks whose ends are just out of the water. You can cover the plants and tub with a sheet of clear plastic, set your bathroom light on a timer to give 12 hours of light a day, and they will be in pretty good shape when you get back. Be sure that the faucet doesn't drip and that your overflow drain works.

• Your large floor plants will survive your absence beautifully if you water them well before you go and pull them back out of the strong light. In the wintertime you can lower your thermostat (if you're sure it's reliable) to 60°, and this, with the decrease in light, will cut down on the plants' need for water. However, unless *all* your plants like invigorating temperatures, you'd better not push the thermostat much below that. If you do everything you can do to slow down growing while you're gone, they may not even know you've been away.

• Self-watering pots and plant waterers can water your plants while you're away. But self-watering pots and plant waterers are great only for certain plants — generally those that like to be kept evenly moist. They're not the thing to get just before you go off on a long trip since some work and others don't. They're often good for African violets and begonias but too wet for geraniums and succulents. If you're interested, try them and see, but do it while you'll be around to throw out a lifeline in case it's needed.

## Summer Camp

Plants that have been growing inside during the winter can often get a real pick-me-up by moving outside during the summer. Where they go depends on the amount of light they can tolerate. The bright light of a sunny window is often the equivalent of open shade outside. Plants that have spent the winter indoors are usually palefaces that have to get used to the outdoor light gradually. They sunburn, too, if they get too much at one time. Plan on taking about two weeks to move them from the protected interior to where you intend to keep them.

Although a summer outdoors can be invigorating and give plants an active period of growth that they can draw on during the winter, there are a few things to consider. Plants outdoors need more frequent watering than plants indoors, and they grow more rapidly. If you take the plants out of their pots for the summer, you may not be able to coax them back into them in the fall. If you put the plant in its pot in the ground, you'll have to turn it or lift it several times during the summer so the roots don't grow out of the bottom, requiring major surgery when you want the plant to come back inside.

Large plants probably keep better if you keep them above the ground so they don't collect so many baddies with the goodies. When these plants first go outside, they are so tender and juicy that varmints will come from miles around just to sink their teeth into them. Also watch out for strong winds, heavy rains, and softball games.

If you are a procrastinator, don't take them out because the pain of bringing them all in just before a hard freeze is frightful. If you are well-organized, start hardening them to the realities of the harsh life inside as soon as the days start cooling at the end of summer. Pass them through one quarantine station after another to get rid of the many little friends they have picked up during the summer and finally bring them in — refreshed and ready to give pleasure for another season.

# Size and Growing Habits

What you do with your plants inside is really, within certain limitations, just a matter between you and the plants. You can put them anywhere that is mutually agreeable, and even from time to time move them about into new combinations and arrangements. In the chapters "Plants Are Living Organisms" and "Plant Descriptions," there are some suggestions for possible uses; but there is no aesthetic reason why a terrarium can't hang from the ceiling or a "floor plant" be placed on a table. There may be, of course, a few practical problems: a tiny plant on the floor might get stepped on unless it's protected by a larger plant or a barricade of some sort, and a very tall plant might get the bends if perched too high.

If you want to obtain a certain effect with your plant, start with one that is already close to the size you'll need because plants never grow as fast as you think they're going to when you purchase them. The following five lists are groupings for specific purposes of the best-rated plants (see "Rating the Plants"). As you and your plant get better acquainted, you may both decide on another group location.

## Tops in Growing from the Table to the Floor

When a plant gets too large for the windowsill or table then you might want to give it a small platform of its own or promote it to a place on the floor.

| Botanical Name | Common Name |
| --- | --- |
| BEAUCARNEA recurvata | Pony Tail |
| CYCAS revoluta | Sago Palm |
| DRACAENA deremensis | |
| DRACAENA draco | Dragon Tree |
| DRACAENA fragrans massangeana | |
| DRACAENA marginata | Red Margined Dracaena |
| DRACAENA sanderiana | |
| EUPHORBIA tirucalli | Milk Bush. Pencil Cactus |
| OPUNTIA species | |
| PANDANUS veitchii | Screw Pine |
| SANSEVIERIA trifasciata | Snake Plant, Mother-in-Law's Tongue. Bowstring Hemp |
| SYNADENIUM grantii rubra | |

## Tops in Floor Plants

Of course, there is no reason why a plant generally thought of as a floor plant can't be used very dramatically on a table. Many times an ordinary floor plant will look magnificent at new heights.

| Botanical Name | Common Name |
| --- | --- |
| ARAUCARIA bidwillii | Monkey-Puzzle Tree |
| ARAUCARIA heterophylla | Norfolk Island Pine |
| CARYOTA mitis | Fishtail Palm |
| CHAMAEDOREA elegans 'bella' (Neanthe bella) | Parlor Palm |
| CHAMAEDOREA erumpens | Bamboo Palm |
| FICUS elastica | India Rubber Plant. Rubber Plant |
| FICUS elastica variegata | Variegated Rubber Plant |
| FICUS lyrata | Fiddle-Leaf Fig |
| HOWEIA forsteriana | Kentia Palm, Paradise Palm. Thatch Leaf Palm |
| MONSTERA deliciosa | Hurricane Plant. Swiss Cheese Plant. Split Leaf Philodendron |
| PHILODENDRON selloum | Saddle Leaf Philodendron |
| RHAPIS excelsa | Lady Palm |

## Tops in Table Plants

Many plants are quite satisfied with their station in life and don't aspire to heights or depths. They look well and do well on a table or sill.

| Botanical Name | Common Name |
| --- | --- |
| AECHMEA fasciata (BILLBERGIA rhodocyanea) | Vase Plant, Urn Plant |
| AGAVE victoriae-reginae | Queen Victoria Century Plant |

| Botanical Name | Common Name |
| --- | --- |
| ASPIDISTRA elatior | Cast Iron Plant. Parlor Palm |
| CEPHALOCERUS senilis | Old Man Cactus |
| CRYPTANTHUS zonatus 'Zebrinus' | Zebra Plant |
| ECHEVERIA derenbergii | Painted Lady |
| ECHEVERIA elegans | Mexican Snowball |
| ECHINOCACTUS grusonii | Golden Barrel Cactus |
| EUPHORBIA splendens (EUPHORBIA milii splendens) | Crown of Thorns |
| FAUCARIA tigrina | Tiger Jaw |
| GASTERIA hybrids | |
| GASTERIA verrucosa | Oxtongue Gasteria |
| HAWORTHIA species | |
| PEPEROMIA caperata | Emerald Ripple |
| PEPEROMIA metallica | |
| PEPEROMIA obtusifolia | |
| PEPEROMIA sandersii 'Argyreia' | Watermelon Peperomia. Watermelon Begonia |
| SANSEVIERIA trifasciata 'Hahnii' | Birdnest Sansevieria |
| SEDUM rubrotinctum (SEDUM guatemalense) | Christmas Cheer |
| SPATHIPHYLLUM floribundum | Spathe Flower |
| STAPELIA grandiflora | Starfish Flower, Carrion Flower |

## Tops in Hanging Plants

Some plants that start out on a table or sill eventually overflow their space. hanging down all around. and then need either a pedestal. a hanging basket. or a hoop or trellis to curl up around.

| Botanical Name | Common Name |
| --- | --- |
| CEROPEGIA woodii | String of Hearts. Rosary Vine. Chinese Lantern Plant |
| CHLOROPHYTUM capense (CHLOROPHYTUM elatum) | Spider Plant |
| CHLOROPHYTUM comosum | Spider Plant. Airplane Plant. Ribbon Plant |
| HOYA carnosa | Wax Plant |
| HOYA carnosa variegata | Variegated Wax Plant |
| PLECTRANTHUS australis | Swedish Ivy |
| PLECTRANTHUS oertendahlii | Candle Plant, Swedish Ivy |
| RHIPSALIS species | Mistletoe Cactus |
| SEDUM morganianum | Burro Tail, Donkey's Tail |
| TRIPOGANDRA multiflora | Tahitian Bridal Veil |

## Tops in Table Plants That Grow Long and Viny

Finally, there are plants that grow long and viny. They can either be staked up like a tree or allowed to hang down like a vine. In time however there can be a lot of naked stem hanging around, and occasionally the best thing is to cut them back and start a number of new plants.

| Botanical Name | Common Name |
|---|---|
| AGLAONEMA commutatum | |
| AGLAONEMA modestum | Chinese Evergreen |
| DIEFFENBACHIA amoena | Dumb Cane, Tuftroot, Charming Dieffenbachia, Mother-in-Law Plant |
| DIEFFENBACHIA exotica | Exotic Dieffenbachia |
| DIEFFENBACHIA picta (DIEFFENBACHIA brasiliensis) | Variable Dieffenbachia |
| DIEFFENBACHIA sequina | |
| PHILODENDRON bipinnatifidum | |
| PHILODENDRON oxycardium (formerly PHILODENDRON cordatum) | Heart Leaf Philodendron |
| PHILODENDRON panduraeforme | |
| PHILODENDRON radiatum | |
| PHILODENDRON squamiferum | |
| PHILODENDRON wendlandii | |
| SCINDAPSUS aureus | Pothos, Devil's Ivy, Golden Pothos |
| SYNGONIUM podophyllum | |

Remember that an avocado will never look like an African violet nor a sansevieria look like a fern; plants don't change their basic appearance and structure any more than people do. The important thing is that you both should have fun growing together.

# Who Is Going to Adjust?

**P**ersonality clashes don't enter into the picture — it's just a fact that some plants do better than others indoors with people, pets, and even other plants. There are plants to fit most indoor situations and personal needs and some that don't.

Some plants are casual about their needs and others are very precise. Some plants do beautifully as long as you do things their way (50°F at night and plenty of fresh air), but mope at 65° and slip away at 75°. Others are so comfortable to have around that they get less than their share of time and attention because they are always in there pitching for you. As a result, these undemanding plants often look less than their best.

Have fun with your plants; not every plant is for every person. If you have a perfectly good plant that makes you feel inferior, give it away. If you have one that bores you or takes too much time (nothing you like to do takes too long) give it away, recycle it, or trade it in.

Choose a plant that likes the same things you do. You can add lights, increase or decrease temperature and humidity, or just let the plant fend for itself. The "Plant Descriptions" will give you some general hints about plants' preferences, but each plant is unique, and there is no substitute for asking yourself some hard questions before putting out the hard cash: Do I like big plants, small plants, green plants, flowering plants, soft plants, bony or thorny plants? Do I like to water, dust, putter, or prune? Do I like plants or do I want a decorative element?

### How to Foil Pets — and Pests

When a plant is taken inside, there are adjustments to be made on both sides. The plant has to adjust to you and your environment, and you and yours have to adjust to the plant. Sometimes more than introductions all around is necessary. If you have small children, suggest to them that it's bad manners and messy to nibble on the plants. If you're a permissive parent, then avoid certain plants that bite back, like dieffenbachia, or have tiny spines that break off inside the fingers.

If a cat lets you live with it, be sure you don't put a new plant on its place in the sun. Or if your dog likes to hail people out the window, it's wisest to leave that spot free. If your animals eat the plants, offer them some of their own. Cats like grass — the legal kind — and many times a box of their very own, planted with sod, will keep them happy. But don't try to grow your own grass from seed. The cat will use that nice box of dirt for other things before the grass ever gets a chance to sprout.

If cats are digging in the soft soil around your plants and adding too much nitrogen, you can try to meet the challenge by putting sharp white stones over the top of the soil, or fitting chicken wire or hardware cloth over the top of the pot and around the plant.

If the plants are getting pushed around, find another location for them. It's easier to move the plant than to re-train the household. If the plant keeps getting knocked (or pushed) over, try double potting — that is, putting the plant and its original pot inside another larger pot with rocks or gravel between the two. Sometimes this is all that is needed to stabilize the interaction among plants, pets, and people.

**Plants Can Be Dangerous**

However, there are times when the fault is not with the people, but is with the plant. Contrary to popular opinion, plants *can* be dangerous. A six-foot schefflera dropped on your foot can be very painful, and a lurking *AGAVE americana* can rip your leg open, not to mention ruining a brand new pair of slacks. Some plants are dangerous under certain conditions, and a few are trouble under nearly all conditions.

In addition to mechanical injury from prickles, spines, and thorns, some plants, under certain conditions, can have poisonous effects, such as causing allergic reactions, skin irritation due to direct or indirect contact with the plant, and internal poisoning from eating all or part of the plant.

Poisonous plants are scattered throughout natural plant families, but the following families have more than their share of troublesome species: Anacardiaceae (Cashew Family), Araceae (Arum Family), Compositae (Composite Family), Ericaceae (Heath Family), Euphorbiaceae (Spurge Family), Leguminosae (Pulse Family), Liliaceae (Lily Family), Ranunculaceae (Crowfoot Family), Solanaceae (Nightshade Family), and Umbelliferae (Parsley Family).

Allergic reactions to plants are a very personal kind of response. People with a tendency toward allergy should proceed carefully, one plant at a time, perhaps avoiding those with broad shiny leaves that need frequent dusting and ones with bad reputations. Relatively few plants produce poisoning by contact, but in those that do, this reaction can range from temporary irritation to painful inflammations with blisters that can persist for weeks. The severity of the reaction depends on the plant and the susceptibility of the individual. By far, the most common cause of plant dermatitis in the United States is poison ivy. This is generally not grown as a house plant, but it does have lovely berries and is sometimes collected by the unsuspecting for dried flower arrangements.

The following plants have bad reputations. It should be pointed out that the fact that a plant (or person) is occasionally irritating to someone is no reason to bring a general indictment against it. This is a selective list of baddies, but all can be documented for having produced contact dermatitis in at least one person.

| Botanical Name | Common Name |
|---|---|
| AGAVE americana | Century Plant |
| ALLIUM sativum | Garlic |
| ANACARDIUM occidentale | Cashew (fruit and raw husks) |
| ASPARAGUS officinalis | Asparagus |
| BORAGO officinalis | Borage |
| BUXUS sempervirens | Box |
| CACTUS grandiflorus | Night-Blooming Cereus |
| CAPSICUM fastigiatum | Red Pepper |
| COLCHICUM autumnale | Meadow Saffron |
| CONVALLARIA majalis | Lily of the Valley |
| EUPHORBIA species | Spurges |
| FICUS species | Figs |
| GELSEMIUM sempervirens | Yellow Jessamine |
| HEDERA helix | Ivy |
| HELIANTHUS annuus | Sunflower |
| HIBISCUS esculentus | Okra |
| JUNIPERUS virginiana | Red Cedar |
| LEPIDIUM sativum | Garden Cress |
| LILIUM species | Lilies |
| MANGIFERA indica | Mango |
| NARCISSUS species | Daffodils |
| NERIUM oleander | Oleander |
| PICEA canadensis | White Spruce |
| PRIMULA species | Primroses |
| RUTA graveolens | Rue |
| SEDUM acre | Mossy Stone Crop |
| SYRINGA vulgaris | Lilac |
| THUJA occidentalis | Arbor Vitae |
| TROPAEOLUM majus | Nasturtium |

If you can manage it, get someone else to crush the garlic and red peppers, and perhaps clean the asparagus. But whatever else you do, *never* let anyone roast hot dogs or marshmallows on oleander twigs!

While you're at it, you'd better make a list to remind yourself not to eat the following:

| Botanical Name | Common Name |
| --- | --- |
| ANACARDIUM occidentale | Cashew |
| CALADIUM species | Elephant Ear |
| COLCHICUM autumnale | Meadow Saffron |
| COLOCASIA antiquorum | Elephant Ear |
| CONVALLARIA majalis | Lily of the Valley |
| DATURA species | Angel's Trumpets |
| DIEFFENBACHIA species | Dumb Cane |
| EUPHORBIA species | Spurgus |
| HEDERA helix | Ivy |
| ILEX species | Holly |
| NARCISSUS species | Daffodils |
| NERIUM oleander | Oleander |
| NICOTIANA glauca | Tobacco |
| PHILODENDRON species | Elephant Ears |
| RHEUM rhaponticum | Rhubarb |
| RHODODENDRON species | Azaleas |
| RICINUS communis | Castor Oil Bean Plant |
| SOLANUM pseudo-capsicum | Jerusalem Cherry |
| TAXUS species | Yew |

Not all poisonous plants have been recognized, and certainly with all the new exotics constantly being introduced in plant stores, one should be cautious. If you tend to be allergic, stick to plants of good family.

In the literature on plant poisoning, fact and fiction are often woven together, and what appears in writing is often quite different from reality. Guilt by association can, at times, be carried a bit far. Some euphorbias are extremely poisonous and others are merely irritating. However, authors who write that children have been "fatally poisoned by poinsettias *(EUPHORBIA pulcherrima),* brought into so many homes at Christmas," will find it impossible to document this statement with more than a single case involving a two-year-old, reported in Hawaii in 1919.*

*Arnold, H. C. "Poisonous Plants of Hawaii," Honolulu, 1944.

## Simple Precautions

If you don't want to live dangerously:
1. Know your plants (family, genus, species), especially those with a shady background.
2. Keep toxic seeds, plants, and bulbs away from animals and young children (who are expensive and hard to replace).
3. Teach your children about the potential danger of certain plants.
4. Look up the number and address of your local poison control center right now and write it down: _____
   _____
   _____

If you need help in locating your local poison control center, the National Clearinghouse for Poison Control Centers is located at 7315 Wisconsin Avenue N.W., Washington, D.C. 20016. Telephone (301) 495-6327.

While you're at it, fill in the address and phone number of your local emergency ward, just in case your grip slips on that schefflera: _____
_____
_____

# Why Did it Die?

**N**ine times out of ten, plants indoors die of unnatural causes. For indoor plants, people are the greatest pests or hazards they have to endure. Trapped in a pot, there's no place they can go, and being confined, they are dependent on people for food and water. People just don't believe that a plant can take care of itself — with just a *little* help — and either kill them with kindness or neglect.

The number-one cause of indoor plant deaths is overwatering. However, a lot of water, by itself, doesn't do it. If the soil is porous and the pot drains well, in fact, plants can be watered every day. It's poor drainage, soggy soil, and sitting in saucers of stale water that weakens a plant to the point that it will succumb to any rotter that comes along.

Another major cause of plant death is underwatering — either because not enough water is given at a time or none is given for a long period of time. Some people believe in sprinkling rather than immersion, and although they do a watering every day, the few drops on top are not enough to keep the root ball moist. Other people are forgetful and don't remember to water until the plants are brown or flat on the floor.

Too much fertilizer is probably number three. Proud plant parents push food on their plants to make them grow big and strong. Nothing is too good for their plant, and they can afford to give it the very best. If a teaspoonful is good, then a cup should be better.

Not enough light and too much light, not enough humidity and too much humidity, and temperatures that are too high or too low are other causes for death. Some plants are never happy indoors, and there's nothing that can be done to keep them. And others die because they have no roots. This is the case when large plants which haven't rooted

Healthy Plant    Sick Plant

Dead Plant

yet are sold and moved from the humid environment of the greenhouse to the drier atmosphere of the average house or apartment.

Some plants die of old age. They come to the end of their allotted span and just stop. This often happens when the plant feels assured that its kind will continue. This is the reason for keeping the flowers cut off and keeping the plant from going to seed — the plant never feels confident that its species will endure and keeps on living, trying to plant a seed.

*Aphid*

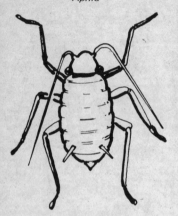

*Aphid*

## Pests

Insects and other pests have been around for a long time and are well ahead of people in the race for survival, an important thing to remember when you try to put anything over on them. Many insects are useful. They pollinate 85 percent of our fruits and vegetables, produce honey, and police picnic areas. Since non-selective chemicals have been used, we're finding out how much these "helpers" were doing in controlling the harmful pests. Although there are innumerable pests (Dr. Wescott lists over 200 different aphids in her *Gardener's Bug Book*) five kinds are responsible for almost all the problems of the indoor gardener. Since these generally are very small, here is a large portrait of each kind with some biographical information to help in recognizing and undermining them. But if you really want to get to know them,

*Aphids on underside of leaf.*

you'll need a 10- or 20-power hand lens.

**Aphids** (also known as plant lice) are small green, pink, lavender, grey, black, or red insects usually found clustered on the most succulent new growth or on the undersides of leaves. They are pear-shaped, soft-bellied insects with six legs and a hollow beak (rostrum) through which they suck up the plant juices. The plant sap, which is rich in sugar, is eventually secreted as honeydew, a by-product of digestion, out the other end. This honeydew is very attractive to ants and sooty mold. Aphids can also be recognized by a pair of cornicles (wax-secreting tubes) projecting from their back end.

Aphids have a very complicated family life. An egg hatches and produces a wingless female which can, without the benefit of fertilization, produce living young which are either wingless or winged females (which can fly off

*Mealybug*

*Mealybugs look like cottony fluffs.*

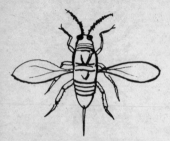

*Adult Winged Male Scale*

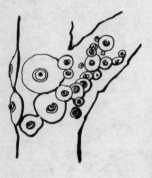

*Scale*

to another plant). Outdoors this goes on all summer, but toward autumn, males (either winged or wingless) appear and mate, producing an over-wintering egg. Under warm conditions in the South or indoors, the female living young are produced continuously at temperatures of 70°F, producing twice as many as are produced at 50°F. The tender young are easy to wash off, so the higher the temperatures, the more frequently the plant should be sprayed with water.

**Mealybugs** (really a soft scale) are small, cottony fluffs which appear along the veins of leaves or at the joining of the leaves to the plant. When the young hatch out, they are often six-legged insects with smooth bodies, and they crawl out all over the plant and suck sap, just like the Aphids. Soon after they start hatching, transformation takes place, and a waxy filament starts forming, covering their bodies and radiating out from them. At this time, they become sluggish.

The mature female is a wingless, stay-at-home who keeps on eating. But the mature male (an active two-winged insect) dies soon after it mates because it traded in its mouth parts for an extra pair of eyes. The 300 to 600 eggs laid by each female hatch out in about 10 days, and 99 percent of the babies are also females — each of whom will also eventually lay 300 to 600 eggs.

**Scale** (or barklouse) is a relative of the Mealybug, the main difference between them being that Scale have a hard, usually shiny shell rather than a furry or cottony one. If you have ferns, don't panic; the similar-looking brown spots found on the backs of fern leaves are spores and not Scale.

**Spider Mite, Red Spider** or **Two-Spotted Spider Mite** are small (the female is about 1/50th-of-an-inch long, and the male is much smaller); oval, yellow, green, red or brown spiders with a few hairs arranged in longitudinal rows down their backs. They are generally found on the underside of leaves where they suck and scrape. When the six-legged young hatch, they eat for a day or two before they rest and change their shape (which includes adding two legs). The males do this twice, and the females do this three times before becoming adult. Mating takes place a few minutes after the female reaches the adult form. The females lay eggs whether they mate or not. But if mating doesn't take place, the eggs hatch into males only.

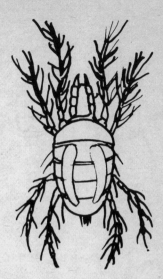

*Spider Mite*

*Spider Mites on the underside of leaves.*

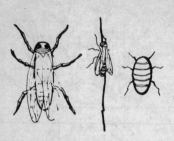

*White Fly*

*White Flies on leaf.*

The length of time to produce a generation decreases with increases in temperature. At 75°F, the adult stage is reached in 5 days; at 55°F, it takes 40 days.

**White Fly** is a minute sucking insect (the adult is about 1/16 of an inch long) that looks like a tiny moth. They are often present in great numbers on the undersides of the leaves and are rarely noticed unless the plants are disturbed. Eggs hatch in 4 to 12 days, and the crawlers move about avoiding the light. These are sapsuckers that in their first stage look like Aphids, in their second stage look like Scale, and in their third stage look like flies. They are easiest to get rid of in the first stage, and this can be done by washing the plant or giving the plant a bath.

Harmful insects don't limit their attacks just to direct action; they can also raise problems by carrying diseases along with them. Plant diseases are just as much a part of nature as sun, wind, rain, weeds, and insects.

There are more than 80,000 plant diseases, and some are always about ready to strike your plant. Diseases due to fungi, bacteria, and virus can often be confused with each other and with problems due to plant injuries, insecticides, over- and under-fertilization, and air pollution. Often diseases and other problems are combined, and even the experts have trouble fingering the main culprit. If you want to expand your horizons of ignorance read Dr. Shurtleff's book, *How to Control Plant Diseases in House and Garden*.

**Pest Control**

Pests and diseases are threats only to weak and feeble plants that don't have the strength to fight; a strong, healthy plant can live with them. So the first line of defense against pests and diseases is to keep the plant as healthy as possible by giving it the best possible growing conditions. The second line of defense is to keep the pests and diseases out from the start. Check plants and cut flowers before bringing them into the house or apartment. Isolate new plants for a couple of weeks before you introduce them to the rest. It can really bug you if you don't.

Washing plants off is one of the most effective ways of keeping down dust and insects. It's a good idea to give each shiny-leaved newcomer a warm bath under the sink spray. Then dry off the leaves with a soft towel. If you have reason to believe that a plant may be housing guests (but still want to add the plant to your collection), fill the sink with warm, soapy water, hold the plant upside down with your hand over the pot and swish the plant around. Always dry the leaves off carefully afterwards. Most of the time, a weekly bath with a soft brush or damp cloth will be all that is necessary to keep pests under control or to remove Aphids, Mealybugs, and Scale.

Plants with furry leaves, however, shouldn't be washed. Take a soft brush or one of the plant's own leaves, and wipe it gently over the plant.

Aphids or Mealybugs can often be wiped off with a cotton-wrapped toothpick. Scale can be scraped off with a fingernail, but this is not easy to do without injuring the plant. And plants with Red Spider, at a temperature of 72°F, respond well to three baths per week. It's always easier to keep these varmints out in the first place.

Here are other forms of control for handling pests:

**Natural control,** in the form of varying the temperature or the humidity, can be quite successful under the proper conditions. Biological control includes ladybugs and other "helpers" doing what comes naturally to them. This form of control also includes such sneaky methods as the sterilization of male insects to make the eggs infertile. A recent method, the pheromone phenomenon, draws on odors to achieve its effect. If the essential odor of a harmful female insect can be reproduced this odor can then be used to attract male insects into a trap — Perfume can snare bugs, too.

**Control by exclusion** is accomplished mainly by quarantine. The Plant Quarantine Act of 1912 authorizes the Secretary of Agriculture to impose quarantine restrictions on both plants and plant products in order to prevent the spread of insect infestations and plant diseases. The Act authorizes the Department's inspectors to search (without a warrant) persons coming into the United States and vehicles coming in from any country or traveling between states. They can be really wicked if you try to cross the border with bromeliads in your baggage. Because of the Act, plants which will travel must be carefully treated to prevent pests.

Sometimes plant material imported from abroad may be so well-treated against all possibilities of insects and diseases that it will arrive at its destination pure — but dead. But considering that crop loss due to insects runs about four billion dollars a year, and that fresh new bugs with-

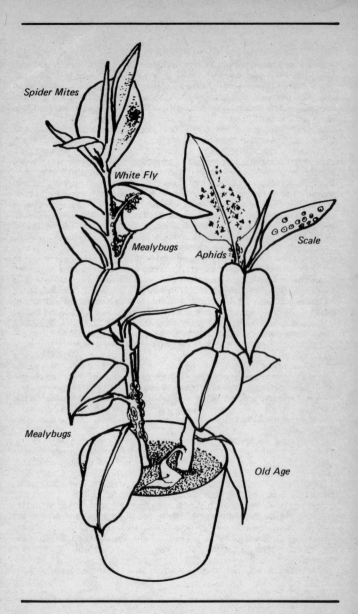

Spider Mites

White Fly

Mealybugs

Aphids

Scale

Mealybugs

Old Age

out any resident natural enemies can spread destruction quickly and widely, one can understand why the inspectors take their work very seriously.

**Cultural control** involves keeping the plant clean by removing dead stems and leaves and other breeding places and by arranging to make things as difficult as possible for the insects to maintain a comfortable life-style.

**Chemical control** includes all the various poisons that work in many different ways. Some people feel that, "If you have to spray, throw it away," on the basis that if a plant is so infested that it can't be controlled by bathing then it's too far gone to save. Pesticides, although they are often effective, may very well be hazardous, especially in an enclosed space. But if you're going to use a dip or spray, make sure it's a pest or disease and not a cultural weakness you're trying to cure.

If you decide you need a pesticide, the best buy is the smallest size package that will do the job. Don't stock pile! But if you do keep a pesticide on hand, make sure that it stays in the original container and out of reach of children and pets.

Before buying dips or sprays, read all the fine print on the label. Make sure it will control the pests or diseases that are plaguing your plant — and be sure the plant will be able to survive the treatment. Often you will find after your plant has died, that it said in fine print way down at the bottom: "Not to be used on ferns or African violets." If it's a no-no for African violets, it probably won't do other members of the African violet family (gesneriads) much good either.

Before opening the package or the bottle, READ THE LABEL AGAIN. Use the chemicals as directed. More isn't better. Sometimes it's a very small difference in the amount that will kill or cure a plant.

Be prepared in case you spill, inhale, or ingest the chemical. Don't eat, drink, or smoke until after you have washed up. Avoid, even if you can get them, chemicals that require a respirator, protective clothing, or come with directions to wash clothing after every use. Remember, you can often do more damage in a minute with a misused dip or spray than the pest or disease can do in a year!

# Requirements for Growing

# Light

Light is one of the three essentials for the growth of green plants. Green plants use sunlight or other light to convert water and carbon dioxide into sugar. This process is called *photosynthesis (photo —* light, *synthesis —* putting together), a light manufacturing process permitted even in the most exclusive residential areas. The manufactured sugar is the stored energy that not only feeds plants, but in turn, feeds most of the other living things on earth. In addition to its use as food, we also use the energy stored by plants — in the form of fossil fuels — to heat houses, run automobiles, and even to grow more plants.

This process of energy storage can be carried on by plants only in the presence of light and is dependent on the carbon dioxide concentration, the temperature, and the kind of plant. On the other hand, a plant can use this stored energy at any time of day or night. This means that if a plant doesn't get enough light, it will start using its stored energy, and when it has used it all, it will start consuming itself. Lack of light results in weak, stunted, or spindly growth; thin, pale stems; and smaller leaves. It also causes yellowing and dropping of leaves, especially at the bottom of the plant.

Light intensity usually is measured in foot candles. That is the amount of light in a totally dark room thrown by a candle on a square foot of surface one foot away, or the amount of light produced on a piece of paper by an evenly burning paper match four inches away. This may sound like a complicated way to measure light intensity, but plants can tell the difference between bright, filtered, and shady levels of light without playing with matches. An easier way for you to test light intensity is to place a sheet of white paper in the area where you want to put a plant. Hold your right or left hand (depending on whether you're right or left-

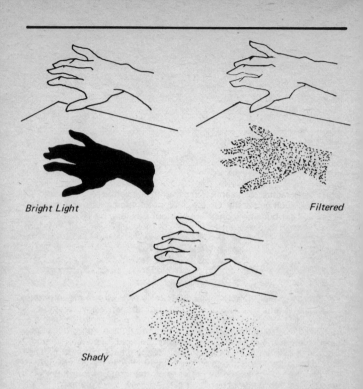

*Bright Light*

*Filtered*

*Shady*

handed) a foot above the sheet, and see if there's a sharp, well-defined shadow of your hand. If there is, you have bright light. If the result is a fuzzy, but recognizable shadow-hand, you have filtered light. If all you get is a blur on the paper, your light condition is shady, and you will have to select your plants with great care or else think about the addition of a periodic or permanent light.

Most plants that grow flowers or fruits like bright light. This is true of most succulents as well. Filtered light is good for gesneriads, figs, ferns, ivies, and palms. Philodendrons, aspidistra, dracaenas, peperomia, and spathiphyllum are happy in shade. Plants with thickened root stalks, bulbs, and tubers need light while they are actively growing, but during their period of dormancy, they need a lot less light. In fact, if they die back to a bulb or tuber, you can keep them in the dark.

Most house plants need light the year around. But the intensity of the light striking your plants will change depending on where you and your plants move to, as well as on the season of the year. As winter approaches, the sun casts its rays at a smaller and smaller angle. As the seasons change, then, you will want to move your plants either closer to or farther from the window.

If the plants have to stay in the same place (or if you like them where they are) you will have to adjust your watering and feeding habits. Reduce watering by increasing the length of time between waterings. Water the plant only enough to prevent wilting. Cut down on the amount of fertilizer to one-fourth of that recommended for actively growing plants. And you should also lower the temperature. Poorly lit plants do better at 60° than they do at 75°

Lower levels of light (for example, winter days or moving the plant further from the light source) makes some plants go into dormancy (a state of resting). However, these same low light levels on other plants, if the temperature is below 50°, will promote flower bud formation. Christmas cactus, chrysanthemums, and poinsettias are splendid examples of such perversity. On the other hand, bromeliads and many annuals will set buds only on 12- to 16-hour day lengths.

To a certain extent, plants will move, by themselves, to light. This turning toward the light is called *phototropism*. If you leave a plant in the same position on the windowsill, it will start leaning toward the light. You can frustrate this movement and keep the plant standing straight by turning the pot a quarter of the way round every once in a while.

## Light Solutions

If your plants seem to be suffering from not enough light, there are several things you can do to improve the situation:

**Wash the windows.** Dirty windows can cut down on light transmittal by as much as 40 percent. The human eye is able to adjust to the ever-decreasing light, but the plant can't. People can move about, but plants (within limits) have to stand and take it.

**Move the plants.** Let each plant have its day in the sun. Move them about so that each plant has a chance, and also turn the plant around so that each side has an equal chance to grow.

**Add artificial light** to extend the day length. A longer period of weak light will have the same effect as a shorter period of strong light. For dramatic effects, instead of hanging the light above the plant, place it under the plant, so that it's lit from the side or underneath. But when you change lighting conditions for a plant, do so by stages so that the plant will have a suitable opportunity to adjust.

**Increase light reflection** by using aluminum foil, or you can use sharp white rocks in the tops of pots. The rocks have the dual purpose of reflecting light and making it an uncomfortable place for the cat to sit.

Generally too much light is not a problem inside the house or apartment where it is very easy to move the plant back from the light or to close sheer curtains or blinds. It is a problem though, when one takes them outside on a pleasant day for a little refreshment. Too much light may cause the leaves to burn, look grey, scorched, or bleached, and can cause the plant to wilt, shrivel, and die. Plants and people both have to be toughened up to go out into the noonday sun. Remember, the light in open shade outdoors is about equal to what the plants consider bright light inside.

**Indoor Gardening**

Plants don't need sunlight to survive; they just need light. For additional information on gardening with artificial lights, get in touch with the closest chapter of the Indoor Light Gardening Society of America.

### Indoor Light Gardening Society of America, Inc.

Delaware Chapter ILGSA
Mrs. James H. Keen
2618 Cayuga Rd., Dartmouth Wood
Wilmington, Delaware 19810

Kingwood Chapter ILGSA
Mr. John C. Williams
Graham Road, Rte 8
Lexington, Ohio 44904

New England Chapter ILGSA
Mrs. Richard Pearson
Rocky Brook Rd.
Dover, Mass. 02030

Potomac Valley Chapter ILGSA
Mr. Richard McClellan
6211 Frontier Dr.
Springfield, Va. 22150

Twin City Chapter ILGSA
Mrs. Michael J. Rummenie
1508 West 87th Street
Bloomington, Minn. 55431

Cleveland Chapter ILGSA
Mrs. James Land
7261 Barton Cir.
Cleveland, Ohio 44129

Philadelphia Chapter ILGSA
Mrs. Ann L. Conroy
604 Hillcrest Avenue
Glenside, Pa. 19038

Indianhead Chapter ILGSA
Mrs. Wilbur Patterson
Route 5, Box 213
Chippewa Falls, Wisconsin 54729

Toronto Chapter ILGSA
Mr. Art C. Drysdale, Associate Dir.
The Civic Garden Centre
Don Mills, Ontario M3C 1P2, Canada

Hudson-Mohawk Chapter ILGSA
Mrs. Eldon Pullar
411 New Karner Road
Albany, New York 12205

Metropolitan Chapter ILGSA
c/o The Horticultural Society of N.Y.
128 West 58th Street, New York, 10019

Oregon Chapter ILGSA
Mrs. R. D. Morrison
5305 S.W. Hamilton Street
Portland, Oregon 97221

Long Island Chapter ILGSA
Mrs. Zelda Isaacs
560 West Beech Street
Long Beach, New York 11581

Rock Valley Chapter ILGSA
Mrs. Paul D. Pullin
1811 Oxford
Rockford, Illinois 61103

Cincinnati Chapter ILGSA
Mr. Robert Kranz
3127 Lookout Circle
Cincinnati, Ohio 45208

Greater Chicago Chapter ILGSA
Mrs. G. E. Christoph
90 Evergreen Ct.
Deerfield, Ill. 60015

If there is no chapter near you and you are interested in forming one write to:

Mrs. R. D. Morrison
5305 S. W. Hamilton St.
Portland, Oregon 97221

# Water, Watering, and Humidity

Every living thing must have water to live. People are about 65 percent water, pineapples and potatoes are about 80 percent water, and tomatoes and watermelon check in at about 95 percent water. Water keeps plants from collapsing (remember the celery that was out of the refrigerator for a couple of days), carries food to the different parts of the plant (water is a great solvent), and can almost be considered a nutrient itself since it is essential (with carbon dioxide and light) in the production of the sugars and starches that the plant uses for growing.

**How Much and How Often**

New plant parents often ask "How much water should I give it?" and "How often should I water?" These are easy questions to answer: "As much as it needs." and "Whenever it needs it." Deciding how much it needs and when it needs it, though, can be tough. Probably 90 percent of plant problems indoors are caused by over- or under-watering.

Some plants can take their soil dry or wet. Others like it one way and not the other. In the chapters "Plants are Living Organisms" and "Plant Descriptions," each plant's preference is indicated. A plant's preference often depends on it's native growing conditions. Plants originating in deserts and dry areas usually like to be drenched and then permitted to dry out. This can be done by soaking the plant (submerging it's pot in a bucket or sink filled with tepid water until all the air bubbles have come out), and then draining. Wait to rewater until the surface of the soil is dry to the touch. Most of the plants that are hairy, thorny, or waxy-leaved, and have coarse white roots prefer drenching and drying.

Many of the plants that originated in woods and jungles like to be kept evenly moist. These plants have delicate hairlike roots that rot if they get too wet, or dry up and die if they get too dry. There are a few plants that originally came from bogs and marshes that like to be kept wet, and although most of them do not like to sit in water all the time, there are a few that do.

Watering requires judgment, skill, knowledge, and experience. It is an art that everyone must learn for himself. There is no single answer. The amount and frequency depend on the temperature of the room, the kind of pot (clay or plastic), the size of the plant, the amount of light, and the kind of plant. Here are some of the conditions that affect frequency of watering:

**Water more often if:**
pot is clay
temperature is above 65°F
light is bright (sunny)
humidity is low
windy, good air circulation
plant is actively growing
pot is filled with roots
large plant in small pot
plant has large thin leaves
stems are thin or woody
old plant
plant is healthy

**Water less often if:**
pot is plastic or glazed clay
temperature is below 65°F
light is dim (cloudy)
humidity is high
air is still, poor circulation
plant is dormant or resting
plant has few roots in pot
small plant in large pot
plant has spines, thick leaves
stems are thick and succulent
new plant
plant is sick

**How and With What**

When you water, water slowly and thoroughly until the water runs out the bottom of the pot. If you have the plant in a saucer, empty the saucer after the plant finishes draining. The watering process forces the air out of the root ball. Most plants will suffer serious root damage and die if they are kept constantly wet. (In a spirit of fairness they will do the same if kept constantly dry.)

Use water that has been sitting for some time. It will be at room temperature (there are a few plants that don't like cold water — African violets for one) and a lot of the chlorine will have evaporated. If you have an ion exchange water softener get your plant water from the tap before it goes into the softener. Plants don't like softened water.

A long-spouted watering can is useful since it makes it possible for you to put the water where you want it on the soil, and avoids the soaking of the leaves and centers of plants that tend to rot if they get too wet. Adding water at the top of the pot reduces the amount of mineral salts that accumulate on the top of the soil and also reassures you that the drainage system is working. Drainage can be improved by enlarging the hole in the bottom of the pot, using more crocking (broken clay pots), or putting more sand or perlite in your potting mix.

*Place pots on a layer of pebbles to increase humidity.*

There are a number of self-watering pots and plant waterers available on the market. They work by means of wicks, gravity, or capillary action, and if used should be used with plants that prefer to be evenly moist or wet. Some of them do a beautiful job on water-loving plants, but they are not satisfactory for plants that like to get a bit dry between waterings. Test them carefully before turning a plant over to them.

**Overwatering and Underwatering**

Sometimes it's hard to tell just by looking if the plant is suffering from overwatering or underwatering. In both cases the leaves may darken and the plants may wilt.

If the problem is underwatering, the plant will look slightly dry and shrivelled, like a carrot left out on the counter overnight. The soil will be dry rather than wet. Sometimes you can water every day and have the plant wilt from underwatering. If you dribble a little water over the top of the plant and call it watering, the root ball dries out, the soil shrinks away from the side of the pot, and the next watering (even if a lot of water is used) finds the water running down between the soil and the pot. One way to get the plant back on the track is to sink the pot in tepid water until all the air bubbles come out.

On the other hand, if the problem is overwatering and the roots and stem are rotting, the plant will look plump and sloppy, like a stalk of celery left too long in the crisper. There isn't much you can do to revive a rotting plant; you can't bring a dead plant back to life. The only thing you can do is start from scratch and try again. Cut the still-healthy leaves or stems from your dying plant, and root them to start new plants (see the windowsill gardening directions in "Fun With Plants").

Plants that often suffer from underwatering are bog plants, ferns, figs, and ivies. Plants that suffer from overwatering are the succulents, begonias, impatiens, peperomias, and pileas. Coleus and impatiens may wilt from lack of water, but they will forgive you and come back completely when they get a drink. Other plants, such as camellias, azaleas, and pomegranates, suffer permanent injury if they get too dry. All in all it's probably safer to underwater than to overwater, and many plants can be slowly trained to use less water, especially if they are going to be existing in a room without too much light.

**Humidity**

People, plants, and antiques all would do better with higher humidity. People would sleep better, have less skin trouble, and feel more comfortable if the humidity in their homes were higher. Many houses and apartments are much drier than the Sahara, and that low humidity can affect even the desert plants. (In the desert, they at least have the benefit of dew condensing on them every night.)

Humidity for plants can be increased by several means. You can place them closer together so they fog each other's glasses. You can put a layer of pebbles or perlite in a metal or plastic pan, place the pots on the pebbles, and keep enough water in the pan so it is just below the bottoms of the pots. Or you can increase the amount of moisture in the air by using misters or foggers.

Misting is a chancy operation because it's also a great way to transmit diseases from one plant to another. If you're going to mist, do it so the moisture will evaporate by afternoon, be sure the water is warm, and don't let it collect in hairy foliage or in the center of plants susceptible to rot. For plants that need a high humidity, it's usually easier in a home to keep them in a terrarium or a plastic tent.

# Air and Temperature

Since air and temperature generally are not visible, few people give them much thought when they are growing plants. Even those who give the temperature some consideration don't give the air much thought. However, this "out of sight, out of mind" attitude leads to overlooking some interesting and important facts.

**Air**

Air contains one of the three essentials for plant growth — carbon dioxide. The primary work of photosynthesis is to use the energy from light to decompose water so that its hydrogen atom can get together with the carbon dioxide to form a carbohydrate molecule which the plant can use for food. However, the amount of carbon dioxide in the air (about three percent) is below the maximum at which plants are geared to work. This means that photosynthesis in plants is more often restricted by lack of carbon dioxide than by the supply of light energy. The owners of some greenhouses have extra carbon dioxide pumped in to accelerate plant growth.

The free movement of air is necessary to allow the exchange of these materials between the atmosphere and the cells inside the leaves. But indoor plants are often put in protected places, out of traffic patterns and drafts, so they are often deprived of this necessary movement of the air. This is not usually a problem for outside plants or for your plants when you put them outside for the summer.

In order to get movement of the air without chilling the plants, you can sometimes open a window slightly at the top. This lets some of the warm air out and creates an air current behind it from which the plants can benefit. Of course this won't work in a modern apartment building whose windows don't have top halves. or in an old house where the top half of the window is painted shut. Forced air heating also moves air but this can create problems by drying plants out because of low humidity (see the chapter on Water. Watering. and Humidity).

**Temperature**

When speaking of temperature. we have to be specific. We can't say that a plant likes "warm" temperatures or "cool" temperatures because temperature is a relative matter. For example, some texts state that cattleyas need to be kept warm, and that 55°F is the preferred night temperature. What person living in the United States in the second half of the twentieth century is going to consider a 55°F night temperature warm? In most cities that is a temperature at which you would take your landlord to court.

Plants have different preferences and tolerances when it comes to temperature. Some tropical plants can be hurt if the temperature falls below 50° But other tropical plants. like *PHILODENDRON oxycardium.* *PHILODENDRON selloum,* and *MONSTERA deliciosa* (the Swiss cheese plant), can tolerate temperatures down to freezing. Fortunately, the less hardy tropicals are usually protected because their owners tend to start screaming before the temperature approaches the danger point. Just be careful about turning the thermostat down too far when you're getting ready to go on vacation.

If your tropical plants are near a window and the weather turns subzero. the answer is simply to find a warmer place for them even though this means moving them away from the spot where they are displayed to their best advantage. Another trick is to cover the window with a thin sheet of plastic to slow up the loss of heat radiation from the room. Incandescent bulbs provide a still better answer since they give off infrared radiation which raises the temperature. (For this purpose fluorescent tubes are worthless.) A single incandescent bulb suspended three feet above the plants will heat a circle three feet in diameter. Since tropical plants are not sensitive to the photoperiod (length of daylight). these lights can be left on as long as they are needed.

On the other hand, there are many plants that prefer brisk evenings. Some of the most deceptive plants like it cold at night (40-45°F.). and they are quite intolerant if they are kept too warm. just like those people who insist on having the bedroom window open every night of the year. Here's a list of plants that prefer a cold. bracing rest at night.

| Botanical Name | Common Name |
|---|---|
| ACER palmatum | Japanese Maple |
| ACORUS gramineus variegatus | Calamus Root. Dwarf Japanese Sweet Flag. Sweet Flag |
| BEGONIA species | |
| CALCEOLARIA herbeohybrida | Pocketbook Plant |
| CAMELLIA japonica | |

| Botanical Name | Common Name |
|---|---|
| CHRYSANTHEMUM morifolium (CHRYSANTHEMUM hortorum) | Mum |
| CROCUS | |
| CYCLAMEN persicum | Florist's Cyclamen. Alpine Violet |
| FATSHEDERA lizei | Tree Ivy. Fat Lizzie |
| FATSIA japonica | Japanese Aralia |
| FUCHSIA hybrids | Lady s Eardrops |
| HEDERA helix | English Ivy |
| HYACINTHUS orientalis | Hyacinth |
| LANTANA camara | |
| NARCISSUS jonquilla | Jonquil |
| NARCISSUS pseudo-narcissus | Daffodil. Lent Lily |
| NARCISSUS tazetta | Paper White Narcissus |
| NOTOCACTUS leninghausii | Golden Ball Cactus. Ball Cactus |
| OXALIS rubra | Grandmother's Shamrock |
| PELARGONIUM hortorum | Geranium |
| PELARGONIUM peltatum . | Ivy Geranium |
| PODOCARPUS macrophylla | |
| REBUTIA species | |
| RHODODENDRON | Azalea |
| SAXIFRAGA sarmentosa | Strawberry Begonia. Mother of Thousands |
| SEMPERVIVUM tectorum | Hens and Chickens. Roof-Houseleek |
| SENECIO articulatus | Candle Plant |
| SENECIO cruentus | Cineraria of florists |
| STREPTOCARPUS hybridus | |
| TULIPA hybrids | Tulip |

The following plants also like chilly evenings. but they are a little easier to live with. Their favorite nighttime range is 50-55°F.

| Botanical Name | Common Name |
|---|---|
| ABUTILON hybridum | Chinese Bellflower. Flowering Maple. Parlor Maple |
| AEONIUM arboreum | Saucer Plant |
| AEONIUM canariense | Giant Velvet Rose |
| AGAPANTHUS africanus | Blue African Lily. Lily of the Nile. Love Flower |
| AGAVE americana | Century Plant |
| AGAVE victoriae-reginae | Queen Victoria Century Plant |
| ALOE arborescens | Candelabra Aloe |
| ALOE variegata | Partridge Breast. Tiger Aloe |
| ALOE vera | Medicine Plant. Lily of the Desert. Burn Plant |
| ARAUCARIA heterophylla (ARAUCARIA excelsa) | Norfolk Island Pine |

| Botanical Name | Common Name |
|---|---|
| ARDISIA crispa (ARDISIA crenulata) | Coral Berry |
| ASPARAGUS meyeri | Foxtail Asparagus Fern |
| ASPARAGUS plumosus | Asparagus Fern |
| ASPARAGUS sprengeri | Asparagus Fern |
| ASPIDISTRA elatior | Cast Iron Plant, Parlor Palm |
| BEAUCARNEA recurvata | Bottle Palm, Elephant Foot, Pony Tail |
| BELOPERONE guttata | Shrimp Plant |
| CALLISIA elegans (SETCREASEA striata) | Wandering Jew, Striped Inch Plant |
| CALLISIA fragrans | |
| CARISSA grandiflora | Natal Plum |
| CEROPEGIA debilis | |
| CEROPEGIA radicans | |
| CEROPEGIA woodii | String of Hearts, Rosary Vine, Chinese Lantern Plant |
| CHAMAEROPS humilis | European Fan Palm |
| CHLOROPHYTUM capense (CHLOROPHYTUM elatum) | Spider Plant |
| CHLOROPHYTUM comosum | Spider Plant, Airplane Plant, Ribbon Plant |
| CISSUS antarctica | Kangaroo Vine, Kangaroo Ivy, Treebine, African Tree Grape |
| CISSUS rhombifolia | Grape Ivy, Treebine |
| CITRUS limon 'Ponderosa' | American Wonderlemon |
| CITRUS mitis 'Calamondin | Calamondin Orange |
| CITRUS paradisi | Grapefruit |
| CITRUS sinensis | Sweet Orange |
| CLIVIA miniata | Kafir Lily |
| CRASSULA arborescens | Silver Dollar |
| CRASSULA argentea | Jade Plant, Chinese Rubber Plant |
| CRASSULA pyramidalis | |
| CYANOTIS somaliensis | Pussy Ears |
| CYCAS revoluta | Sago Palm |
| CYPERUS alternifolius | Umbrella Plant |
| CYPERUS papyrus | Egyptian Paper Plant |
| ECHEVERIA derenbergii | Painted Lady |
| ECHEVERIA elegans | Mexican Snowball |
| ECHINOCACTUS grusonii | Golden Barrel |
| ERIOBOTRYA japonica | Loquat, Japan Plum |
| FAUCARIA tigrina | Tiger Jaw |
| FICUS carica | Common Edible Fig |
| GASTERIA hybrids | |
| GASTERIA verrucosa | Oxtongue Gasteria |

| Botanical Name | Common Name |
|---|---|
| GREVILLEA robusta (GREVILLEA banksii) | Silk Oak |
| HAWORTHIA species | |
| HELXINE soleirolii | Baby Tears, Irish Moss |
| HIPPEASTRUM (AMARYLLIS) hybrids | Amaryllis |
| HOWEIA forsteriana | Kentia Palm. Paradise Palm. Thatch Leaf Palm |
| HOYA bella | Wax Plant |
| HOYA carnosa | Wax Plant |
| HOYA carnosa variegata | Variegated Wax Plant |
| IMPATIENS walleriana sultanii | Patient Lucy. Busy Lizzie |
| IRESINE herbstii | Bloodleaf |
| KALANCHOE blossfeldiana | Air Plant |
| KALANCHOE daigremontiana (BRYOPHYLLUM daigremontianum) | Air Plant |
| KALANCHOE pinnata | |
| KALANCHOE tomentosa | Panda Plant. Pussy Ears |
| LAMPRANTHUS emarginatus | Ice Plant |
| LITHOPS species | Living Stones |
| LIVISTONA chinensis | Chinese Fan Palm |
| MAMMILLARIA species | Pincushion Cactus |
| NERIUM oleander | Oleander |
| ORCHIDACEAE genus. species | |
| OXALIS hedysaroides rubra | Firefern |
| PASSIFLORA caerulea | Passion Flower |
| PASSIFLORA coccinea | Red Passion Flower |
| PERSEA americana | Avocado. Alligator Pear |
| PHOENIX dactylifera | Date Palm |
| PITTOSPORUM tobira | |
| PITTOSPORUM tobira 'Variegatum' | |
| PLECTRANTHUS australis | Swedish Ivy |
| PLECTRANTHUS oertendahlii | Candle Plant. Swedish Ivy |
| PLUMBAGO capensis | |
| PORTULACARIA afra | Elephant Bush |
| PRIMULA malacoides | Fairy Primrose. Baby Primrose |
| PUNICA granatum | Pomegranate |
| PUNICA granatum 'Nana' | Dwarf Pomegranate |
| RHAPIS excelsa | Lady Palm |
| RHOEO spathacea | Moses in the Cradle. Moses in the Bullrushes. Man in a Boat. Oyster Plant |
| SEDUM morganianum | Burro Tail. Donkey's Tail |
| SEDUM rubrotinctum (SEDUM guatemalense) | Christmas Cheer |
| SENECIO mikanioides | Parlor or German Ivy |

| Botanical Name | Common Name |
|---|---|
| SETCREASEA purpurea | Purple Heart |
| STAPELIA grandiflora | |
| STRELITZIA reginae | Bird of Paradise |
| THUNBERGIA alata | Black-Eyed Susan |
| TILLANDSIA usneoides | Spanish Moss |
| TOLMIEA menziesii | Piggy-back Plant. Mother of Thousands |
| TRADESCANTIA blossfeldiana | |
| TRADESCANTIA sillamontana | White Velvet |
| VRIESEA carinata | |
| VRIESEA splendens | Painted Feather |
| YUCCA elephantipes | Spineless Yucca |
| ZANTEDESCHIA elliottiana | Calla |
| ZEBRINA pendula | Wandering Jew |

The mind adjusts easily to the thought that spring bulbs like it cold. but cineraria *(SENECIO cruentus)*, the pocketbook plant *(CALCEOLARIA herbeohybrida)*, and cyclamen — which all look like hot house plants — object to too-warm temperatures in the same way: their leaves start looking limp and yellowish. If you aren't prepared for this jaundiced response. you may think that they need more water and act accordingly. This wetness enables these fussy plants to continue their decline and eventually. when they have convinced you that you've killed them. they can die happy. These plants have very high standards and never want to look less than their very best — no old bathrobes or hair-in-curlers for them.

One of the more tolerant of the cold lovers is the piggy-back plant, *(TOLMIEA menziesii)*. In its native habitat on the Pacific coast north of California and up into Alaska. this grows wild in the woods — which is a far cry from most house conditions.

Fifty years ago it was important that plants not get too cold. But with the change in heating systems. the major consideration these days is that the temperature doesn't stay too warm. If your favorite plants are those that like cooler temperatures at night. why not invest in a green sweater and turn down the thermostat?

# Fertilizing

**P**lants need fertilizer to replenish what was once available in the soil. Since house plants can't send their roots out very far in their search for nutrients, you have to provide them. However, as with people, too much food can make your plant sick. Using too much fertilizer can stunt some plants and kill others.

## How Much?

The general answer to "how much" is "a lot less than you think." More plants die of indigestion than starvation. Don't think that if one teaspoon per gallon is good, then ten will be better. If you do this, your plant may look so bad that you will think it needs *more* fertilizer. The end of this cycle is a dead plant.

There isn't a fixed level of light, water, temperature, and nutrients that a plant needs for good growth. It functions on many different levels, but the important idea is "balance" at each level. What this means is simply that when the light on your plants lessens during the winter, you should decrease the amount of food and water you give it — to keep the plant in balance at its new light level.

The amounts of fertilizer suggested on fertilizer labels were established for plants that are grown in greenhouses with almost ideal amounts of light and humidity. Plants growing in your house or apartment are probably getting too little light, too much heat, very low humidity, and possibly too much watering. This means that you have to adjust what the label recommends to fit your situation.

Too high a concentration of fertilizer can pull the water out of the roots and leaves of a plant. This damages the tissues of the plant and leads to a condition called "burning." Generally a rule of thumb is to start with one quarter of the amount recommended or reduce the frequency of fertilizing. You can always add more fertilizer later or fertilize more often if necessary, but you probably won't have to.

## When?

When do you fertilize? Let's start off by being negative. Don't fertilize a plant that's sick or droopy. Don't fertilize a plant that's just been brought home from the store or greenhouse. Don't fertilize a plant that's just been moved, transplanted, or repotted. Don't fertilize a plant that's resting.

The best single answer to when to fertilize is to let the plant tell you. If the plant is stunted or if the lower leaves are becoming pale yellow and the edges are turning rusty brown, then the plant is probably saying it needs nitrogen. If the plant is growing slowly and has spindly stems, then it probably needs phosphorus, although those symptoms may also indicate that the plant is suffering from a lack of light. If the edges of the leaves look scorched, the stems are weak, and the seeds or fruits become shrivelled, then the plant probably needs more potassium.

## With What?

There are all sorts of fertilizers on the market — powders, liquids, pills, and even "instant" little green beads. You will save yourself a lot of problems if you use a water-soluble fertilizer and apply it when you are watering. This puts the chemicals into a solution that the plants can use right away. Dry fertilizers aren't as good indoors because they don't dissolve completely, will build up, and may eventually kill the plant. Even when you use a soluble fertilizer you may notice a build up in the form of a white crust on the surface of the soil. This should be removed along with a little of the surface soil, and should be replaced with new soil.

Organic or natural fertilizers — forms of matter that were once alive (manure, bones, blood, leaves, fish, etc.) — also are not ideal for indoor plants. They are very complex materials. The nutrients in them generally are not easily available to plants; they have to be broken down into simpler forms by bacteria, which is a slow process. Also, since you are not sure of the state of the bacteria's health, it is hard to know how much of the nutrients is actually being made available at any given moment.

Chemical and synthetic fertilizers, on the other hand, are concentrated and quick-acting. They go into solution quickly, and their availability to the plants does not depend on bacteria. Organic fertilizers are good for slow release, and the chemical fertilizers are good for a quick pick-up. Some people like to combine both, but they must make sure that the total of the nutrients available is less than the amount that would cause burning.

If you want to do something special for your plants you can give them dried blood (high in nitrogen), grind up some eggshells (these contain calcium and some nitrogen), or you can take a banana skin (high in potassium), dice it very small, and work it into the soil.

Coffee, tea, and left-over martinis are not good for growing plants. Neither are cigar and cigarette ashes, which will stunt their growth.

## Why?

Green plants don't "eat" food, they make it. Plants use solar energy to transform water and carbon dioxide into food. In fact, 95 percent of the plant's food comes from carbon, oxygen, and hydrogen through photosynthesis.

Fertilizer packages "tell" about their quantities of nitrogen (N), phosphorus (P), and potassium (K). Many texts picture collapsed or unhappy plants suffering from shortages of one or more of these three major elements. And yet plants can exist without these three. But without carbon, hydrogen, and oxygen, the plants wouldn't just be droopy or dead — they wouldn't even exist.

Ten elements play major roles in plant growth. The three vital elements — carbon, hydrogen, and oxygen — generally come from air and water. Iron, calcium, sulphur, and magnesium are usually available from the soil. Trace elements — copper, cobalt, boron, zinc, and manganese — are elements needed by plants in very small quantities. This leaves nitrogen, phosphorus, and potassium to be supplied by fertilizers. In order to be absorbed by a plant, all these nutrients, except carbon dioxide, have to be in a water solution.

**Nitrogen** is important for leaf growth and photosynthesis and is an essential element in chlorophyll. Nitrogen is the "growth element." It is often in the soil, but not in a form that is available to the plant. When the plant gets too much nitrogen the result will be soft, lush, sometimes flabby growth, and in flowering plants there will be lots of leaves and no flowers.

**Phosphorus** is needed for cell division, stiff stems, and flower and seed formation. It is a tricky chemical since it has a habit of quickly locking itself into the soil in an insoluble form so the plant can't get it.

**Potassium** is useful in photosynthesis as a catalyst. This means that it has to be there to get the other elements to work. It is also essential in the formation of starch, for the movement of sugars within the plant, and for seed formation.

The numbers on a container of fertilizer, for example, 0-12-1 (bone meal) or 5-1-1 (fish emulsion) give you the percentages of nitrogen, phosphorus, and potassium by weight. In the past, fertilizers often had low percentages of nutrient elements in order to keep the price per pound low. Today, since freight and packaging costs have skyrocketed, the trend is toward higher proportions, or "high analysis" mixtures. A 20-20-20 mixture has twice the concentration of a 10-10-10, and so you would use only half as much.

You should read the labels on the packages carefully to be sure you're getting what the plant needs. After you have read the labels of several brands of fertilizer, you may ask yourself, "Why is there the same analysis on each package. but the one with the pretty pictures on the package costs twice as much as the others?'' There is a real chance to save here — unless. of course. you collect pretty packages.

Differences in the proportions of a fertilizer mixture, however, are not just the result of economics. There are legitimate reasons based on the growth pattern and type of plant. Different plants need different proportions for proper growth. and each type of plant will have different needs at different stages of growth. Just remember: fertilizing should be scaled to the slower tempo of indoor growth. And no matter how much you want to do for your plants. less is better than more.

# Catalog of Plants

# Old Faithfuls

**P**lants vary in the care they need, but there is no such thing as a care-free plant. Even plastic plants have to be dusted sometimes and kept out of the bleaching light of the sun. The amount of care a plant needs depends a great deal on environmental factors such as temperature, light, humidity, and an individual's inclination to water. In an apartment or a house, success with a plant can depend as much on the choice of the plant (one that tolerates living with people) as on the skill of the individual. Some plants take much less care than others, and, generally speaking, well-established mature plants are much easier than small immature plants. There are some plants that are tolerant, self-sufficient, and great teachers because they sustain the owner's ego and build confidence while forgiving errors of commission or omission.

The Chinese evergreen (*AGLAONEMA modestum*) will go on and on and on. They will exist under poor light, but if they can be given a little light refreshment every week, they will look even better. However, this will make the dust on their leaves show up, so you might combine a warm bath with their weekend under the light. Your plants might even reward you by growing a little faster. When the canes get too long, chop off the tops and stick them back into the pot. Some people have been doing successive cuttings for over 50 years and have become quite talented at raising canes.

The monkey-puzzle tree (*ARAUCARIA bidwillii*) and the Norfolk Island pine (*ARAUCARIA heterophylla*) are real charmers. Bill is prickly, and Phil tends to baldness by losing his lower branches. Bill and Phil control themselves very nicely in most home situations although outside they can shoot up to 200 feet. Some people use them as living Christmas trees and put sterling silver snowflakes on them. These give off lively sparkles without overheating the tree. Since they grow slowly, it's possible to keep up the payments on the silver without having to add too many flakes in any one year.

The cast iron plant *(ASPIDISTRA elatior)* is the queen of house plants. It will survive for a generation without feeding or re-potting. Although it responds well to regular dusting and warm showers, it will tolerate shade, gas fumes, and dry air and soil — almost everything except bright light. In other words, this plant does exceptionally well in house conditions.

The pony tail *(BEAUCARNEA recurvata)* keeps its silhouette whether it's one or thirty feet high. It's a cheerful plant that will go without watering for a long time, and, although it prefers bright light, it will tolerate much less.

The bamboo palm *(CHAMAEDOREA erumpens)* is an elegant plant with bamboolike stems and leaves that keep growing out near the bottom. This is one of the few tall-growing floor plants that doesn't need to have other plant material added to fill the sparse places near the bottom.

The spider plant or ribbon plant *(CHLOROPHYTUM comosum)* is a neat and tidy plant that, when growing well, can give the appearance of gay abandon. Although it shoots little plantlets out all over the place, it doesn't drop any leaves or make a mess. The plantlets are easy to pot up as gifts, which will leave you with a provident feeling. This is an old-timer (Goethe thought it was great in 1828), and is highly tolerant — although it also responds well to care.

The sago palm *(CYCAS revoluta)* is a slow grower with disciplined foliage that wears like iron. Since each leaflet is important to the plant's overall appearance (and they don't grow back in), they must be protected from mechanical injury.

The corn plant *(DRACAENA fragrans massangeana)* is an attractive table specimen although it'll grow as tall as you let it. Generally, however, in house situations, it will lose all its lower leaves, which is what gives it the cornstalk look. If it gets too long in the stem, you can move it behind other plants. When it hits the ceiling and begins to bend, you can chop it back.

Crown of thorns *(EUPHORBIA splendens)* has an interesting shape and can be trained around a window. It will remain in flower for months, and, if watered regularly, it will keep right on growing. Occasionally it will drop its leaves, which is simply a subtle way of saying that it would like a rest. Hold off the watering for a month and then start over again. While this is a plant for people who like success, it's not a plant for those who like something soft and cuddly.

The milk bush or pencil cactus *EUPHORBIA tirucalli)* has dark green cylindrical, pencil-shaped stems that provide an intriguing silhouette. This plant will exist for months without leaves, especially if it isn't watered. Both the milk bush and the crown of thorns should be handled carefully since the one has spines and both have sap that affects some people.

The India rubber plant *(FICUS elastica)* and the fiddle leaf fig *(FICUS lyrata)* are two "get them and forget them" plants. They grow straight up unless the top is cut out and, in a bright light, can hit the ceiling in a couple of years. These are good ones to buy small and watch them grow tall. You can use the money you saved by buying small ones to purchase a larger specimen of a slower growing plant.

Wax plants *(HOYA carnosa* and *HOYA carnosa variegata)* are vining plants with shiny leaves and delicate, waxy pink flowers. Since they need to be root-bound before they flower, they can stay for years in the same pot.

The Swiss cheese plant *(MONSTERA deliciosa)* isn't for everyone, with its huge, perforated leaves and the look of the jungle about it, but it does accommodate to indoor living. Nothing short of a freeze seems to hurt it. With support, it can be trained up a wall; without support it will spread out almost indefinitely. If you want it to ramble over a large area, feed it well but make sure that your machette is well-sharpened so you can carve a path to your other plants.

The philodendrons *(PHILODENDRON oxycardium* and *PHILODENDRON selloum)* are such great indoor plants that many people automatically think of them when they hear the term house plant. The heart-leafed philodendron *(PHILODENDRON oxycardium)* will continue to exist under almost any indoor condition. Many people think of it as that long bare stem with a couple of leaves at the end that they see marching across the fireplace or giving a jaunty touch to an old chianti bottle. The saddle-leafed philodendron *(PHILODENDRON selloum)* represents the other type of philodendron, the one that gets wider rather than longer. Although its leaves may make it a bit large for many homes, it's great in the lobbies of modern office buildings because of its size and because it tolerates any temperature above a solid freeze.

Swedish ivy (PLECTRANTHUS australis) is a lush green plant that, despite its common name, comes from Australia and the South Pacific. It's great for hanging in windows to provide privacy without appearing to do so. It reproduces easily and will be able to take care of the needs of many of your friends.

Mother-in-law's tongue (SANSEVIERIA trifasciata) is very patient of almost any kind of treatment. It's resistant to drought and tolerant of shade, so it's probably the best plant for forgetful people. The only thing that really seems to get to it is overwatering. When it's well-grown it can have five foot long, shiny, swordlike leaves that give dramatic accents in a modern setting. If they were harder to grow, more people would grow them just because of this striking appearance.

If you want a plant that really hangs in there, try golden pothos *(SCINDAPSUS aureus).* In its youth, it looks a lot like the  heart-leafed philodendron, and in its maturity, the leaves look like those of a Swiss cheese plant. It grows slowly, though, so don't expect results next year. Easy to keep and easy to reproduce, this is another plant that often looks worse than it should because it's so accommodating. But it's one plant that will stick with you while you learn.

The burro tail *(SEDUM morganianum)* is a great hanging basket plant, and if it can be left undisturbed high in a window, some of the chains of blue-green leaves will grow down to the floor. If you don't get up to water it though, the plant will remind you. The plump little leaflets will begin to shrivel. If you disregard this warning, the leaflets will fall off, but even then, if you do water it, the leaves will grow back. However, the stems will look bald in spots for a long time. The stems are brittle and break off easily, so if one breaks off, pot it up and give it to a friend.

*SYNADENIUM grantii rubra* is a fleshy-stemmed shrub with purple, red, and green leaves. This plant has been known to survive without light or water for nine months in a basement. It looks a bit like a round-leaved croton. But if you are sensitive to sappy-plants, this one is a relative of the poinsettia and the crown of thorns and should be avoided.

*SYNGONIUM podophyllum* is another relative of the philodendrons and is great for adding another leaf shape and size to the green on green in your indoor garden. The immature plants have arrow-shaped leaves with ears at each side of the base, and in the mature plants the leaves develop a fingerlike appearance.

Tahitian bridal veil *(TRIPOGANDRA multiflora)* is one of the happy wanderers that doesn't get as leggy as some of the others. A full-looking plant in a hanging basket, it can be used to obstruct the view without seeming to do so. This is a delicate plant that is easy to grow.

# A Touch of Color: Foliage Plants

**E**verything goes well with green. But there's no such thing as a plain or ordinary green. There are greens of every shade, texture, and feeling. There are strong, bold greens, such as the color of the rubber tree, the saddle leaf philodendron, and the euphorbias. There are soft-looking, feathery, and fluffy greens, such as the asparagus, the Boston fern, and the selaginella. There are also greens with a touch of color: blue-greens, yellow-greens, cloudy greens, and frosted greens. There are plants whose leaves and stems sport subtle stripes, bold spots, and even the suggestion of a plaid, such as in some of the calatheas and marantas.

Plants with colorful foliage prefer to be in the limelight, needing more light than their green relatives. In fact, some plants acquired because of their colorful markings will revert to green if the light intensity is below what they need to shine. This is because without enough light, they have to put all of the leaf to work. However, plants with colorful foliage don't need as much light to keep their leaves colorful as flowering plants need to produce flowers.

### PLANTS WHOSE LEAVES ARE MARKED WITH YELLOW, GREY, WHITE, OR SILVER

| Botanical Name | Common Name |
|---|---|
| ABUTILON hybridum | Chinese Bellflower, Flowering Maple, Parlor Maple |
| ACORUS gramineus variegatus | Calamus Root, Dwarf Japanese Sweet Flag, Sweet Flag |

| Botanical Name | Common Name |
|---|---|
| AECHMEA fasciata (BILLBERGIA rhodocyanea | Vase Plant, Urn Plant |
| AGAVE victoriae-reginae | Queen Victoria Century Plant |
| AGLAONEMA species | |
| ANANAS comosus variegatus | Variegated Pineapple |
| APHELANDRA squarrosa 'Louisae' | Zebra Plant |
| BEGONIA species | |
| CALADIUM hortulanum | Fancy Leaved Caladium |
| CALATHEA insignis | |
| CALATHEA makoyana | Peacock Plant |
| CALATHEA ornata 'Sanderiana' | |
| CALLISIA elegans (SETCREASEA striata) | Wandering Jew, Striped Inch Plant |
| CALLISIA fragrans | |
| CEPHALOCEREUS senilis | Old Man Cactus |
| CEROPEGIA woodii | String of Hearts, Rosary Vine, Chinese Lantern Plant |
| CHLOROPHYTUM comosum | Spider Plant, Airplane Plant, Ribbon Plant |
| CODIAEUM (CROTON) species | Croton |
| COLEUS blumei | Coleus |
| CYANOTIS somaliensis | Pussy Ears |
| DIEFFENBACHIA species | |
| DRACAENA species | |
| EUPHORBIA lactea | Milk Striped Euphorbia, Dragon Bones |
| FICUS elastica variegata | Variegated Rubber Plant |
| FITTONIA argyroneura | Silver-nerved Fittonia |
| HEDERA species and varieties | |
| HOYA carnosa variegata | Variegated Wax Plant |
| KALANCHOE tomentosa | Panda Plant, Pussy Ears |
| NOTOCACTUS leninghausii | Golden Ball Cactus, Ball Cactus |
| PANDANUS veitchii | Screw Pine |
| PEDILANTHUS tithymaloides variegatus | Devil's Backbone |
| PELARGONIUM hortorum varieties | Geranium |
| PELARGONIUM peltatum varieties | Ivy Geranium |
| PEPEROMIA obtusifolia | |
| PEPEROMIA sandersii 'Argyreia' | Watermelon Peperomia, Watermelon Begonia |
| PILEA cadierei | Aluminum Plant, Watermelon Plant |
| PITTOSPORUM tobira 'Variegatum' | |
| PLECTRANTHUS oertendahlii | Candle Plant, Swedish Ivy |

| Botanical Name | Common Name |
| --- | --- |
| SAINTPAULIA ionantha | African Violet |
| SANSEVIERIA trifasciata | Snake Plant. Mother-in-Law's Tongue. Bowstring Hemp |
| SAXIFRAGA sarmentosa | Strawberry Begonia. Mother of Thousands |
| SCINDAPSUS aureus | Pothos, Devil's Ivy, Golden Pothos |
| TILLANDSIA usneoides | Spanish Moss |
| TRADESCANTIA blossfeldiana | |
| TRADESCANTIA sillamontana | White Velvet |
| ZANTEDESCHIA elliottiana | Calla |
| ZEBRINA pendula | Wandering Jew |

## PLANTS WHOSE LEAVES ARE MARKED WITH RED, PINK, MAGENTA, BROWN, OR PURPLE

| Botanical Name | Common Name |
| --- | --- |
| ANANAS comosus variegatus | Variegated Pineapple |
| BEGONIA species and varieties | |
| CALADIUM varieties | |
| CALATHEA insignis | |
| CALATHEA makoyana | Peacock Plant |
| CALATHEA ornata 'Sanderiana' | |
| CALLISIA elegans (SETCREASEA striata) | Wandering Jew, Striped Inch Plant |
| CALLISIA fragrans | |
| CODIAEUM (CROTON) species | Croton |
| COLEUS blumei | Coleus |
| COLUMNEA gloriosa | |
| COLUMNEA hirta | |
| CORDYLINE terminalis | Red Dracaena, Ti Plant |
| CRYPTANTHUS zonatus 'Zebrinus' | Zebra Plant |

| Botanical Name | Common Name |
|---|---|
| DRACAENA marginata | Red Margined Dracaena |
| ECHEVERIA derenbergii | Painted Lady |
| EPISCIA cupreata | Flame Violet |
| EPISCIA lilacina | |
| EPISCIA reptans | |
| EUPHORBIA pulcherrima | Lobster Flower, Mexican Flame Leaf, Poinsettia |
| FITTONIA verschaffeltii | Red-Nerved Fittonia |
| GUZMANIA lingulata | |
| GYNURA aurantiaca | Velvet Plant, Purple Passion Plant |
| HOYA carnosa variegata | Variegated Wax Plant |
| IRESINE herbstii | Bloodleaf |
| OXALIS hedysaroides rubra | Firefern |
| PEDILANTHUS tithymaloides variegatus | Devil's Backbone |
| PELARGONIUM hortorum varieties | Geranium |
| PEPEROMIA metallica | |
| PILEA involucrata | Pan-American Friendship Plant, Panamiga |
| RHOEO spathacea | Moses in the Cradle, Moses in the Bullrushes, Man in a Boat, Oyster Plant |
| SAXIFRAGA sarmentosa | Strawberry Begonia, Mother of Thousands |
| SEDUM rubrotinctum (SEDUM guatemalense) | Christmas Cheer |
| SETCREASEA purpurea | Purple Heart |
| SYNADENIUM grantii rubra | |
| TRADESCANTIA blossfeldiana | |
| ZEBRINA pendula | Wandering Jew |

# Flowering Plants

**W**hen you think of a flower you usually think of something that's colorful, showy, and perhaps has a nice smell. Cut or left attached to their plants, flowers can be used to brighten up any room or decorate a dinner table. But don't be hurt when your flowers disappear. Usually the really colorful flowering plants, like the azaleas, cyclamen, cineraria, mums, and spring flowering bulbs, are charming guests that can only visit a short time inside. Getting them to bloom takes the right conditions, which usually include stronger light than is available inside and special day lengths and temperatures. And the cyclamen, cineraria, and pocketbook plant all need such cold night temperatures to keep their blooms that they usually have to be treated like a potted bouquet. The closer you come to satisfying their needs, the longer they will last, but at average house temperature they will hold out only a bit longer than cut flowers.

Some plants are annuals that bloom only once a year, and some of these, such as poinsettia, fuchsia, and mums can be rather unattractive in their resting period. Bringing plants back into bloom can be fun and can produce the greatest feeling of satisfaction, but it usually takes so much time, space (where do you put them while they're looking tacky), and self discipline that it's easier to buy them in bud and enjoy the pleasure of their company while they last.

Some plants can never be coaxed to rebloom. The bromeliads, for example, bloom only once and die after flowering. But they are not just one-time plants, their offshoots keep on coming and, under ideal conditions, will also bloom.

The following plants are ones you buy at the greenhouse because of their beautiful flowers. Unfortunately, the flowers soon disappear, never to be seen again. You should buy these for the pleasure of their company, but be aware that you'll probably be glad to wish them farewell after a while.

## BUY IN BUD OR BLOOM

| Botanical Name | Common Name |
| --- | --- |
| AECHMEA fasciata (BILLBERGIA rhodocyanea) | Vase Plant, Urn Plant |
| ANANAS comosus (ANANAS sativus) | Pineapple |
| ANANAS comosus variegatus | |
| APHELANDRA squarrosa 'Louisae' | Zebra Plant |
| CALCEOLARIA herbeohybrida | Pocketbook Plant |
| CAPISCUM annuum 'Conoides' | Christmas Pepper |
| CHRYSANTHEMUM morifolium (CHRYSANTHEMUM hortorum) | Mum |
| CROCUS | Crocus |
| CRYPTANTHUS zonatus 'Zebrinus' | Zebra Plant |
| CYCLAMEN persicum | Florist's Cyclamen, Alpine Violet |
| EUPHORBIA pulcherrima | Lobster Flower, Mexican Flame Leaf, Poinsettia |
| FUCHSIA hybrids | Lady's Eardrops |
| GUZMANIA lingulata | |
| HIPPEASTRUM (AMARYLLIS) hybrids | Amaryllis |
| HYACINTHUS orientalis | Hyacinth |
| NARCISSUS jonquilla | Jonquil |
| NARCISSUS pseudo-narcissus | Daffodil, Lent Lily |
| NARCISSUS tazetta | Paper White Narcissus |
| PRIMULA malacoides | Fairy Primrose, Baby Primrose |
| RHODODENDRON species | Azalea |
| SENECIO cruentus | Cineraria of florists |
| TILLANDSIA cyanea | |
| TULIPA hybrids | Tulip |
| VRIESEA carinata | |
| VRIESEA splendens | Painted Feather |
| ZANTEDESCHIA elliottiana | Calla |

Because of their special requirements in terms of day length, temperature, or dormancy, the following plants bloom only on a once-a-year basis. If you are in to them and want to badly enough, you can hasten their blooming. This is called forcing. But it's a lot easier to let them do it their way and just sit back and enjoy.

## PLANTS THAT BLOOM ONCE A YEAR

| Botanical Name | Common Name |
|---|---|
| AGAPANTHUS africanus | Blue African Lily, Lily of the Nile, Love Flower |
| ANTHURIUM andreanum | Flamingo Flower Flamingo Plant |
| ANTHURIUM crystallinum | |
| CLIVIA miniata | Kafir Lily |
| CRASSULA argentea | Jade Plant, Chinese Rubber Plant |
| EPIPHYLLUM oxypetalum | Queen of Night |
| FAUCARIA tigrina | Tiger Jaw |
| GYNURA aurantiaca | Velvet Plant Purple Passion Plant |
| HELICONIA humilis | Lobster Claw |
| HOYA carnosa | Wax Plant |
| HOYA carnosa variegata | Variegated Wax Plant |
| HYDROSME rivieri (Amorphophallus) | Devil's Tongue, Voodoo Plant |
| MUSA nana (MUSA cavendishii) | Dwarf Banana, Dwarf Jamaica Banana |
| ORCHIDS | |
| PLUMERIA rubra (PLUMERIA acuminata) | Frangipani tree |
| RHIPSALIS species | Mistletoe Cactus |
| SCHLUMBERGERA bridgesii | Christmas Cactus |
| STAPELIA grandiflora | Starfish Flower, Carrion Flower |
| STRELITZIA reginae | Bird of Paradise |
| ZYGOCACTUS truncatus | Thanksgiving Cactus |

Actually, most green plants grown inside, except for ferns and a few other "lower" plants, have flowers. For some plants, such as the century plant *(AGAVE)* it may take years, even out of doors under ideal conditions, to produce a flower, and they may never feel up to it at all indoors. On other plants, the flower is so subtle and understated (green on green) that it doesn't make much difference to anyone except the plant.

The following plants are exciting to have about since they have flowers that look like flowers, and when well-adjusted, can bloom at almost any time. The more ideal conditions, the more bloom. For example, some happy African violets bloom almost all the time.

## PLANTS THAT BLOOM FROM TIME TO TIME

| Botanical Name | Common Name |
|---|---|
| ABUTILON hybridum | Chinese Bellflower, Flowering Maple, Parlor Maple |
| ARDISIA crispa (ARDISIA crenulata) | Coral Berry |
| BEGONIA species | |
| BELOPERONE guttata | Shrimp Plant |
| BOUGAINVILLEA glabra | |

| Botanical Name | Common Name |
|---|---|
| CAMELLIA japonica | |
| CARISSA grandiflora | Natal Plum |
| CITRUS limon 'Ponderosa' | American Wonderlemon |
| CITRUS mitis 'Calamondin' | Calamondin Orange |
| CITRUS paradisi | Grapefruit |
| CITRUS sinensis | Sweet Orange |
| COFFEA arabica | Coffee |
| COLUMNEA gloriosa | |
| COLUMNEA hirta | |
| EPISCIA cupreata | Flame Violet |
| EPISCIA lilacina | |
| EPISCIA reptans | |
| EUPHORBIA splendens | Crown of Thorns |
| (EUPHORBIA milii splendens) | |
| GARDENIA jasminoides | |
| HIBISCUS rosa-sinensis | Chinese Rose, Shoeflower |
| HIBISCUS schizopetalus | Hibiscus |
| IMPATIENS walleriana sultanii | Busy Lizzie, Patient Lucy |
| LANTANA camara | |
| MIMOSA pudica | Sensitive Plant |
| NERIUM oleander | Oleander |
| OXALIS rubra | Grandmother's Shamrock |
| PASSIFLORA caerulea | Passion Flower |
| PASSIFLORA coccinea | Red Passion Flower |
| PELARGONIUM hortorum | Geranium |
| PELARGONIUM peltatum | Ivy Geranium |
| PLUMBAGO capensis | |
| PLUMBAGO indica coccinea | |
| PUNICA granatum | Pomegranate |
| PUNICA granatum 'Nana' | Dwarf Pomegranate |
| RHOEO spathacea | Moses in the Cradle, Moses in the Bullrushes, Man in a Boat, Oyster Plant |
| SAINTPAULIA ionantha | African Violet |
| SAXIFRAGA sarmentosa | Strawberry Begonia, Mother of Thousands |
| SINNINGIA pusilla | |
| SINNINGIA speciosa | Gloxinia |
| SPATHIPHYLLUM floribundum | Spathe Flower |
| STREPTOCARPUS hybridus | |
| THUNBERGIA alata | Black-Eyed Susan |
| TRIPOGANDRA multiflora | Tahitian Bridal Veil |

# Plant Descriptions

The plants described in this book are rated on a scale from "Five" (tolerant and easy) down to "One" (very finicky and a real challenge). Ratings are based on how well a plant will do in an average house or apartment where no modifications have been made to benefit the plant.

*ABUTILON hybridum*

**Botanical name:** ABUTILON hybridum

**Common names:** Flowering Maple, Parlor Maple, Chinese Bellflower

**Origin:** Tropical America

**Description:** Bushy plant with maple-shaped leaves. In the variety 'Aureomaculatum,' the green leaves are blotched with yellow. (This is the work of a virus, but it doesn't hurt the plant and sometimes it's localized in just part of the plant.) The flowers look like single hollyhocks and are mostly yellow, white, or pink. Grows fast.

**Requirements:** Bright light and even moisture. Heavy soil with good drainage. Abutilons don't like soggy soil, and they prefer plenty of fresh air. They do best with a cool night temperature. If they get four hours full sun in the winter or are grown under artificial light, they will flower almost all year round.

**Propagation:** Seeds, Cuttings
**Use:** Floor, Table
**Rating:** 2

**Botanical name:** ACER palmatum
**Common name:** Japanese Maple
**Origin:** Japan, Korea
**Description:** Small tree with dark red, maple-shaped leaves. This plant is often trained and grown as a bonsai.
**Requirements:** Bright light; drench let dry. Needs cold nights, good air circulation, and requires a period of dormancy. It is best kept outside in a protected place in the winter. Although it may not survive a winter outside, it would be very unhappy inside.
**Propagation:** Seeds
**Use:** Floor, Table
**Rating:** 1

*ACORUS granineus variegatus*

**Botanical name:** ACORUS gramineus variegatus
**Common names:** Calamus Root, Dwarf Japanese Sweet Flag, Sweet Flag
**Origin:** Japan
**Description:** A grassy-looking

plant with flat 8- to 10-inch leathery green and white leaves. A bog plant, it grows in clumps and is used in terrariums even though it prefers good air circulation.

**Requirements:** It likes filtered light and wants to be kept constantly wet. Heavy soil, good air circulation, and cold nights also make it happy.

**Propagation:** Division
**Use:** Table, Terrarium
**Rating:** 2

*ADIANTUM species and varieties*

**Botanical name:** ADIANTUM species and varieties
**Common name:** Maidenhair Fern
**Origin:** Worldwide
**Description:** Attractive fern with wiry black stems and wedge-shaped emerald green leaflets. However, unless there is high humidity in the air, the leaflets curl and turn brown.
**Requirements:** Shady location, constant moisture, and high humidity. Tolerates house temperature, but does better with cool nights. Needs soil with high organic content. If you get scale on a strong, mature plant, reduce watering and put it in a cool place for about a month. Then cut off all the leaf stems (fronds), bring it back to a warmer location, start watering more frequently, and, when growing, start fertilizing.
**Propagation:** Division
**Use:** Table, Terrarium
**Rating:** 1

**Botanical name:** AECHMEA fasciata (BILLBERGIA rhodocyanea)

**Common names:** Vase Plant, Urn Plant

**Origin:** Rio de Janeiro (Brazil)

**Description:** Stocky, leathery, grey-green leaves arranged in a vaselike shape, about a foot-and-a-half tall. The leaves are banded with a silvery-white tiger stripe, and blue flowers are carried in a rose-colored glob which stands high in the center of the plant.

**Requirements:** Filtered light with even moisture. The vase of the plant should always contain water, but the roots shouldn't be kept wet. Prefers light soil with excellent drainage, and can take dry air and house temperatures. Although the plant dies after flowering, there are always new offshoots to carry on. So if someone admires your blooming plant, be generous and give it to them, but keep the little ones. If you use this vase for cut flowers be careful that the stems don't puncture the bottom, and change the water before it smells.

**Propagation:** Offshoots

**Use:** Table, Hanging Basket

**Rating:** 5

*AECHMEA fasciata*

**Botanical name:** AEONIUM arboreum

**Common name:** Saucer Plant

**Origin:** Morocco

**Description:** Succulent with a thick, bare stem topped with rosettes of green leaves. Flowers are golden yellow, and the plant dies after it blooms. This plant often goes dormant in the wintertime and drops all of its leaves. But you know it's just resting because it hasn't bloomed.

**Requirements:** Filtered light; drench and let dry out between waterings. In the winter when they are dormant, they need much less water. They prefer cool nights, good air circulation, and heavy soil with excellent drainage. A dramatic-looking plant when in full leaf, it's hard to keep from doing something to it when it's dormant.

**Propagation:** Seeds, Cuttings
**Use:** Floor, Table
**Rating:** 3

*AEONIUM arboreum*

**Botanical name:** AEONIUM canariense

**Common name:** Giant Velvet Rose

**Origin:** Tenerife (Canary Islands)

**Description:** Succulent with a thick bare stem and large rosettes of floppy, light green, waxy leaves. The flowers are pale yellow, and the plant dies after blooming. This plant often goes dormant in the winter. A well-grown single plant is as dramatic as a piece of good sculpture, but while it's dormant it has a reproachful air.

**Requirements:** Filtered light. Normally, they like to be drenched and let dry between waterings, but while they are dormant during the winter, they need less water. They like heavy soil, but the drainage should be excellent if you don't want them to rot. They prefer cool nights and good air circulation.
**Propagation:** Seeds, Cuttings
**Use:** Table
**Rating:** 3

**Botanical name:** AGAPANTHUS africanus
**Common names:** Blue African Lily, Lily of the Nile, Love Flower
**Origin:** Cape of Good Hope (Africa)
**Description:** Large clump of dark green, straplike leaves about two feet long. The flowers are light blue and grow in a bunch at the top of a straight two- to two-and-a-half-foot stalk.
**Requirements:** Bright light and even moisture. When in bloom, they take a lot more water and need extra fertilizer. They like heavy soil, dry air, and a beauty sleep in the winter time when it's just above freezing. They like to be crowded, so repotting should only be done when they're breaking out of the pot. They get very heavy to lug about, so if you're keeping them, break the gang up every once in awhile.

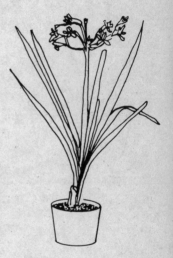

*AGAPANTHUS africanus*

**Propagation:** Root Division (roots break apart more easily if they're soaked in water for a few hours first), Seeds
**Use:** Floor, Table
**Rating:** 2

**Botanical name:** AGAVE americana
**Common name:** Century Plant
**Origin:** Mexico
**Description:** A large rosette of fleshy grey-green leaves that end in a sharp needlelike spine, which in Mexico is used with the attached fiber to sew up heavy sacks. The edges of the leaves are armed with sharp brown hooks. A succulent that dies after flowering, it's still a good buy since it may take 20 years or longer for it to flower inside.
**Requirements:** Bright light but will tolerate less; drench and let dry between waterings. Prefers a heavy soil with good drainage, and circulating dry air. This is a very tough plant that will last for years in less than ideal situations. It has a dramatic, decorative appearance but it does get large (four- to five-foot leaves) and needs a lot of room because of its stiffness and very sharp spines. Fortunately, the pot can be kept relatively small since they prefer to be a bit root-bound.
**Propagation:** Seeds, Offsets
**Use:** Floor, Table
**Rating:** 4

*AGAVE americana*

**Botanical name:** AGAVE victoriae-reginae
**Common name:** Queen Victoria Century Plant
**Origin:** North Mexico
**Description:** Pom-pom of thick green leaves (triangular in cross section) that have smooth white edges and a dark blunt spine at the end. The leaves look a bit like six-inch-long flattened crayons. This is a slow-growing succulent that will sit and look attractive for a long time.
**Requirements:** Prefers bright light, but will tolerate much less; drench and let dry between waterings. It would rather have cool nights, but it does well in house temperatures and dry air.
**Propagation:** Offshoots
**Use:** Table
**Rating:** 5

AGAVE victoriae-reginae

**Botanical name:** AGLAONEMA commutatum
**Origin:** Philippines, Ceylon
**Description:** A cluster of large, oblong, dark green leaves that are shaded with grey and that have a long stem. The leaves grow off a stem that grows and grows to the point where the top has to be cut off and rerooted. There is a white flower that looks like a small calla lily. A very satisfying plant to have around.
**Requirements:** It likes to be

evenly moist or wet and will even live in water for a time. It prefers heavy soil, but will take anything. It's very happy with dry air, house temperatures, and shade. When it gets too tall and floppy, either stake it or cut off the top and start over.

**Propagation:** Cuttings
**Use:** Table
**Rating:** 5

*AGLAONEMA modestum*

**Botanical name:** AGLAONEMA modestum
**Common name:** Chinese Evergreen
**Origin:** Kwantung (China)
**Description:** An erect plant with large, long, oval, pointed, dark green, leathery leaves. The flower is creamy white and looks like a small calla lily. This plant will grow very tall, losing its lower leaves. But if you chop off the top and reroot it, not only will you get a new plant from the cutting, but new leaves will grow from the cut stem of the original plant. You can keep going this way for years and years.
**Requirements:** Will tolerate very low light intensity, house temperatures, and dry air. But it likes heavy soil with good drainage. This is one of the most faithful indoor plants. It will grow for quite some time in water alone and, unless abandoned, will grow for 35, 50, or

even more years in the same pot.

**Propagation:** Cuttings
**Use:** Table
**Rating:** 5

**Botanical name:** ALOE arborescens
**Common name:** Candelabra Aloe
**Origin:** South Africa
**Description:** Succulent plant with blue-green tapering leaves (up to two feet long) that have teeth along the edges. As the plant grows older, it gets a number of side branches. It has red flowers that appear around the first of the year in bunches at the end of long stems. This is a very interesting-looking plant with strong definite lines.
**Requirements:** Bright light, but will tolerate much less. Drench and let dry. Needs more water in the summertime than in the winter. It likes dry air and cool night temperatures and can take it just above freezing in the winter, but it also does alright at house temperature. Needs light to flower. Drainage is more important to it than the type of soil, so it does well with broken bricks in the bottom of the pot.
**Propagation:** Cuttings, Offshoots (needs very little water while rooting)
**Use:** Floor, Table
**Rating:** 4

*ALOE arborescens*

*ALOE variegata*

**Botanical name:** ALOE variegata
**Common names:** Partridge Breast, Tiger Aloe
**Origin:** Cape of Good Hope (Africa)
**Description:** One of the most attractive aloes, this has white-spotted, blue-green leaves — that grow to 10 inches — with warty, saw-toothed edges. The leaves are triangular in cross section and arranged in three neat stacks or ranks. The salmon-red tubelike flowers grow on the end of a long stem.
**Requirements:** Bright light, but will tolerate much less. Watch out for sunburn and too much light, which can cause pale leaves. Type of soil is not as important as good drainage. Give it almost no water in winter, and not too much water in the summer. Prefers dry air and a cool night temperature, but does well at house temperature.
**Propagation:** Cuttings, Offshoots (needs very little water while rooting)
**Use:** Table
**Rating:** 4

**Botanical name:** ALOE vera
**Common names:** Medicine Plant, Lily of the Desert, Burn Plant
**Origin:** Cape Verde and Madeira (Portugal), Canary Islands (Spain)
**Description:** Succulent plant with grey-green leaves that can get over a foot long. These water-

looking, irregularly splotched leaves have feeble, fleshy spines along the edges. Squashed leaves are used to relieve burns, chapping, and other skin irritations.

**Requirements:** It prefers bright light, but is tolerant of dim light. To water, drench it and then let it dry. Good drainage is more important than the type of soil. Although it tolerates house temperatures well, it prefers cool nights and dry air. The aloe is a tolerant, accommodating plant whose death is usually due to overwatering; it needs more water in summer, but practically none in winter.

**Propagation:** Offsets
**Use:** Table
**Rating:** 4

*ALOE vera*

**Botanical name:** ANANAS comosus (ANANAS sativus)
**Common name:** Pineapple
**Origin:** Bahia (Salvador), Mato Grosso (Brazil)
**Description:** Pineapples were the symbol of hospitality among the natives of the Caribbean before Columbus arrived, and the Europeans took the idea up with enthusiasm. The plant is made up of a rosette of long, stiff, more or less rough-edged, sword-shaped leaves. The violet flowers are bunched in a small pineapplelike cluster on top of a stiff stem. The fruit from pineapples, when grown inside,

doesn't have much flavor and is pretty bony.

**Requirements:** Bright light and even moisture. They like a rich organic soil with excellent drainage (about one-half sand), and adore regular showers. They like a warm temperature. Cold drafts and low humidity will produce brown edges on the leaves, and if its bad enough, the whole leaf will quit.

**Propagation:** A fresh pineapple top can be planted in peat moss and sand and, if kept warm and moist, will grow into a new plant.

**Use:** Floor, Table

**Rating:** 3

*ANANAS
comosus variegatus*

**Botanical name:** ANANAS comosus variegatus

**Common name:** Variegated Pineapple

**Description:** Like *ANANAS comosus*, except that it has wide cream-colored bands on the leaves, red spines, and red in the center of the rosette.

**Requirements:** Bright light and even moisture. Rich organic soil with excellent drainage (about one-half sand), and regular showers. It likes to have warm temperatures and high humidity.

**Propagation:** Offshoots

**Use:** Floor, Table

**Rating:** 3

**Botanical name:** ANTHURIUM andraeanum

**Common names:** Flamingo Flower, Flamingo Plant

**Origin:** S.W. Colombia

**Description:** Plant with long, pointy, heart-shaped leaves and a flower that is backed up by a brilliant red, white, or pink patent-leather spathe (sheath) that lasts a long time.

**Requirements:** In the summer, it needs filtered to shady light and must be kept constantly moist. In the winter, it should be kept dryer. Does well in house temperatures but needs humid air. The soil should be high in organic matter and kept heaped over the spots where the leaves join the underground stems to keep the thick succulent roots from drying out. The drainage must be good or it will rot. Not a bad sort though if you give it a sympathetic environment.

**Propagation:** Division

**Use:** Table

**Rating:** 3

*ANTHURIUM andraeanum*

**Botanical name:** ANTHURIUM crystallinum

**Origin:** Colombia, Peru

**Description:** Large, beautiful, velvety green, heart-shaped leaves with contrasting silvery-white veins. The flowers are insignificant, and the spathe (sheath) is green.

**Requirements:** It likes a shady location, organic soil, and con-

stant moisture. Drainage
should be excellent, so the pot
should contain pieces of broken
clay pots in the bottom. Anthurium does well in house
temperatures but prefers humid
air. Don't pot the plant too deep,
but the aerial roots that form at
the base of each leaf should be
kept covered with moist sphagnum moss to keep the plant
from going into a slow decline.
**Propagation:** Division
**Use:** Table
**Rating:** 3

*APHELANDRA*
*squarrosa 'Louisae'*

**Botanical name:** APHELANDRA
squarrosa 'Louisae'
**Common name:** Zebra Plant
**Origin:** Brazil
**Description:** An erect plant with
large, dark green leaves whose
veins are outlined in white. In
addition to the beautiful leaves,
it has a stunning yellow flower
spike made up of yellow scales
and flowers. A wow plant that
starts its decline at the moment
of purchase, it has given many
green thumbers an inferiority
complex.
**Requirements:** It needs filtered
light, evenly moist organic soil,
and high humidity to flower. But
after flowering, it likes it dry —
but not too dry. Since the plant
you bought or were given was a
nice compact tip end cutting,
the long, scrawny, bare stem
that develops can be a bit of a
jolt. Like coleus and purple

passion plants, they are better looking when young. Brown thumbers will enjoy its striking beauty, but many green thumbers will swear with frustration.

**Propagation:** Cuttings
**Use:** Table
**Rating:** 1

**Botanical name:** ARAUCARIA bidwillii
**Common name:** Monkey-Puzzle Tree
**Origin:** Queensland, Australia
**Description:** A straight tree with branches that appear in starlike layers. Similar to the Norfolk Island pine except that it has small, sharp, dark green leaves instead of needles. Known as "bunya-bunya" in Australia, "Bill" is one of the best and handsomest trees for pots. It will eventually grow as tall as you let it inside, but its size can be controlled by holding down the pot size and fertilizer.
**Requirements:** Filtered light and even moisture in an organic soil with good drainage. Prefers cool nights and dry air, but will take house temperatures. Because the symmetry of its growth is affected if it is crowded, give it plenty of room. Plants raised from seeds have much greater distances between the layers of branches than those raised from cuttings. If making a cutting, the cutting should be taken from the top

*ARAUCARIA bidwillii*

(the leader) or the new shoot will not be symmetrical. Fortunately, when the top is cut out, a number of new leaders appear, all of whom will grow into symmetrical plants.

**Propagation:** Cuttings, Seeds
**Use:** Floor, Table
**Rating:** 5

**Botanical name:** ARAUCARIA heterophylla (ARAUCARIA excelsa)

**Common name:** Norfolk Island Pine

**Origin:** Norfolk Island

**Description:** A straight tree with branches that appear in star-like layers. Small, stiff, scale-like leaves cover all the branches uniformly. A handsome pot tree, it is making a comeback as an indoor Christmas tree. Hung with sterling stars or snowflakes it will save a lot of energy.

**Requirements:** Filtered light and even moisture in an organic soil with good drainage. Prefers cool nights and dry air but will take house temperatures. Because the symmetry of its growth is affected if it's crowded, give it plenty of room. You can't iron out an araucaria after it has a crimp in it. Too much light or too little light causes it to drop its lower leaves and branches, so move it one way or another when the

*ARAUCARIA heterophylla*

*ARAUCARIA bidwillii*

lower branches start looking dry or peaked.

**Propagation:** Leader Cuttings for symmetrical trees (branch cuttings won't reproduce the star shape)

**Use:** Floor, Table

**Rating:** 5

*ARDISIA crispa*

**Botanical name:** ARDISIA crispa (ARDISIA crenulata)

**Common name:** Coral Berry

**Origin:** China, Malaya

**Description:** A small shrub with dark green, thick, shiny leaves. The pinky-white flowers are followed by hollylike berries (especially if the pollen has been brushed about). When the plants get to be about three years old, they often start losing their leaves and getting leggy.

**Requirements:** Filtered light, even moisture, heavy soil, and cool, circulating air. New plants can be made from the bushy tops by air layering. When the plants start to flower, keep water off the tops until the berries are set.

**Propagation:** Cuttings, Air Layering

**Use:** Table

**Rating:** 3

**Botanical name:** ARECASTRUM romanzoffianum (COCOS plumosa)

**Common name:** Queen Palm

**Origin:** Bahia to Argentina and Bolivia

**Description:** A palm with graceful plumy leaves that starts out about two-and-a-half feet tall and can grow to over 30 feet outside, but it does it slowly. The first leaves, which look like fins and fish tails, have an entirely different look than the later ones, which are like fringe on a curving stem.

**Requirements:** It likes filtered light, house temperature, and high humidity. Although it likes a lot of moisture and never wants to dry out, it doesn't like wet feet. If the humidity is low, the ends of the leaves turn brown (these can be cut off); if there isn't enough water, the leaves turn a sickly yellow.

**Propagation:** Seeds

**Use:** Floor, Table

**Rating:** 3


**Botanical name:** ASPARAGUS meyeri

**Common names:** Foxtail, Asparagus Fern

**Origin:** South Africa

**Description:** Erect foxtail-like stems to two feet long, made up of dense, bright green, needlelike foliage. It has rather stiff stems that don't hang like the other asparagus. It lacks functional leaves — those little green things on the stems that are usually considered leaves are actually called cladodes.

**Requirements:** Filtered light with evenly moist, heavy soil. Prefers a cool night temperature and good air circulation.

**Propagation:** Division (use an ax, sharp knife, or a hatchet)

**Use:** Table, Hanging Basket

**Rating:** 4 (would have rated higher if it wasn't such a cladode dropper)

*ASPARAGUS plumosus*

**Botanical name:** ASPARAGUS plumosus

**Common Name:** Asparagus Fern

**Origin:** South Africa

**Description:** A climber with bright green, flat, fernlike "leaves" that grow in a horizontal plane on green wiry stems on which are concealed a number of little claws. Actually, they have no functional leaves; the little green things on the stems are cladodes. At one time the plant was seen in every bride's bouquet and on every banquet table because it was able to hold up so well without wilting.

**Requirements:** Filtered light and evenly moist heavy soil. It prefers a cool night temperature and good air circulation. If you let the plant dry out or if the temperature gets too hot, the cladodes turn yellow and drop like mad. Every once in awhile, to make sure the entire root ball is moist, sink the whole pot into water until all the air bubbles come out.

**Propagation:** Seed, Division (use a hatchet or machete)

**Use:** Table, Hanging Basket

**Rating:** 4

**Botanical name:** ASPARAGUS sprengeri

**Common name:** Asparagus Fern

**Origin:** West Africa, Natal

**Description:** A fluffy-looking plant with many branching stems covered with bright green "needles" (cladodes). Often has tiny white flowers that are followed by red berries.

**Requirements:** Filtered light and evenly moist, heavy soil. Prefers a cool night temperature and good air circulation. It drops its "needles" if the temperature gets too warm or if the plant dries out. The heavy mat of roots sometimes causes the water to run off the top, so sink the whole pot in water every once in awhile.

**Propagation:** Seeds, Division (use a heavy knife or a hatchet)

**Use:** Table, Hanging Basket

**Rating:** 4

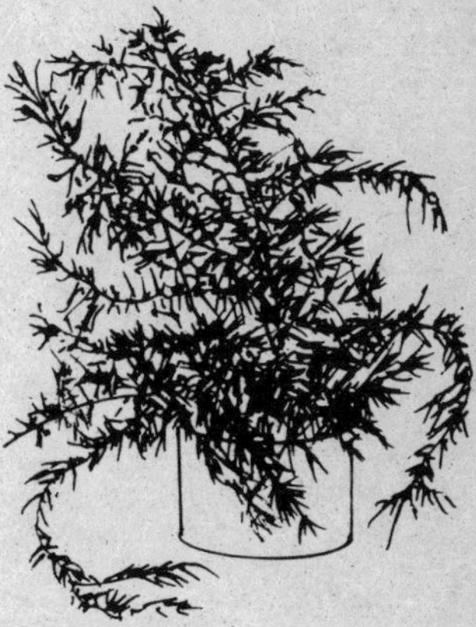

*ASPARAGUS sprengeri*

**Botanical name:** ASPIDISTRA elatior

**Common names:** Cast Iron Plant, Parlor Palm

**Origin:** China

**Description:** Pot plant with large (to two feet), oblong, dark green, leathery leaves. A great favorite with the Victorians, it fell out of favor and is now hard to find. A slow grower.

**Requirements:** Will tolerate very low light intensity. It likes heavy soil, preferably with good drainage, that is kept evenly moist. Although it will grow under almost any conditions inside, it prefers cool nights and dry air. Aspidistras will take dust, heat, cold, and drought — more adverse conditions than almost any other plant inside. However, under these conditions, it just stands there. If you expect it to grow, you have to show you care.

**Propagation:** Division
**Use:** Table
**Rating:** 5

*ASPIDISTRA elatior*

**Botanical name:** ASPLENIUM nidus
**Common names:** Birdnest-Fern, Spleenwort, Shuttlecock
**Origin:** India to Queensland and Japan
**Description:** A fern that doesn't look like one, it has long, wide, bright green leaves growing in a funnel-shaped rosette that will grow 18 inches high. It is a strong, definite-looking plant with a great deal of character.
**Requirements:** Should be firmly planted in an organic mix. It likes a shady location with the roots kept constantly wet, but it will turn brown in the winter if

there's too much humidity in the air. It does well at house temperature if it doesn't get above 75°F. Bathe it regularly, but keep water out of the rosette or you may have a problem with rot.

**Propagation:** Division, Spores
**Use:** Table, Terrarium
**Rating:** 2

**Botanical name:** ASPLENIUM viviparum
**Common name:** Mother Fern
**Origin:** Mauritius
**Description:** A compact fern with lacy, dark green leaves on which little plants sometimes grow from little "bulblets."
**Requirements:** It likes shade and organic soil kept wet. It also likes cool nights. In the winter, it will sometimes turn brown if the air is too wet. This asplenium is easy to propagate from the small plantlets that grow on the edge of the leaves. When the small plants look about ready to leave home, remove them with a part of the mother fern's leaf and plant them in a mix that's one-third garden soil, one-third peat, and one-third sand. Plant it so the old leaf is packed in, holding the young plant up until the roots form in about two weeks.
**Propagation:** Plantlets on the leaves
**Use:** Table, Terrarium
**Rating:** 2

*ASPLENIUM nidus*

*BEAUCARNEA recurvata*

**Botanical name:** BEAUCARNEA recurvata

**Common names:** Pony Tail, Bottle Palm, Elephant Foot

**Origin:** Mexico

**Description:** A treelike plant with a trunk swollen at the base topped by a rosette of long, thin straplike leaves. In time, it will grow to be a large-sized floor plant.

**Requirements:** It likes bright light and to be drenched and allowed to dry out between waterings. This succulent can exist for a long time on the water it stores, which makes it a great plant for people who have to be away a lot. Although a very tolerant plant, it prefers heavy soil with good drainage, dry air, and cool nights. An excellent house plant, it keeps its shape without having to be pinched, pruned or prodded.

**Propagation:** Seeds or Offshoots. But if you really want one, buying it is best; because the seeds are hard to come by and it may take longer to shoot off than you want to wait.

**Use:** Table, Floor

**Rating:** 5

**Botanical name:** BEGONIA species and varieties

**Origin:** South America

**Description:** There are many different kinds of begonias that grow well indoors. Some are grown for the beauty of their leaves, which come in many different shapes and are often marked with colors and metallic sheens, and others are grown for their flowers, which are rose, pink, red, salmon, yellow, and white.

**Requirements:** Like filtered light and to be kept evenly moist. Generally, they prefer house temperatures although some prefer cooler evenings, humid air, and good circulation. When you're making stem cuttings take them from the bottom of the plant, because plants grown from cuttings with flowers or buds on them usually don't shape up too well. Since the seeds are so very small, it's usually easier to reproduce plants from cuttings.

**Propagation:** Seeds, Cuttings, Division

**Use:** Table, Hanging Basket

**Rating:** 3

*BELOPERONE* guttata

**Botanical name:** BELOPERONE guttata

**Common name:** Shrimp Plant

**Origin:** Mexico

**Description:** A rank-growing, viny bush with dark green leaves. It has scales (bracts) the color and shape of boiled shrimp at the end of the branches. Sometimes an insignificant white flower appears between the scales. This is a sprawly plant that needs a lot of room.

**Requirements:** It likes bright light and to be drenched and allowed to dry. But it dries out very quickly. so it needs to be watered frequently. Don't hesitate to cut the plant back. or it will sprawl and look very ratty. It also prefers heavy soil with good drainage. cool night temperatures. and good air circulation. This is a plant that likes to rest after it has bloomed. and it often will droop and turn yellow. Sensitive to too little or too much water. it's a picky plant for growing inside.

**Propagation:** Cuttings
**Use:** Table. Hanging Basket
**Rating:** 1

*BOUGAINVILLEA glabra*

**Botanical name:** BOUGAIN-VILLEA glabra
**Origin:** Brazil
**Description:** A climbing shrub with dark green leaves and stout spine. The flowers are small and cream-colored. but they're set off by bright magenta or purple tissue-paperlike bracts. Although gorgeous when happy, it sulks easily. dropping its leaves and bracts. It will come back. though. if you do things its way.
**Requirements:** Bright light. When not blooming. it should be watered well and allowed to dry out a bit between waterings.

When it's blooming, it should be kept evenly moist. It also likes house temperatures, heavy soil, and good air circulation. After blooming, cut it back to encourage growth of new shoots and to keep it under control — if it's happy, it tries to take over. What it doesn't like is change, so if you want to move one, try to do it slowly, by stages, so it can become used to the new location.

**Propagation:** Cuttings
**Use:** Table, Hanging Basket
**Rating:** 2

**Botanical name:** BRASSAIA actinophylla (SCHEFFLERA actinophylla)
**Common names:** Australian Palm, Australian Umbrella Tree, Octopus Tree, Schefflera
**Origin:** Queensland (Australia), New Guinea, Java (Indonesia)
**Description:** A tree with large leaves made up of large leaflets arranged like spokes on an umbrella. Very bushy when young, it tends to lose lower leaves with age (as well as lack of light). It will grow as tall as you'll let it inside and will eventually be very bare with a tuft of leaves at the top.
**Requirements:** Likes bright light but will tolerate very low light. Prefers a good watering with the soil drying out quite a bit between each watering. It also likes heavy soil with good drainage, house temperatures,

*BRASSAIA actinophylla*

and dry air. Although an excellent house plant, some people can't forgive it for the lanky look of adolescence. This is easily remedied by planting in a pot with smaller plants that like a bit of shade.

**Propagation:** Cuttings
**Use:** Floor, Table
**Rating:** 4

**Botanical name:** BROMELIA-CEAE genus and species
This is a large family. For descriptions of particular plants within this family, see ANANAS, CRYPTANTHUS, GUZMANIA, TILLANDSIA, VRIESEA.

*CALADIUM hortulanum*

**Botanical name:** CALADIUM hortulanum
**Common name:** Fancy Leaved Caladium
**Description:** Stocky plants grown for the beautiful colors and markings on their large heart- or arrow-shaped leaves. The seedlings are all green, and it isn't until the fourth or fifth leaf that they begin to show their true colors.
**Requirements:** Filtered light, humid air, and to be kept evenly moist while they are actively growing. After they have lost their leaves and are resting, they don't need as much water, and the air can be dry. They

also prefer organic soil with a bit of sand to improve the drainage. If you plan to take them outside, choose green plants. The ones with all the color don't do as well as those that are mostly green.

**Propagation:** Seeds, Tubers
**Use:** Table
**Rating:** 1

**Botanical name:** CALATHEA insignis
**Origin:** Brazil
**Description:** Bushy plant with long, oval, wavy-edged leaves that grow to 18 inches. The top of the leaf is pale green marked with long and short blotches of dark green. The underside is a dark maroon. A healthy plant has the appearance of fine metalwork.
**Requirements:** Likes filtered light and to be kept evenly moist. Favorite soil is organic with about half sand for good drainage. It likes temperatures above 65°F and prefers high humidity although it does quite well in the average house and will survive a good deal of neglect.

**Propagation:** Division
**Use:** Table
**Rating:** 3

*CALATHEA insignis*

**Botanical name:** CALATHEA makoyana
**Common name:** Peacock Plant
**Origin:** Minas Gerais

**Description:** Bushy plant with broad, oblong, light olive-green leaves marked with dark green stripes and blotches on top and with purplish-red underneath.

**Requirements:** Filtered light and even moisture. The organic soil should have good drainage (about half sand), and they prefer a temperature over 65°F. If they don't get sufficient moisture, the leaves can turn brown around the edges and sometimes die off, but they will usually come back if their watering is attended to in a more orderly fashion.

**Propagation:** Division

**Use:** Table

**Rating:** 3

*CALATHEA makoyana*

**Botanical name:** CALATHEA ornata 'Sanderiana'

**Description:** Bushy plant with long oval leaves that are a glossy, leathery, dark olive-green on top and a plum-red below. The leaves of the immature plant are striped with bright rose. The stripes turn white in adolescence and disappear in maturity.

**Requirements:** Filtered light, good drainage, and even moisture. They like organic soil that is about half sand, and they prefer temperatures over 65°F and high humidity.

**Propagation:** Division

**Use:** Table

**Rating:** 3

**Botanical name:** CALCEOLARIA
herbeohybrida
**Common name:** Pocketbook
Plant
**Origin:** Cool Andes of Chile
**Description:** A pot plant with
balloonlike red, yellow, or
orange spotted flowers that
grow in a cluster over bright
green leaves. A plant to be en-
joyed as one would a bunch of
cut flowers since it is very
unhappy in ordinary house
situations.
**Requirements:** Likes to be
drenched and let dry with
filtered light, organic soil, and a
night temperature of 50°F. If you
can give them cold nights, they
will keep longer, but they are
annuals and once through
flowering they will not bloom
again.
**Propagation:** Purchase (seeds are
very small and in a house situation the young plants are very
weak and tend to rot)
**Use:** Table
**Rating:** 1

*CALCEOLARIA herbeohybrida*

**Botanical name:** CALLISIA
elegans (SETCREASEA striata)
**Common names:** Wandering Jew,
Striped Inch Plant
**Origin:** Oaxaca (Mexico)
**Description:** Enthusiastic vining
plant that stays close to the
ground. It has olive-green
leaves that are striped with
white on top and purple under-

neath. And it has small white flowers.

**Requirements:** Filtered light, even moisture, heavy soil, and circulating air. It prefers cool night temperatures, but is quite tolerant of house temperatures.

**Propagation:** Cuttings

**Use:** Table, Hanging Basket

**Rating:** 4

*CALLISIA elegans*

**Botanical name:** CALLISIA fragrans

**Origin:** Oaxaca (Mexico)

**Description:** Fresh, glossy, green plant with long vining runners. Sometimes, in a strong light, they turn purplish at the edges. It also has white flowers.

**Requirements:** Filtered light, even moisture, heavy soil with good drainage, and well-circulating air. Although it prefers cool night temperatures, it's pretty tolerant.

**Propagation:** Cuttings

**Use:** Table, Hanging Basket

**Rating:** 4

**Botanical name:** CAMELLIA japonica

**Origin:** Mountains of Japan and Korea

**Description:** Well-shaped, small, ornamental tree with glossy, dark green, leathery, evergreen leaves. The flowers are single or double and are white, pink, red, or combinations of these colors.

**Requirements:** Filtered light and plenty of water. The organic soil should contain sand to help the drainage. Camellias are very particular plants, requiring cold night temperatures and good air circulation. The plants with double flowers often drop all their buds, and they all resent being moved when their buds are forming. If you have to move one, mark the plant so that it can be relocated with the same side to the light.

**Propagation:** Cuttings
**Use:** Floor, Table
**Rating:** 1

*CAMELLIA japonica*

**Botanical name:** CAPSICUM annuum 'Conoides'
**Common name:** Christmas Pepper
**Origin:** South America
**Description:** A dense, bushy plant with bright green leaves. The white flowers are followed by one-inch whitish peppers which turn bright red. The peppers are edible but quite hot, and care should be taken not to rub the eyes with fingers that have been bruising them.
**Requirements:** Bright light, even moisture, and heavy soil, with good air circulation at regular house temperatures. Although it sometimes lives longer, this

pepper is usually treated as an annual.
**Propagation:** Seeds
**Use:** Table
**Rating:** 1

**Botanical name:** CARISSA grandiflora
**Common name:** Natal Plum
**Origin:** Natal (Africa)
**Description:** A sprawly shrub with dark green, shiny leaves. The fragrant, star-shaped, white flowers are sometimes followed by red plumlike fruit. This plant can be used as an instant bonsai by pruning away some of the branches.
**Requirements:** Bright light, even moisture, heavy soil and cool temperatures with good air circulation. Frequent showering helps keep the leaves shiny.
**Propagation:** Cuttings, Seeds
**Use:** Table
**Rating:** 3

*CARYOTA mitis*

**Botanical name:** CARYOTA mitis
**Common name:** Fishtail Palm
**Origin:** Burma, Malaya, Indonesia
**Description:** A palm with many suckers growing up from the base. The dull, dark green leaves look as if they were covered with triangular, ragged-edged fish tails.
**Requirements:** Filtered light, heavy soil kept wet, dry air, and house temperatures. If the tem-

perature goes down, the watering should be cut down too because the cool temperature and too much water can cause the roots to rot, especially in the winter.

**Propagation:** Seeds, Offshoots
**Use:** Floor, Table
**Rating:** 5

**Botanical name:** CEPHALOCEREUS senilis
**Common name:** Old Man Cactus
**Origin:** Mexico
**Description:** A cylindrical cactus with white bristles that are two to four inches long and look like hair. As it gets older, it also gets strong yellowish spines. The flowers are rosy purple and quite beautiful.
**Requirements:** Bright light, heavy soil with good drainage, and house temperatures, though tolerant of dry air. Normally likes to be drenched and let dry between waterings, but needs less water in the wintertime. It's hair can be brushed with a soft toothbrush or left natural.
**Propagation:** Cuttings, Offshoots
**Use:** Table
**Rating:** 5

**Botanical name:** CEROPEGIA debilis
**Origin:** Nyassaland (Africa)
**Description:** A threadlike vine with narrow pointed leaves. It

*CEPHALOCEREUS senilis*

has small, thin, lanternlike flowers.

**Requirements:** Filtered light, organic soil with good drainage, dry air, and cool night temperatures. Normally it should be drenched and let dry, but it needs much less water during its resting period. It's not a showy plant, but it doesn't get upset if it isn't watered for a long time. The stems may drop off, but usually new shoots will start again when watering is restarted.

**Propagation:** Division, Cuttings
**Use:** Table, Hanging Basket
**Rating:** 3

*CEROPEGIA debilis*

**Botanical name:** CEROPEGIA radicans

**Description:** Succulent hanging vine with pointed, opposite, spadelike leaves. Flower looks like a small green and white (with a touch of purple) lantern. A small plant with a long life.

**Requirements:** Filtered light, organic soil, drench and let dry. Needs good drainage and much less water during its resting period. This plant takes a long period without water and will usually come back when watering is restarted. Dry air and cool night temperatures.

**Propagation:** Cuttings, Division
**Use:** Table, Hanging Basket
**Rating:** 4

**Botanical name:** CEROPEGIA woodii

**Common names:** String of Hearts, Rosary Vine, Chinese Lantern Plant

**Origin:** Natal

**Description:** Threadlike vine with opposite heart-shaped, silver-marked leaves. The vine will grow very long and will tangle easily so some people keep them wound up on a hoop. Flowers look like small purplish baskets or lanterns.

**Requirements:** Filtered light, organic soil, drench and let dry. Needs good drainage and less water during its resting period and can go a long time without water. The name rosary vine comes from the small storage beads (along the stem) that help the plant get through long periods of neglect. Good dry air circulation and cool night temperatures.

**Propagation:** Cuttings, Division

**Use:** Table, Hanging Basket

**Rating:** 5

**Botanical name:** CHAMAE-DOREA elegans 'Bella' (Neanthe bella)

**Common name:** Parlor Palm

**Origin:** Mexico

**Description:** A slow-growing dwarf palm with graceful, thin stems and leathery, dark green leaves. The flowers are reddish orange.

**Requirements:** It will tolerate low light intensity, but it is insistent

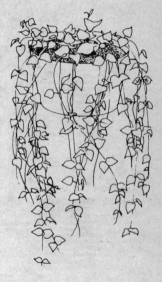

*CEROPEGIA woodii*

*CHAMAEDOREA elegans 'Bella'*

that its heavy soil be kept evenly moist and have good drainage. It's happy with house temperatures and dry air. Although it flowers without too much difficulty, you need both a male and a female plant to produce a seed. Since it's impossible to tell which is which until it blooms, you may end up buying two male plants. Therefore, the best way to get a plant that blooms is to start with the seed.

**Propagation:** Seeds
**Use:** Floor, Table
**Rating:** 5

**Botanical name:** CHAMAE-DOREA erumpens
**Common name:** Bamboo Palm
**Origin:** Honduras
**Description:** Bushy erect palm with clumps of bamboo-like canes and papery, dark green leaves that grow all the way down to the bottom of the plant. A mature, well-established plant does very well inside — really makes itself at home. This is one of the few plants that doesn't lose all its bottom leaves in poor light.
**Requirements:** Will tolerate low light intensity. Likes heavy soil with good drainage and likes to be kept evenly moist. It also prefers house temperatures and dry air.
**Propagation:** Seeds
**Use:** Floor, Table
**Rating:** 5

*CHAMAEDOREA erumpens*

**Botanical name:** CHAMAEROPS
humilis

**Common name:** European Fan
Palm

**Origin:** Mediterranean. South
Europe, North Africa

**Description:** Bushy palm with stiff
leaves in the shape of large
fans. A tolerant, rather slow
growing plant that will keep its
place.

**Requirements:** Bright light (will
survive with less). wet, with less
water in winter if your house is
kept cold. Heavy soil, one-third
sand for good drainage. Prefers
good air circulation and cool
temperatures but is very accommodating. Since it grows low
and bushy it should have space
so it can be appreciated.

**Propagation:** Seeds. Offsets

**Use:** Floor. Table

**Rating:** 4

*CHAMAEROPS humilis*

**Botanical name:** CHLOROPHY-
TUM capense (CHLOROPHY-
TUM elatum)

**Common name:** Spider Plant

**Origin:** South Africa. E. Cape Province

**Description:** Rosette of straplike.
bright green leaves. White
flowers appear in open clusters
at the ends of stems.

**Requirements:** Evenly moist,
heavy soil. cool night temperatures. and good air circula-

tion. They prefer filtered light.
but are tolerant of low light.
**Propagation:** Division, Plantlets
**Use:** Table, Hanging Basket
**Rating:** 5

**Botanical name:** CHLOROPHY-
TUM comosum
**Common names:** Spider Plant.
Airplane Plant. Ribbon Plant
**Description:** Rosettes of green-
and white-striped, strap-shaped
leaves. Loose clusters of
flowers appear on the end of
long stems which later are
followed by clusters of leaves
which develop into little plants
with roots ready to pot.
**Requirements:** Filtered light.
even moisture. heavy soil. and
good air circulation. They
prefer cool night temperatures.
but are very tolerant of house
conditions.
**Propagation:** Division. Plantlets
**Use:** Table, Hanging Basket
**Rating:** 5

*CHLOROPHYTUM comosum*

**Botanical name:** CHRYSANTHE-
MUM morifolium (CHRYSAN-
THEMUM hortorum)
**Common name:** Mum
**Origin:** China
**Description:** A many branched
plant with woody stems and
fragrant (smelly) leaves. It has
showy flowers in every color ex-
cept blue.

**Requirements:** Bright light and even moisture. Likes heavy soil, cold nights, and fresh air. It should be treated as a transient guest rather than a member of the family since, in addition to falling apart in a warm environment, it needs short days to flower. The most elegant ones are not hardy in the North.

**Propagation:** Cuttings, Root Division

**Use:** Table

**Rating:** 1

*CHRYSANTHEMUM morifolium*

**Botanical name:** CIBOTIUM schiedei

**Common name:** Mexican Tree Fern

**Origin:** Mountains of Mexico and Guatemala

**Description:** Large fern with lacy, light green, leathery fronds which range from 18 inches to 3 feet long, and which will eventually, after many years, form a trunk.

**Requirements:** Filtered light, even moisture, and organic soil with good drainage. It is tolerant of dry air.

**Propagation:** Purchase

**Use:** Floor, Table

**Rating:** 4

**Botanical name:** CISSUS antarctica

**Common names:** Kangaroo Vine, Kangaroo Ivy, Treebine, African Tree Grape

**Origin:** New South Wales

**Description:** A shrubby plant with climbing branches that help themselves along with tendrils. It has firm, shiny, green leaves with brown veins and stems.

**Requirements:** Filtered light, heavy soil with good drainage, and dry air. Drench it and then let it dry. It prefers cool night temperatures, but it can take the heat. A friend of red spider, especially when kept dry, it also loses its leaves when not watered for a long period of time.

**Propagation:** Cuttings

**Use:** Table, Hanging Basket

**Rating:** 4

**Botanical name:** CISSUS rhombifolia

**Common names:** Grape Ivy, Treebine

**Origin:** West Indies, Northern South America

**Description:** A vinelike plant with hairy brown branches that climb with the help of tendrils. The three-part, shiny, green leaves have brown veins, and the undersides of the leaves are covered with thin white felt, as in the new young growth.

**Requirements:** Filtered light, heavy soil with good drainage. To water, drench it and then let it dry. It likes good air circulation, cool to house night temperatures. It grows well on end tables under lamps that are lit

*CISSUS antarctica*

at night. It attracts red spider when kept too dry, and the dead leaves must be picked out of the tangled mass of vines. Its leaves turn brown when it isn't watered regularly. This is an excellent plant for organized people, but it can be a lot of work if you are not.

**Propagation:** Cuttings
**Use:** Table, Hanging Basket
**Rating:** 4

*CISSUS rhombifolia*

**Botanical name:** CITRUS limon 'Ponderosa'
**Common name:** American Wonderlemon
**Description:** Small tree (to eight feet) with shiny, leathery, green leaves and stout spines. Flowers are waxy white and very fragrant. Fruit is large, looking a bit like a grapefruit.
**Requirements:** Bright light. Let the soil partially dry out between waterings in winter. This plant uses more water in summer. Heavy soil with good drainage and cool night temperature with good air circulation. A strong plant, it will grow for years in a large tub without many problems except scale. Fruit is encouraged by using a soft watercolor brush to spread the pollen about. Most of the small fruit drops off, leaving one to grow to maturity.
**Propagation:** Cuttings
**Use:** Floor, Table
**Rating:** 3

**Botanical name:** CITRUS mitis 'Calamondin'

**Common name:** Calamondin Orange

**Origin:** Philippines

**Description:** A dwarf shrub with shiny, green, leathery leaves. It has fragrant, white, waxy flowers and small sour oranges which are generally less than one inch in diameter, and have a sweetish skin like a kumquat.

**Requirements:** Bright light, heavy soil, cool night temperatures, and good air circulation. In the winter, it likes watering that lets the soil partially dry out; but in the summer it needs more even moisture. The oranges make a great marmalade if you can get enough of them together at any one time.

**Propagation:** Seeds, Cuttings

**Use:** Table

**Rating:** 3

*CITRUS mitis 'Calamondin'*

**Botanical name:** CITRUS paradisi

**Common name:** Grapefruit

**Origin:** West Indies

**Description:** A small tree with large, shiny, leathery, dark green leaves. The white, fragrant flowers are larger and thicker than those of the other citrus. The fruit is large, round, and pale yellow.

**Requirements:** Bright light. Let the soil partially dry out between waterings in the wintertime. It needs even moisture during its active growing season in the summer. Likes heavy soil with good drainage, cool night temperatures, and good air circulation. They're easy to grow in small groves from seeds left over from breakfast (see "Fun With Plants").

**Propagation:** Seeds, Cuttings
**Use:** Floor, Table
**Rating:** 2

**Botanical name:** CITRUS sinensis
**Common name:** Sweet Orange
**Origin:** Kwangtung, Viet Nam
**Description:** A tree with regular branches and dark green, shiny, leathery leaves. It has waxy, white, fragrant flowers and an orange-colored fruit. Sometimes it has spines that are slender, flexible, and rather blunt.
**Requirements:** Bright light. Let the soil partially dry out between waterings in wintertime, with more even moisture in the summer. Heavy soil with good drainage, cool nights, and good air circulation. It is more cold resistant than lemons or limes. Easy to grow from seeds, it makes a good pot plant, either singly or in clumps.
**Propagation:** Seeds, Cuttings
**Use:** Floor, Table
**Rating:** 2

**Botanical name:** CLIVIA miniata
**Common name:** Kafir Lily
**Origin:** Natal (Africa)

**Description:** A large plant with leathery, straplike, bright green leaves. Red-orange, bell-shaped flowers appear in a cluster on top of a long stalk. It has thick, fleshy roots like an agapanthus and keeps its leaves all year round.

**Requirements:** Filtered light, heavy soil with good drainage, cool night temperatures, and good air circulation. It likes being drenched and then allowed to dry. Propagate them by dividing the old plants that have become very crowded in their pots. This is a great plant if there is plenty of room.

**Propagation:** Division
**Use:** Floor, Table
**Rating:** 2

*CLIVIA miniata*

**Botanical name:** CODIAEUM (CROTON) variegatum
**Common name:** Croton
**Origin:** Southern India, Ceylon, Malaya
**Description:** A lush, leafy shrub with brightly colored leaves. It's available in a great variety of leaf shapes and colors. The colors range from almost pure white, through the yellows, oranges and reds. These colors are often combined with each other and with green. Crotons are real favorites of red spiders and mealybugs.
**Requirements:** Bright light and even moisture. Use a heavy soil with excellent drainage. They

need warm temperatures, good circulation, and high humidity. If they don't get enough humidity the leaves drop off. This is beautiful outdoors in the tropics or inside in a warm greenhouse, but it's hardly ever happy in a house or apartment.

**Propagation:** Cuttings
**Use:** Floor, Table
**Rating:** 1

*COFFEA arabica*

**Botanical name:** COFFEA arabica
**Common name:** Coffee
**Origin:** Ethiopia, Angola
**Description:** A small slender tree with shiny, leathery, dark green leaves. White, fragrant flowers grow out at the base of the leaves and are followed by cranberry-looking berries. It often has flowers and both red and green berries on branches at the same time.
**Requirements:** Filtered light, even moisture, and good air circulation. It prefers house temperatures although it can take it quite cool at night. In the same family as the citrus trees, they can be grown together for the breakfast table.
**Propagation:** Seeds, Cuttings
**Use:** Floor, Table
**Rating:** 3

**Botanical name:** COLEUS blumei
**Common name:** Coleus
**Origin:** Java (Indonesia)
**Description:** A brightly colored plant with square stems and op-

posite leaves. There is great variety in the leaf shapes and coloring. The most important thing for their good looks is youth. Old plants get scrawny and lose the full look of the young plants.

**Requirements:** Bright light, even moisture, heavy soil, house temperatures, and circulating air. To encourage fuller growth, the ends should be cut back regularly. These cuttings can be used to start new plants — which should be done regularly if you like the look of the plant you bought or were given.

**Propagation:** Seeds, Cuttings

**Use:** Table, Hanging Basket

**Rating:** 3

*COLEUS blumei*

**Botanical name:** COLUMNEA gloriosa

**Origin:** Costa Rica

**Description:** A good basket plant. It has weak, hanging stems covered with small, oval, opposite leaves that are covered with reddish-brown hair. The red and yellow flowers are trumpet-shaped.

**Requirements:** Filtered light, even moisture, and organic soil with good drainage. Prefers high humidity, but will survive in the ordinary house situation. It does best in a hanging basket; however, keeping it evenly moist up there can be a

bit of a problem.
**Propagation:** Cuttings
**Use:** Table, Hanging Basket, Terrarium
**Rating:** 2

**Botanical name:** COLUMNEA hirta
**Origin:** Costa Rica
**Description:** A creeping plant with stems that are covered with red hairs. It has shiny, oval, reddish leaves, and red flowers that are marked with orange. The flowers are smaller than those of *COLUMNEA gloriosa* but are more plentiful.
**Requirements:** Filtered light, organic soil that is kept evenly moist, house temperatures, and a humid atmosphere.
**Propagation:** Cuttings
**Use:** Table, Hanging Basket, Terrarium
**Rating:** 2

*COLUMNEA hirta*

**Botanical name:** CORDYLINE australis, DRACAENA indivisa of florists
**Common name:** Grass Palm
**Origin:** New Zealand
**Description:** Large cluster of long, narrow, leathery, bronze green leaves that come out of the top of an erect stem. It looks a lot like a dracaena, but you can tell them apart by looking at the roots. Those of the cordyline are white while those of the dracaena are yellowish.

Also, after flowering the cordyline has a lot of seeds in each fruit while the dracaena has only one.

**Requirements:** Filtered light, even moisture, heavy soil with good drainage, house temperatures, and good air circulation. The lower light and humidity in most house situations cause them to lose their lower leaves.

**Propagation:** Seeds, Stem Cuttings.

The stem, from which all the leaves have been removed is laid flat and barely covered with soil with good drainage. They should be kept moist and at about 80°F. When the shoots develop about five leaves, they are separated and potted separately.

**Use:** Floor, Table

**Rating:** 3

**Botanical name:** CORDYLINE terminalis

**Common names:** Red Dracaena, Ti Plant

**Origin:** India, Malaysia to Polynesia

**Description:** Clusters of rosy-red to dark-red leaves on the top of a canelike stalk. The young winter leaves are the lighter color. The flowers are lavender and are followed by red berries.

**Requirements:** Filtered light, even moisture, heavy soil with good drainage, and house temperatures with good air circula-

*CORDYLINE terminalis*

tion. Lower light and humidity cause them to lose most of their lower leaves.

**Propagation:** Stem Cuttings laid flat in moist soil kept at about 80°F. When the shoot develops about five leaves, they should be potted up separately.

**Use:** Floor, Table

**Rating:** 3

**Botanical name:** CRASSULA arborescens

**Common name:** Silver Dollar

**Origin:** Cape Province, Natal (Africa)

**Description:** A treelike succulent with thick, grey stems and flat, fleshy, grey-green, opposite leaves that are dotted with red. The flowers are white but turn pink with age. This is often called *CRASSULA argentea* by growers.

**Requirements:** Filtered light and heavy soil with good drainage. (Place some broken brick in the bottom of the pot.) It likes to be drenched and let dry, cool night temperatures and good air circulation. Not a fussy plant, it can take almost any house condition, except too much water.

**Propagation:** Cuttings

**Use:** Floor, Table

**Rating:** 4

**Botanical name:** CRASSULA argentea

**Common names:** Jade Plant, Chinese Rubber Plant

*CRASSULA arborescens*

**Origin:** Cape Province. Natal (Africa)

**Description:** Much branching, thick-stemmed treelike succulent that has thick, fleshy, glossy, jade green leaves. The top of the leaves, which turn reddish in the sun, are padded, and the bottoms are flat. The flowers are very light pink. This plant is often called *CRASSULA arborescens* by growers.

**Requirements:** Filtered light, heavy soil with good drainage (a few pieces of broken brick in the pot helps), cool night temperatures, and good air circulation. It likes to be drenched and let dry. Unless watered too much, it will grow to a splendid old age, four or five feet tall on a very heavy trunk.

**Propagation:** Cuttings

**Use:** Floor. Table

**Rating:** 4

**Botanical name:** CRASSULA pyramidalis

**Origin:** Cape Province. Namaqualand (Africa)

**Description:** Small, bright green, succulent plant with equal-sized triangular, flat leaves stacked one on top of the other like pancakes. The whitish flowers appear at the top of the stack.

**Requirements:** Filtered light, heavy soil with good drainage, cool night temperatures, and good air circulation. It likes to

*CRASSULA argentea*

be drenched and let dry.

**Propagation:** Cuttings
**Use:** Table
**Rating:** 4

**Botanical name:** CROCUS species
**Origin:** Mediterranean
**Description:** A plant with thin straplike leaves four to seven inches long. It has cheerful lilylike flowers in white, lavender-blues, yellows, and combinations. Saffron, probably the world's highest priced food, is obtained from the pollen of *CROCUS sativus*. About 4300 flowers are needed to produce an ounce of the subtle flavoring essential to many Mediterranean dishes.
**Requirements:** Bright light, even moisture, and heavy soil. A period of dormancy is needed when they must be kept cold but not allowed to dry out. When forced for indoor use, they do best if they are kept on the cool side in good air circulation.
**Propagation:** Bulbs
**Use:** Table
**Rating:** 1

*CRYPTANTHUS
zonatus 'Zebrinus'*

**Botanical name:** CRYPTANTHUS zonatus 'Zebrinus'
**Common name:** Zebra Plant
**Origin:** Pernambuco
**Description:** A beautiful bromeliad with a bronzy purple, wavy rosette of leaves that are marked with silvery to light

brown horizontal bands. They are sometimes called earth stars because they grow in the ground. They look their best when they can be viewed from on top. The flower is whitish and pretty much hidden.

**Requirements:** Filtered light, organic soil with good drainage, house temperatures and dry air. It likes its soil to be drenched and allowed to dry, but at the same time, it wants its "vase" kept filled with water at all times.

**Propagation:** Remove offshoots or plantlets called "pups," which appear between the leaves of the older plant, and pot separately.

**Use:** Table

**Rating:** 5

**Botanical name:** CYANOTIS somaliensis

**Common name:** Pussy Ears

**Origin:** Somaliland (Africa)

**Description:** A viny plant that looks like a furry wandering Jew. It has glossy green leaves covered with soft white hair. The flowers are purple. It makes a compact hanging basket and is interesting combined with other similar plants.

**Requirements:** Bright light, drench and let dry between waterings. If you wait too long to water, the little green leaves turn brown. Likes heavy soil with good drainage, cool

*CYANOTIS somaliensis*

nights, and good air circulation.
**Propagation:** Cuttings
**Use:** Table, Hanging Baskets
**Rating:** 3

**Botanical name:** CYATHEA arborea
**Common name:** Tree Fern
**Origin:** Mountains of Puerto Rico to Jamaica
**Description:** A tree fern with a brown trunk whose upper part is covered with brown hair. The fronds are bright green, although paler underneath and are much divided.
**Requirements:** Filtered light, organic soil kept wet, house temperatures, and humid circulating air. The trunk should also be kept constantly moist. It needs a very small pot since it produces very few offshoots.
**Propagation:** Spores
**Use:** Floor, Table
**Rating:** 3

*CYATHEA arborea*

**Botanical name:** CYCAS revoluta
**Common name:** Sago Palm
**Origin:** South Japan to Java
**Description:** Palmlike plant with huge fernlike leaves two to six feet long. The leaves grow in a giant rosette made up of hard, shiny, dark green leaflets that wear like iron. A whole circle of leaves appears at one time. A

very slow growing and well-disciplined plant that needs a lot of room.

**Requirements:** Filtered light, heavy soil with good drainage, cool night temperatures, and dry air. It likes to be drenched and then allowed to dry. If a large plant has to be moved, sometimes the easiest thing to do is to cut off all the leaves and start it up again at its new location since the leaves are so symmetrical and damage to them really shows.

**Propagation:** Seeds.

**Use:** Floor, Table

**Rating:** 5

**Botanical name:** CYCLAMEN persicum

**Common names:** Florist's Cyclamen or Alpine Violet

**Origin:** Greece to Syria

**Description:** Beautiful plants, with large, succulent, heart-shaped leaves marked with silver. They have nodding, single or double flowers of rose, white, salmon, lavender, or red that are held on single stems above the leaves.

**Requirements:** Filtered light, even moisture, organic soil with good drainage, good air circulation, and cold night temperatures — 50°F is ideal when they are flowering. In most situations, should be treated like a potted bouquet — just a short-time visitor. They grow best from seeds (it takes about

*CYCLAMEN persicum*

15 - 18 months) since they don't care to have their tubers dried out. A certain number of the seedlings will just sit and sulk and refuse to grow, and nothing you can do will tempt them. To avoid excess frustration, throw them out. This is a very challenging plant to try and grow.

**Propagation:** Seed (preferably) Tubers

**Use:** Table

**Rating:** 1

*CYPERUS alternifolius*

**Botanical name:** CYPERUS alternifolius

**Common name:** Umbrella Plant

**Description:** Clumps of one-and-a-half to four-foot green three-angled stems with long grasslike umbrella spokes around the top. The flowers are green to brown fuzzies that come out at the top of the stem.

**Requirements:** Filtered light, heavy soil, dry air, and cool night temperatures. The plant is happiest when sitting in water all day. If it doesn't get enough water, the tips of the leaves turn brown — first the tips and then the plant. The brown end can be cut off, but it's better to keep the plant sitting in water since there's a limit to how far back one can cut them.

**Propagation:** Division

**Use:** Floor, Table

**Rating:** 4

**Botanical name:** CYPERUS papyrus

**Common name:** Egyptian Paper Plant

**Origin:** Egypt

**Description:** Clumps of four- to seven-foot long stout, dark green stems topped with a droopy brush of threadlike leaves. The flowers are light brown. This is a very dramatic plant for an indoor pool.

**Requirements:** Filtered light, and heavy soil kept wet. It's happiest when sitting in water all the time. It also likes cool night temperatures and dry air.

**Propagation:** Division

**Use:** Floor, Table

**Rating:** 4

*CYRTOMIUM falcatum*

**Botanical name:** CYRTOMIUM falcatum (ASPIDIUM falcatum)

**Common name:** Hollyfern

**Origin:** Japan, China, India, Celebes, Hawaii

**Description:** Fern with brownish hairy stalks and shiny dark green leaflets. One of the few ferns that will grow under house conditions.

**Requirements:** Low light intensity to filtered light. Heavy soil with good drainage kept evenly moist. Cool night temperatures with good air circulation. This fern, because of the hard surface on its fronds, will tolerate dry air. Like most ferns, it is happiest with a set routine and not too happy about creative variations in watering, light, temperature, etc.

**Propagation:** Division
**Use:** Table, Terrarium
**Rating:** 3

**Botanical name:** DAVALLIA species
**Common name:** Rabbit Foot Ferns
**Description:** Ferns with creeping stems that look like small paws covered with wooly or hairy scales in brown, black, or white.
**Requirements:** Will tolerate low light. Likes evenly moist organic soil with good drainage. Cool to house night temperatures and good dry air circulation. As they grow older they seem to like more light.
**Propagation:** Division
**Use:** Table, Terrarium
**Rating:** 2

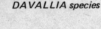

*DAVALLIA species*

**Botanical name:** DIEFFEN-BACHIA amoena
**Common names:** Dumb Cane, Tuftroot, Charming Dieffen-bachia, Mother-in-Law Plant
**Origin:** Colombia, Costa Rica
**Description:** A handsome, thick-stemmed, large-leaved, foliage plant. The oblong pointed leaves are dark green marked with creamy white and have splotchy stripes along the veins.

Biting the stalk can cause very painful swelling of the tongue and mouth, so this is not a plant to keep around pets or children who are liable to taste your plants. The sap is also very painful on cuts.

**Requirements:** Filtered light and heavy soil with good drainage. It should be drenched and let dry but shouldn't be permitted to become soggy. The temperature always must be above 65°F, and it's happy with dry air. It should be kept growing all the time because each individual leaf doesn't last too long. And if there are no new ones, all you'll have in time is a stalk. When the stalk gets too long, cut it off at the top and reroot it; new leaves will come up from the old base also, so you'll end up with two plants.

**Propagation:** Cutting
**Use:** Floor, Table
**Rating:** 5

**Botanical name:** DIEFFEN-BACHIA exotica
**Common name:** Exotic Dieffen-bachia
**Origin:** Costa Rica
**Description:** A handsome, compact plant with long, narrow, dark green leaves splotched with creamy white. Biting the stalk can cause painful swelling of the tongue and mouth. In fact, in Central America, messengers were often given a

*DIEFFENBACHIA exotica*

good chew of dumb cane to keep them from talking till they got to where they were going with the message.

**Requirements:** Filtered light, heavy soil with good drainage which is drenched and let dry, dry air, and temperatures above 65°F. Since the individual leaves are short-lived, the plant should be kept growing. When the stalk gets too long, it can be cut off and rerooted.

**Propagation:** Cuttings

**Use:** Floor, Table

**Rating:** 5

*DIEFFENBACHIA picta*

**Botanical name:** DIEFFENBACHIA picta (DIEFFENBACHIA brasiliensis)

**Common name:** Variable Dieffenbachia

**Origin:** Brazil

**Description:** A thick-stemmed, plant with large, oval-pointed leaves. Each leaf varies in color from dark green, pale green, to creamy white.

**Requirements:** Filtered light, heavy soil with good drainage, dry air, and temperatures over 65°F. It likes to be drenched and let dry. Since the individual leaves are short-lived, keep new leaves coming to slow down the appearance of the naked stalk. The leafy top can be cut off and rerooted, and the excess cane laid on sandy soil where it will send up shoots at each joint. New shoots will probably start up from the base of the old plant where the cutting was made.

**Propagation:** Cuttings
**Use:** Floor, Table
**Rating:** 5

**Botanical name:** DIEFFEN-BACHIA seguina
**Origin:** Puerto Rico, West Indies
**Description:** A strong-growing foliage plant with thick stems and long, oval, dark green leaves. The sap causes swelling and can be painful on a cut or in the mouth.
**Requirements:** Filtered light, heavy soil with good drainage, dry air, and temperatures kept above 65°F. It should be drenched and then let dry. Since the individual leaves are short-lived, the new ones should be kept coming or the plant will go to stalk. When the stalk gets too long, it can be cut off and rerooted.
**Propagation:** Cuttings
**Use:** Floor, Table
**Rating:** 5

**Botanical name:** DIZYGOTHECA elegantissima
**Common names:** False Aralia, Threadleaf, Finger Aralia
**Origin:** New Hebrides

*DIZYGOTHECA elegantissima*

**Description:** Small tree with thin, narrow, bronze-green leaflets that grow from a single stem. It grows to six feet or more inside. In dry air and less than optimum light, it loses its lower leaves, giving it a slender palmlike look that many people prefer over its normal very leafy, fussy-looking appearance.

**Requirements:** Filtered light, even moisture, good air circulation, heavy soil, and house temperatures. It needs less water in the wintertime and at lower temperatures. The roots may rot if they get more water than they want. It's better to keep this plant too dry and lose some leaves than too wet and lose the plant.

**Propagation:** Cuttings

**Use:** Floor, Table

**Rating:** 3

**Botanical name:** DRACAENA deremensis

**Description:** A thick, tall stem that easily grows over eight feet high. It has long, narrow, grey-green leaves with a couple of silvery stripes that are bordered on the outside with dark green. The small flowers, which are dark red on the outside and white on the inside, grow in a large cluster and stink.

**Requirements:** Filtered light, heavy soil with good drainage, house temperatures, and dry air. The plant should be kept wet but not soggy. Keep the leaves dry or you may have leaf spot disease that starts out small but can take over the whole plant, especially if the young leaves are kept wet.

**Propagation:** Seeds, Stem Cuttings, Root Cuttings

**Use:** Floor, Table

**Rating:** 5

**Botanical name:** DRACAENA draco

**Common name:** Dragon Tree

**Origin:** Canary Islands

**Description:** A tree with a heavy trunk and with thick rosettes of fleshy, sword-shaped, sharp, blue-green leaves. It has a red, tasteless, odorless sap that was once sold as genuine dragon's blood and burns with a bright light.

**Requirements:** Filtered light, heavy soil with good drainage, house temperatures, and dry air. The plant likes being kept wet but not soggy.

**Propagation:** Stem Cuttings

**Use:** Floor, Table

**Rating:** 5

*DRACAENA*
*fragrans massangeana*

**Botanical name:** DRACAENA fragrans massangeana

**Description:** A tall stalk with floppy rosettes of dark green leaves striped with lighter green and with a yellow stripe down the middle.

**Requirements:** Filtered light, heavy soil with good drainage, house temperatures, and dry air. Keep the roots wet but the leaves dry.

**Propagation:** Stem Cuttings

**Use:** Floor, Table

**Rating:** 5

*DRACAENA godseffiana*

**Botanical name:** DRACAENA godseffiana

**Common name:** Gold Dust Dracaena

**Origin:** Congo, Guinea

**Description:** A small shrubby plant with thin stems and small, oval, dark green leaves. The leaves have yellow spots which turn creamy when the plant gets older. It has greenish flowers.

**Requirements:** Filtered light, heavy soil with good drainage, house temperatures, and dry air. Keep the soil wet but the leaves dry.

**Propagation:** Cuttings

**Use:** Table

**Rating:** 4

**Botanical name:** DRACAENA marginata

**Common name:** Red Margined Dracaena

**Origin:** Madagascar

**Description:** It has a tall, thin, greyish trunk and branches with thick rosettes of long, thin, pointed, red-edged, dark green leaves at the ends. This is a slow growing, durable plant.

**Requirements:** Filtered light, heavy soil, and good drainage. Keep the roots wet and the leaves dry. It is a very tolerant plant inside, liking house temperature and dry air.

**Propagation:** Cuttings
**Use:** Floor, Table
**Rating:** 5

**Botanical name:** DRACAENA sanderiana
**Origin:** Cameroons, Congo
**Description:** A rosette of white-edged, dark cloudy-green leaves that climb up on a slender cane until it flops over.
**Requirements:** Filtered light, heavy soil with good drainage that's kept wet, and house temperatures. It likes its air dry, but likes it more humid than the rest of the dracaenas do. It can be planted in a large bottle garden, but will eventually come out the top.
**Propagation:** Cuttings
**Use:** Floor, Table
**Rating:** 5

*DRACAENA marginata*

**Botanical name:** ECHEVERIA derenbergii
**Common name:** Painted Lady
**Origin:** Oaxaca
**Description:** Clusters of

rosettes of thick pale green leaves that are tipped with red. Lots of orangy yellow flowers.

**Requirements:** Bright light. Drench, let dry. Prefers good soil drainage (though not too particular about type of soil), cool nights and good air circulation.

**Propagation:** Cuttings

**Use:** Table

**Rating:** 5

**Botanical name:** ECHEVERIA elegans

**Common name:** Mexican Snowball

**Origin:** Hidalgo

**Description:** Fleshy rosettes of waxy blue leaves with translucent margins. The flowers are rosy pink on pink stems. This is a very definite and disciplined-looking plant.

**Requirements:** Bright light, heavy soil with good drainage, cool nights, and good air circulation. Likes to be drenched and then let dry. When making leaf cuttings, make sure the dormant bud next to the leaf goes with the cutting or the leaf will root but you won't get a plant.

**Propagation:** Leaf Cuttings, Offshoots

**Use:** Table

**Rating:** 5

*ECHEVERIA elegans*

**Botanical name:** ECHINOCACTUS grusonii

**Common name:** Golden Barrel
**Origin:** Mexico
**Description:** Large, closely ribbed, light green globe with large golden spines. The yellow flowers grow around the top like a crown.
**Requirements:** Bright light, heavy soil with excellent drainage. Normally, likes to be drenched and then let dry, but needs less water in the winter. It will take cool nights or regular house temperatures, but prefers good air circulation. A well-controlled plant that sits and slowly balloons. It's very easy to keep.
**Propagation:** Seeds
**Use:** Table
**Rating:** 5

**Botanical name:** EPISCIA cupreata
**Common name:** Flame Violet
**Origin:** Colombia
**Description:** Creeping plant with small, crinkly, oval, metallic, copper-colored opposite leaves that are slightly hairy. The tubelike flowers are red and yellow. This is an excellent hanging basket plant if the humidity can be kept high enough.
**Requirements:** Filtered light, even moisture, high humidity, and rich organic soil.
**Propagation:** Cuttings
**Use:** Table, Hanging Basket, Terrarium
**Rating:** 2

*ECHINOCACTUS grusonii*

**Botanical name:** EPISCIA lilacina
**Description:** Creeping plant with coppery, velvet, opposite leaves with lavender flowers.
**Requirements:** Filtered light, even moisture, rich organic soil with good drainage, and high humidity. It prefers house temperatures and is quite sensitive to cold.
**Propagation:** Cuttings
**Use:** Table, Hanging Basket, Terrarium
**Rating:** 2

*EPISCIA lilacina*

**Botanical name:** EPISCIA reptans
**Origin:** Brazil, Guinea, Surinam, Colombia
**Description:** A creeper with puckered, opposite, brown-green leaves that are marked with silvery green. The bright red, tubelike flowers are fringed at the edge. This plant looks good in a hanging basket.
**Requirements:** Filtered light, even moisture, high humidity, house temperatures, and rich organic soil.
**Propagation:** Cuttings
**Use:** Table, Hanging Basket, Terrarium
**Rating:** 2

**Botanical name:** ERIOBOTRYA japonica
**Common names:** Loquat, Japan Plum
**Origin:** China

**Description:** A small tree with glossy green leaves that grow from six to twelve inches long and are covered with a light grey fuzz when they first unfold. Spicy, cream-colored, plumlike blossoms are followed by yellow fruit which contain large brown seeds.

**Requirements:** Bright light and even moisture. It prefers a cool night temperature with good air circulation, but is not at all particular about soil. A decorative and tolerant plant, it even forgives those who can't keep fingers from rubbing off its fuzz.

**Propagation:** Seeds
**Use:** Floor, Table
**Rating:** 3

**Botanical name:** EUPHORBIA grandicornis
**Common name:** Big Horned Euphorbia
**Origin:** Natal to Kenya
**Description:** A bright, pale green, spiny succulent. The spines are one to two inches long and set on the wavy edges of the three-cornered stem. From time to time it has very small ovalish leaves. It has an interesting branching shape and often grows four feet tall.

**Requirements:** Bright light, heavy soil with excellent drainage, and good air circulation at house or cool temperatures. Likes to be drenched and then allowed to dry. Grows best when root

*EUPHORBIA grandicornis*

bound. If it gets top heavy, tipping over can be avoided by double potting — putting the plant in its original pot, inside a second larger pot with perhaps some rocks in the bottom. This is a great house plant for anyone who doesn't have to be concerned about the spines.

**Propagation:** Cuttings (let them dry out a bit before planting in sand)

**Use:** Floor, Table

**Rating:** 4

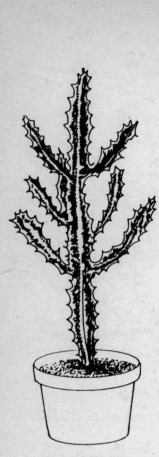

*EUPHORBIA lactea*

**Botanical name:** EUPHORBIA lactea

**Common names:** Milk Striped Euphorbia, Dragon Bones

**Origin:** India, Ceylon

**Description:** A dark green, spiny succulent with a greenish-white marbled area running down the center of each of its branches. The spines are very dark and the three- sometimes four-cornered stems often branch, giving a candelabra form. Because of its rapid growth, it's used as a hedge in temperate climates.

**Requirements:** Bright light, heavy soil with excellent drainage, and good air circulation at house or cool temperatures. Should be drenched and then allowed to dry. Do not put in too large a pot because it likes feeling crowded. If it gets top heavy, tipping over can be avoided by double potting — putting the plant in its original pot, inside a second larger pot with perhaps some rocks in the bottom.

**Propagation:** Cuttings (let them dry out a bit before planting in sand)

**Use:** Floor, Table

**Rating:** 4


**Botanical name:** EUPHORBIA mammillaris

**Common name:** Corn Cob Cactus

**Origin:** Cape Province (Africa)

**Description:** An erect succulent that looks like a green corn cob with spines. The spines, which are one-half to an inch long, give it the look of a cactus — especially when the small, thin leaves are not apparent. Although it doesn't get too big, this is a fun plant to have around as a conversation piece. Young people are fascinated by this non-cactus "cactus."

**Requirements:** Bright light, heavy soil with excellent drainage, good air circulation, and cool or house temperatures. It likes to be drenched and then let dry between waterings.

**Propagation:** Cuttings (let them dry out before planting in sand)

**Use:** Table

**Rating:** 4

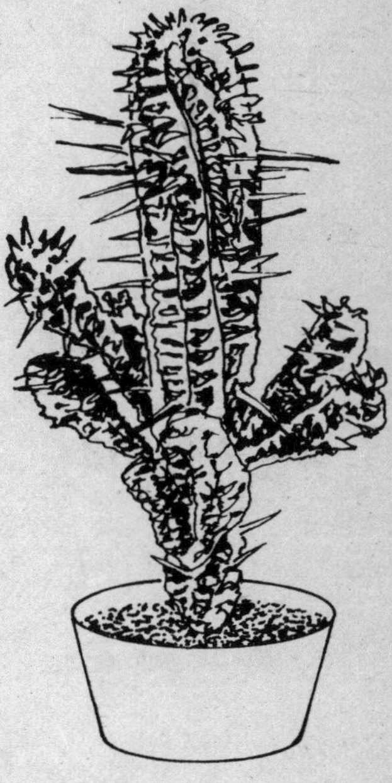

**Botanical name:** EUPHORBIA mauritanica

**Common name:** Milk Bush, Pencil Cactus

**Origin:** South Africa

*EUPHORBIA mammillaris*

**Description:** A much branched shrub with dark green cylindrical branches and very small needlelike leaves that are often absent. Rather similar to *EUPHORBIA tirucalli,* though more open and coarser looking. Some people find the milky sap irritating.

**Requirements:** Bright light, drench and let dry between waterings. Heavy soil with excellent drainage, cool or house temperatures and circulating air. This plant should not be over-potted. Tipping can be avoided by putting rocks in the pot bottom or by putting one pot inside another with rocks between.

**Propagation:** Cuttings (let them dry out before planting in sand)

**Use:** Floor, Table

**Rating:** 4

*EUPHORBIA pulcherrima*

**Botanical name:** EUPHORBIA pulcherrima

**Common names:** Poinsettia, Lobster Flower, Mexican Flame Leaf

**Origin:** Southern Mexico

**Description:** A branching shrub that grows to twelve feet high with woody stems and milky sap. It has dark green leaves except at the ends of the branches where, under the influence of short days, they will turn red, pink, yellow or white, depending on the variety. The flowers are tiny and yellowish.

The plant will often lose all its leaves and go dormant after flowering. In spite of slanderous opinion to the contrary. it is *not* poisonous. Formerly thought of as a Christmas holiday plant it is now being grown almost year round. In Mexico, the story is that the red leaves are a memorial to a young and beautiful princess whose blood splashed the plant when she was sacrificed.

**Requirements:** Normally it likes to be drenched and then allowed to dry out a bit between waterings. but when "flowering." the soil should be kept on the moist side. It likes bright light. heavy soil with good drainage. cool or house temperatures, and good air circulation — but no drafts.

**Propagation:** Cuttings

**Use:** Floor. Table

**Rating:** 2

**Botanical name:** EUPHORBIA splendens (EUPHORBIA milii splendens)

**Common name:** Crown of Thorns

**Origin:** Madagascar

**Description:** A somewhat climbing shrub with grey stems that are one-half to an inch thick and are covered with stout. inch-long spines. It has bright green leaves one to two inches long. Clusters of flowers that have bright red oval bracts appear at the end of the stems.

**Requirements:** Bright light, heavy

*EUPHORBIA splendens*

soil with good drainage, circulating air, and cool or house temperature. It likes to be drenched and then allowed to dry. It sometimes drops all of its leaves unexpectedly due to a lack of water or its inclination to take a little rest. This is a good time to repot the plant if it needs it. Usually light green leaves reappear in about a month, and you can start watering again.

**Propagation:** Cuttings from the tips of the branches

**Use:** Floor, Table, Hanging Basket

**Rating:** 5

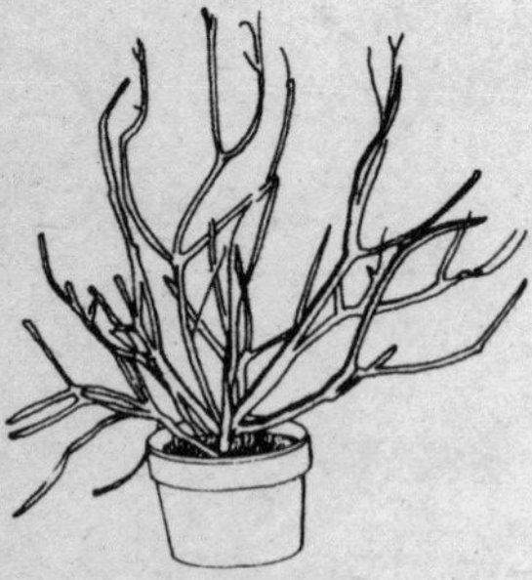

*EUPHORBIA tirucalli*

**Botanical name:** EUPHORBIA tirucalli

**Common names:** Milk Bush, Pencil Cactus, Indian Tree Spurge

**Origin:** Uganda, Congo, Zanzibar (Africa)

**Description:** A small tree with dark green, pencil-thin, cylindrical branches. The narrow leaves usually fall off after appearing, and, unless the air humidity is high, will often go a year without their reappearing. Some people are allergic to the milky sap.

**Requirements:** Bright light, heavy soil with good drainage, and circulating air with cool or house temperature. It likes to be drenched and let dry. Easier to grow than *EUPHORBIA mau-*

*ritanica*, it has an interesting look, grows quickly and doesn't mind people at all. A plant to remember.

**Propagation:** Cuttings
**Use:** Floor, Table
**Rating:** 5

**Botanical name:** FATSHEDERA lizei
**Common names:** Tree Ivy, Fat Lizzie
**Origin:** Cross between *FATSIA japonica* and *HEDERA helix*
**Description:** A tall, thin shrub that usually needs support. It has five-lobed, shiny, leathery, dark green leaves. They are usually potted with three or more in a pot since one always looks a bit scrawny — like a woody, overgrown ivy trying to grow up rather than down.
**Requirements:** Bright light and even moisture. It likes brisk temperatures especially at night, plenty of fresh air, and heavy soil. It always looks better if it has some support.
**Propagation:** Cuttings
**Use:** Floor, Table
**Rating:** 2

**Botanical name:** FATSIA japonica
**Common name:** Japanese Aralia
**Origin:** Japan
**Description:** Shrub with large, ivy-shaped, leathery, dark green leaves. One of the faster grow-

*FATSHEDERA lizei*

ing of the indoor plants. If conditions are met, this makes a dramatic specimen plant.
**Requirements:** Filtered light, evenly moist, heavy soil, good air circulation, and cold night temperatures. Warm temperatures make the leaves turn yellow and drop.
**Propagation:** Cuttings
**Use:** Floor, Table
**Rating:** 2

*FATSIA japonica*

**Botanical name:** FAUCARIA tigrina
**Common name:** Tiger Jaw
**Origin:** Cape Province (Africa)
**Description:** A succulent with thick, bluish green leaves with long slender teeth that give it the appearance of jaws. The flowers are bright yellow.
**Requirements:** It likes to be drenched and let dry. It prefers heavy soil, good air circulation, and cool nights although it will tolerate house temperatures. An interesting plant, it looks good in handmade ceramic pots.
**Propagation:** Seeds, Division
**Use:** Table
**Rating:** 5

**Botanical name:** FICUS benjamina
**Common name:** Weeping Fig
**Origin:** India, Malaya
**Description:** A small tree, that can

grow quite large in time, with
dense, drooping branches
covered with shiny, leathery,
dark green, pointy-oval leaves.
The trunk is grey.

**Requirements:** Filtered light.
Evenly moist, heavy soil, house
temperatures, and dry circulating air. Although a good indoor
plant, it will often drop leaves
when moved. The more light it
gets, the more leaves it will
have; the less light the less
leaves. What this usually
means is that when brought
home directly from a greenhouse, it will lose a lot of
leaves.

**Propagation:** Cuttings
**Use:** Floor, Table
**Rating:** 4


**Botanical name:** FICUS carica
**Common name:** Common Edible
Fig
**Origin:** Mediterranean region,
Asia Minor
**Description:** Small tree with
large, thick, three- to five-lobed
leaves that are rough on top.
You never see the flowers,
which are produced inside the
pear-shaped "fruit." If you
leave the fruit on the tree long
enough, it will become quite
sweet.
**Requirements:** Filtered light,
even moisture, heavy soil with
good drainage, well-circulating
dry air, and cool night temperatures. It grows well in a

large tub and summers well outside.
**Propagation:** Cuttings
**Use:** Floor, Table
**Rating:** 4

*FICUS elastica*

**Botanical name:** FICUS elastica
**Common names:** India Rubber Plant, Rubber Plant
**Origin:** India, Malaya
**Description:** A "house" plant with large, oblong, thick, leathery, dark green leaves. It is usually grown with a single stem, but will branch if cut back — which is the thing to do when it starts to hit the ceiling. The new leaves always start out with a red covering which they discard as soon as they start feeling comfortable.
**Requirements:** Filtered to bright light, dry air, house temperatures, and heavy soil with good drainage. It can stand drying out much better than it can stand too much water which makes the leaves turn yellow and drop. This is a very tolerant plant which will endure much.
**Propagation:** Cuttings, Air Layering
**Use:** Floor, Table
**Rating:** 5

**Botanical name:** FICUS elastica variegata
**Common name:** Variegated Rubber Plant
**Description:** Large house plant

with thick, leathery, dark green leaves blotched with creamy-yellow. Fast growers with almost any kind of care, rubber plants may have to be cut back.

**Requirements:** Filtered light, house temperatures, and dry air. The heavy soil should be kept evenly moist but not wet. If it gets too wet, the leaves drop off; therefore, good drainage is a must.

**Propagation:** Cuttings, Air Layering

**Use:** Floor, Table

**Rating:** 5

*FICUS lyrata*

**Botanical name:** FICUS lyrata
**Common name:** Fiddle-Leaf Fig
**Origin:** Tropical West Africa
**Description:** Tree with large, wavy, fiddle-shaped, leathery, dark green leaves that grow on a woody brown stem.

**Requirements:** Filtered to bright light, house temperatures, and dry circulating air. It likes to be kept evenly moist but not wet, and prefers heavy soil with good drainage. A very tolerant plant, it will take almost any conditions except too much water.

**Propagation:** Cuttings, Air Layering

**Use:** Floor, Table

**Rating:** 5

**Botanical name:** FICUS pumila (FICUS repens)

**Common name:** Creeping Fig

**Origin:** China, Japan, Australia

**Description:** Creeping plant with small, dark green, leathery leaves that are less than an inch long. This plant can cling to a wall like ivy. Nice in a plant room because it's easier to keep inside than ivy.

**Requirements:** Filtered light, even moisture, and warm circulating air. Prefers humidity and is not at all happy with dry air. Unfortunately, it is susceptible to red spider.

**Propagation:** Cuttings

**Use:** Table, Hanging Basket

**Rating:** 2

**Botanical name:** FICUS retusa nitida

**Common name:** Indian Laurel

**Origin:** Malaya

**Description:** Thick-topped tree with waxy, green, shiny leaves that look a lot like FICUS *benjamina* except that the branches are less drooping. This makes a great tub plant that can be easily trimmed and shaped for formal settings.

**Requirements:** Filtered to bright light, even moisture, heavy soil with good drainage, house temperatures, good air circulation, and dry air. It will drop its leaves when moved from a higher to a lower light intensity as part of its readjustment pro-

*FICUS retusa nitida*

cedure. So don't be worried
when it loses leaves after coming to your house from the
greenhouse.
**Propagation:** Cuttings
**Use:** Floor, Table
**Rating:** 4

**Botanical name:** FITTONIA argyroneura
**Common name:** Silver-nerved Fittonia
**Description:** A small trailing plant
with oval leaves that are dark
green and veined with white.
**Requirements:** Filtered light and
evenly moist, heavy soil with
good drainage. It also likes
house temperatures and high
humidity. Does well in a terrarium providing it gets good
air circulation. This plant will
get rather straggly if given its
way, so should be cut back regularly.
**Propagation:** Cuttings
**Use:** Table, Terrarium
**Rating:** 1

*FITTONIA argyroneura*

**Botanical name:** FITTONIA ver-
schaffeltii
**Common name:** Red-nerved Fittonia
**Origin:** Peru
**Description:** Creeping plant with
olive green, oval leaves that are
veined in red. Unspectacular
flowers grow on a terminal
spike, and if this is pinched out

the plant will be less scraggly. This plant is best grown in a bottle garden where it will get the humidity it needs.

**Requirements:** Filtered light, heavy soil with excellent drainage which should be kept evenly moist, house temperatures, and high humidity. This is a beautiful foliage plant when kept under ideal conditions, but it needs to be overhauled every spring, with new plants being started from tip-end cuttings.

**Propagation:** Cuttings
**Use:** Table, Terrarium
**Rating:** 1

*FUCHSIA hybrids*

**Botanical name:** FUCHSIA hybrids
**Common name:** Lady's Eardrops
**Origin:** Peru, Chile to Tierra del Fuego
**Description:** Pot plant to small tree with dark green leaves, often with red stems. The flowers hang like large earrings that look a bit like dancing ladies, and come in combinations of white, pink, red, and purple. Some varieties grow upright, and others have very weak stems and do best in hanging baskets.
**Requirements:** Filtered light and heavy soil kept evenly moist. It needs a lot of water during its growing season, but much less while resting (October-February). It likes cold to cool night temperatures and good air cir-

culation. The flowers drop easily, so it's better to leave the plant put while in bloom. The flowers come on new growth, so the plant has to be cut after dormancy, and each stem should be pinched once or twice. White fly can't leave this beautiful plant alone.

**Propagation:** Cuttings, Seeds
**Use:** Table, Hanging Basket
**Rating:** 1

**Botanical name:** GARDENIA jasminoides
**Common name:** Gardenia
**Origin:** South China
**Description:** A compact, dense shrub with shiny green leaves and very fragrant white flowers that appear from time to time (if the plant's happy). This is a very particular plant. Even when you work very hard to satisfy its every requirement, the best you can get is a shiny green plant that drops buds just as they are about to open. To make matters worse, this is one of the top ten favorites of every plant pest.
**Requirements:** Bright light and even moisture. Gardenias are very particular and most intolerant of any variation from their preferences. They require organic soil and don't appreciate being pot bound. Gardenias require high humidity, good air circulation, and a night temperature that does not go below 65°F. Bathe frequently since

*GARDENIA jasminoides*

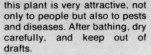

this plant is very attractive, not only to people but also to pests and diseases. After bathing, dry carefully, and keep out of drafts.

**Propagation:** Cuttings (done by someone else)
**Use:** Floor, Table
**Rating:** 1

**Botanical name:** GASTERIA hybrids
**Origin:** California nurseries
**Description:** Plants with thick, succulent, tongue shaped leaves that are arranged in stacks or spirals. Very similar to aloes except that they are flatter and have smooth edges. Dark green leaves covered with white and greenish white lumps.
**Requirements:** Filtered light, heavy soil with good drainage. Drench and let dry. Cool night temperatures and circulating air. If kept dry and cool enough in the winter they sometimes have tubelike red flowers on a long stem.
**Propagation:** Seeds, Offshoots
**Use:** Table
**Rating:** 5

**Botanical name:** GASTERIA verrucosa
**Common name:** Oxtongue Gasteria
**Origin:** South Africa

*GASTERIA verrucosa*

**Description:** Succulent with thick, fleshy, dark grey-green, tongue shaped leaves covered with white warts. Tubelike rosy-red flowers at the top of tall stems appear after a cold dry rest period.

**Requirements:** Filtered light, heavy soil with good drainage. Drench and let dry. Cool night temperature and dry circulating air. A very tolerant plant indoors.

**Propagation:** Seeds. Offshoots

**Use:** Table

**Rating:** 5

*GEOGENANTHUS undatus*

**Botanical name:** GEOGENAN-THUS undatus

**Common name:** Seersucker Plant

**Origin:** Peru

**Description:** A low-growing plant with roundish, fleshy, dark green, quilted leaves. They're marked with parallel, silvery, white bands on top, and are purple-red underneath.

**Requirements:** Filtered light with even moisture, organic soil with good drainage, house temperatures, and dry atmosphere. A very good looking plant, it should be grown in clumps since it often objects to being separated.

**Propagation:** Division, Cuttings

**Use:** Table

**Rating:** 3

**Botanical name:** GREVILLEA robusta (GREVILLEA banksii)
**Common name:** Silk Oak
**Origin:** Queensland, New South Wales, Australia
**Description:** A tree with fernlike leaves that are greyish on one side. Outdoors in temperate climates it will grow over 100 feet tall and have orange brushlike flowers. Indoors it grows easily and makes a great filler in a bright window especially since it doesn't make heavy shade. But it's usually kept only a few years and then disposed of because it loses all its lower leaves and looks quite scrawny.
**Requirements:** Bright light, heavy soil, cool night temperatures, and good air circulation. Likes to be drenched and then let dry. It grows easily from seed and is at its prime as a house plant when about a year and a half old.
**Propagation:** Seeds
**Use:** Floor, Table
**Rating:** 4

**Botanical name:** GUZMANIA lingulata
**Origin:** Central America to Guiana, Ecuador, Bolivia
**Description:** A rosette of smooth, metallic, bright green leaves that are bright red in the inside. The white flowers are carried in a very showy red-orange floral bract.
**Requirements:** Filtered light and

*GREVILLEA robusta*

organic soil with excellent drainage. The base should be kept filled with water. It prefers house temperatures. but will tolerate dry air. After flowering, the rosette from which the flower grew dies, but the plant is always producing new offshoots.

**Propagation:** Offshoots
**Use:** Table. Hanging Basket
**Rating:** 4

**Botanical name:** GYNURA aurantiaca
**Common names:** Velvet Plant, Purple Passion Plant
**Origin:** Java (Indonesia)
**Description:** Plant with velvety leaves that have purple hair and veins. The flowers look like small orange shaving brushes. Once seen, this plant is easy to remember and recognize.
**Requirements:** Bright light. even moisture, heavy soil. house temperatures, and circulating air. It tends to get leggy and should be cut back regularly. The pieces that are cut off root very easily and make welcome gifts. Velvet plant, like coleus, tends to look better when young.
**Propagation:** Cuttings
**Use:** Table. Hanging Basket
**Rating:** 3

**Botanical name:** HAWORTHIA species
**Description:** Thick succulent leaves in crowded rosettes often marked with dots, bars,

*GYNURA aurantiaca*

warts or stripes. The flowers are tubelike in combinations of greens, roses, and red; which hang on long stalks.

**Requirements:** Filtered light, heavy soil with excellent drainage. Drench and let dry. Cool night temperature and dry air. Their interesting shapes make good collector items.

**Propagation:** Seeds. Offsets and Cuttings

**Use:** Table

**Rating:** 5

**Botanical name:** HEDERA helix
**Common name:** English Ivy
**Origin:** Europe. Asia, N. Africa
**Description:** A vine with glossy, leathery, green leaves, that comes in many varieties, sizes, and shapes. They climb, trail, or just hump up on top of themselves.

**Requirements:** Bright light, even moisture, heavy soil, and cold circulating fresh air. A favorite of red spider, they should be bathed frequently because their thick leaves effectively protect from sprays any pests that get into the center of the plant.

**Propagation:** Cuttings

**Use:** Table, Hanging Basket

**Rating:** 2

*HEDERA helix*

**Botanical name:** HELICONIA humilis
**Common name:** Lobster Claw
**Origin:** Trinidad, Brazil
**Description:** A large leafy plant

*HELICONIA humilis*

that looks like a banana tree. It has shiny, green leaves and bright red, boat- or lobster-claw-shaped flower sheaths that have green tips and a greenish yellow ridge. They grow up rather than down like a banana.

**Requirements:** Filtered light, even moisture, heavy soil with good drainage, house temperatures, and good circulating air. This is a big plant that needs a lot of room.

**Propagation:** Division
**Use:** Table, Floor
**Rating:** 3

**Botanical name:** HELXINE soleirolii

**Common names:** Baby Tears, Irish Moss

**Origin:** Corsica, Sardinia

**Description:** A mass of small, roundish, bright green leaves on threadlike branches that mound up nicely in terrariums. It has many, many common names, including Corsican Curse and Mind-Your-Own-Business.

**Requirements:** Filtered light, even moisture, organic soil with good drainage, cool night temperatures with good air circulation, and high humidity. It will dry up if the humidity is too low, and it will rot if kept cooped up

without air. But in the right spot,
it will grow and grow and grow.
**Propagation:** Division
**Use:** Table, Terrarium
**Rating:** 3

**Botanical name:** HIBISCUS rosa-
sinensis
**Common names:** Chinese Rose,
Shoe Flower
**Origin:** Asia, probably China
**Description:** A vigorous, spreading shrub with large, deep,
glossy green leaves. It has
large hollyhocklike flowers,
that are generally red although
there are also varieties with
pink, white, and yellow flowers.
**Requirements:** Bright light, house
temperatures with good air circulation, and even moisture.
They use a lot of water, so the
heavy soil should have good
drainage. To keep the plant
growing and blooming, it
should be fed regularly. But
regular feeding also means that
it has to be cut back regularly
throughout the year, or it will go
through the roof.
**Propagation:** Cuttings
**Use:** Floor, Table
**Rating:** 3

*HIBISCUS schizopetalus*

**Botanical name:** HIBISCUS
schizopetalus
**Common name:** Hibiscus
**Origin:** Tropical East Africa
**Description:** A tall shrub with

drooping branches. The flowers look like large filigree balls hanging on long stems.

**Requirements:** Bright light. heavy soil. house temperatures with good air circulation. and even moisture. They use a lot of water. so the soil should have good drainage. *HIBISCUS schizopetalus* should be fed regularly. and though they don't grow as fast as *HIBISCUS rosa-sinensis*. they need regular pruning to keep them under control. Use the ends that are cut off to make plants for your friends.

**Propagation:** Cuttings
**Use:** Floor. Table
**Rating:** 3

*HIPPEASTRUM (AMARYLLIS) hybrids*

**Botanical name:** HIPPEASTRUM (AMARYLLIS) hybrids
**Common name:** Amaryllis
**Origin:** Africa
**Description:** It has long. leathery. straplike leaves that usually appear after the plant has bloomed. The flowers. which are large and lily-shaped. are in a bunch at the top of a tall thick flower stalk. The leaves turn yellow and die when the plant is ready to rest. After its rest period. the flower stalk shoots up and blooms before the leaves start again.
**Requirements:** While growing, bright light and even moisture. Pot the bulb snugly in heavy soil. Keep in a dark place at 70

to 75°F and water very little until the bud appears. Once the flower bud is well-developed, the plant should be put in a cooler place with good light, but not direct sun. Start watering regularly and give it cool night temperatures. After it flowers, keep watering and start feeding. Keep doing this for six to eight months; then stop completely. The amaryllis may start turning yellow before you stop, or it may not. After a one- or two-month rest start all over again.

**Propagation:** Bulb
**Use:** Table
**Rating:** 1

**Botanical name:** HOWEIA forsteriana
**Common names:** Kentia Palm, Paradise Palm, Thatch Leaf Palm
**Origin:** Lord Howe Island, near Australia
**Description:** The potted palm of Victorian hotel dining rooms has large, dark green, waxy, leathery leaves growing on long slender stalks. Grows to about 60-feet outside but generally stays under six to eight feet inside (probably because they are given away when they get taller).
**Requirements:** Filtered light with even moisture. Heavy soil (though they are not particular), cool night temperatures and dry air. Scale is sometimes a prob-

*HOWEIA forsteriana*

lem, but if it is removed immediately (use a soft tooth brush or fingernail) the leaves will not be marked.

**Propagation:** Seeds
**Use:** Floor, Table
**Rating:** 5

*HOYA bella*

**Botanical name:** HOYA bella
**Common name:** Wax Plant
**Origin:** India
**Description:** A small shrubby vine with small, thick, deep green leaves. The flowers are white with a purple center and appear in a bunch. This is not as large or as vigorous as *HOYA carnosa*.
**Requirements:** Bright light and heavy soil with good drainage. It usually likes to be drenched and let dry, but often rests all winter and needs little water then. Prefers cool night temperatures in the winter and house temperatures the rest of the year. It does best if root bound so don't be in a hurry to repot.
**Propagation:** Cuttings, Layering
**Use:** Table, Hanging Basket
**Rating:** 4

**Botanical name:** HOYA carnosa
**Common name:** Wax Plant
**Origin:** Queensland (Australia), South China
**Description:** A twining plant that has shining, succulent, dark green leaves. The flowers are

fragrant and white with a pink center. They look like a bunch of little wax stars.

**Requirements:** Bright light, heavy soil, cool night temperatures, and good air circulation. Likes to be drenched and let dry. After blooming in the summer, keep the plant semi-dormant and root bound to encourage flowering. After the flowers fall off, don't cut off the stub because this stub will flower again. This plant attracts mealybugs. They can be controlled with regular showers.

**Propagation:** Cuttings, Layering
**Use:** Table, Hanging Basket
**Rating:** 5

**Botanical name:** HOYA carnosa variegata
**Common name:** Variegated Wax Plant
**Description:** A twining plant that has succulent, dark green, cream and pink leaves. The flowers are fragrant, and white with a pink center. They look like a cluster of small white stars.

**Requirements:** Bright light, heavy soil, cool night temperatures, and good air circulation. They like to be drenched and let dry. Keep the plant root bound to encourage blooming. After the flowers drop, it will flower again from the same stubs, so don't cut them off in an effort to

*HOYA carnosa*

tidy up the plant. After it blooms in the summer, the plant should be kept somewhat dormant.
**Propagation:** Cuttings, Layering
**Use:** Table, Hanging Basket
**Rating:** 5

**Botanical name:** HOYA imperialis
**Origin:** Borneo
**Description:** A tall climber with downy stems and shiny, dark green, leathery leaves. The large milkweedlike flowers, which are an inch or more across, are dull purple with cream-colored centers. Although it will grow very tall, it can flower when its 3 to 4 feet high.
**Requirements:** Bright light and good air circulation. Drench and then let it dry a bit between waterings. It likes heavy rich soil and prefers cool temperatures, but a higher temperature than most of the other hoyas. It is very attractive to mealybugs.
**Propagation:** Cuttings, Layering
**Use:** Table, Hanging Basket
**Rating:** 4

**Botanical name:** HYACINTHUS orientalis
**Common name:** Hyacinth
**Description:** Long spikes of fragrant flowers set in bright green straplike leaves. The

*HYACINTHUS orientalis*

flowers are white. blue. pink. rose. red. and yellow.

**Requirements:** Bright light and wet, heavy soil. Hyacinth bulbs will also bloom growing in water. For the best bloom they need cold temperatures and good air circulation. Once a bulb has been forced it won't do much even if planted outside, but their beauty and fragrance is such that their short visit is always worthwhile.

**Propagation:** Bulbs

**Use:** Table

**Rating:** 1

**Botanical name:** HYDROSME rivieri (Amorphophallus)

**Common names:** Devil's Tongue. Voodoo Plant

**Origin:** Indochina

**Description:** Three- to four-foot flower stalk with large brownish red calla lily-like flower (with a strong odor) appears before the leaf. The single leaf stalk divides into three parts. each one looking like a large heavy fern. The tuber can get 8- to 9-inches in diameter. The larger the tuber the larger the plant.

**Requirements:** Bright light. Keep wet April through September. Drench and let dry November through February. The other months are transition periods. Heavy soil (one third each: loam, leaf mold, and sand), house temperatures and cir-

*HYDROSME rivieri*

culating humid air. A great plant to grow in a school classroom since it grows quickly, has a strange look, and a smell that helps cure people of the delusion that all flowers smell sweet.

**Propagation:** Tubers
**Use:** Floor, Table
**Rating:** 2

*IMPATIENS walleriana sultanii*

**Botanical name:** IMPATIENS walleriana sultanii
**Common name:** Patient Lucy, Busy Lizzie
**Origin:** S. E. Africa
**Description:** A plant with a thick watery stem and light green leaves. Under ideal conditions, it flowers continuously. The flowers are red, salmon, pink or white.
**Requirements:** Bright light and even moisture. It prefers a cool night temperature and good air circulation. Use an organic soil, but fertilize infrequently since fertilizing often cuts down on the amount of bloom while producing lush leaves. Insufficient light will also cut down on the amount of bloom. The plant should be frequently cut back to make it bushy. Cut ends root very easily in water. This plant grows quickly. Larger plants may need to be staked because the stems are so brittle.
**Propagation:** Seeds, Cuttings
**Use:** Table, Hanging Basket
**Rating:** 4

**Botanical name:** IRESINE herbstii
**Common name:** Bloodleaf
**Origin:** South Brazil
**Description:** A small plant with round beet-colored leaves. The leaves always look a bit deformed since they are puckered at the end. The older plants grow very leggy. Many people like them because of their distinctive color.
**Requirements:** Bright light and even moisture. Since size and growth habits are similar to coleus, the two can be grown together. Prefers cool nights, circulating air, and heavy soil. To keep it bushy, the ends should be cut back regularly. The cuttings can be used for new plants, so the older plants can be disposed of.
**Propagation:** Cuttings
**Use:** Table
**Rating:** 3

**Botanical name:** KALANCHOE blossfeldiana
**Origin:** Madagascar
**Description:** A compact plant with glossy, succulent, dark green leaves. Clusters of orange-red flowers appear in the winter or whenever there are short days. Because of its sturdiness, it's often used as a holiday gift plant.
**Requirements:** Bright light, heavy soil with good drainage, cool night temperatures, and good air circulation. Likes to be drenched and then allowed to

*KALANCHOE blossfeldiana*

dry. It needs from 9½ to 12 hours of light to flower, but 16 hours of light will produce better seedlings.

**Propagation:** Seeds, Cuttings
**Use:** Table
**Rating:** 4

**Botanical name:** KALANCHOE daigremontiana (BRYOPHYLLUM daigremontianum)
**Common name:** Air Plant
**Origin:** Madagascar
**Description:** An erect plant with fleshy, three-cornered, brown-spotted leaves. Small plantlets often appear in the margins of the saw-toothed leaves. The flowers are greyish green with purple spots.
**Requirements:** Bright light, heavy soil with good drainage, circulating air, and cool night temperatures. Although it likes its soil drenched and then dried out, this is a tough plant and will survive with a minimum of water and almost freezing temperatures.
**Propagation:** Leaves, Stem Cuttings, Seeds
**Use:** Table
**Rating:** 4

**Botanical name:** KALANCHOE pinnata
**Common name:** Air Plant
**Origin:** India and other tropical regions

*KALANCHOE daigremontiana*

**Description:** Erect plant with oval, succulent, green leaves that are tinged with red. Plantlets are produced in the margins of the scalloped leaves. The reddish flowers hang in a loose cluster from a tall flower stalk.

**Requirements:** Bright light and heavy soil with good drainage. It likes to be drenched and let dry between waterings. Actually, this plant will survive with very little water and almost freezing temperatures and will grow almost anywhere, even pinned up on a curtain. But it prefers good air circulation.

**Propagation:** Leaves, Stem Cuttings, Seeds

**Use:** Table

**Rating:** 4

**Botanical name:** KALANCHOE tomentosa

**Common name:** Panda Plant, Pussy Ears

**Origin:** Madagascar

**Description:** A succulent plant with erect branching stems and fleshy, almond-shaped leaves. The leaves are covered with white, furry felt and have brown tips. The flowers are white with brownish stripes.

**Requirements:** Heavy soil with good drainage, cool night temperatures, and good air circulation. Likes to be drenched and let dry. Prefers to be pot-bound, but if it gets top-heavy, it should be double potted — that

*KALANCHOE tomentosa*

is, put the plant in its original pot inside a larger pot with gravel or rocks in between the two. The single leaves root very easily in sand, but if the dormant bud next to the leaf stem isn't snipped off with the leaf, there won't be a new plant.

**Propagation:** Leaves, Cuttings
**Use:** Table
**Rating:** 4

**Botanical name:** LAMPRANTHUS emarginatus
**Common name:** Ice Plant
**Origin:** South Africa
**Description:** A floppy, branching, succulent plant that has long, thin, fleshy, grey-green leaves and magenta, daisylike flowers The plant often looks frozen.
**Requirements:** It likes heavy soil with excellent drainage, so appreciates broken up bricks in the soil mix and as a mulch. Also likes cool night temperatures and wants to be drenched and let dry. Tolerant of very dry air, but wants good air circulation. It grows easily from seeds or cuttings planted in sand, but the cuttings should dry for two or three days before being planted.
**Propagation:** Seeds, Cuttings
**Use:** Table, Hanging Basket
**Rating:** 2

**Botanical name:** LANTANA camara
**Origin:** West Indies
**Description:** A bushy shrub with

*LANTANA camara*

woody stems and pointy, oval leaves that feel quite rough on top and are downy underneath. Sometimes the stems have hooked prickles. Cheerful flat clusters of small bright flowers appear in yellow, red, orange, pink, white, and in combinations. There are some hanging varieties and others that can be trained into trees.

**Requirements:** Bright light. When they're just starting out, they should be kept evenly moist, but at the size when most of them are bought, they should be drenched and then let dry between waterings. They don't mind drought but will bloom well only if they have enough light. They prefer cold night temperatures and good circulating air, but they're not particular about their soil.

**Propagation:** Cuttings (from the soft stems), Seeds

**Use:** Floor, Table, Hanging Basket

**Rating:** 2

**Botanical name:** LITHOPS species

**Origin:** Africa

**Common name:** Living Stones

**Description:** A small succulent plant that looks like a small stone or split rock. It has no stems and is planted quite deep. In its native Africa, it often grows with only the top showing and sometimes that too is covered. It looks interesting planted in small pockets of soil in a large porous rock. The

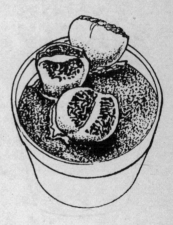

*LITHOPS species*

large daisylike flower is usually bright yellow. although some are white.

**Requirements:** Bright light. and heavy, sandy soil with excellent drainage. It prefers cool nights and good air circulation and likes to be drenched and then allowed to dry.

**Propagation:** Seeds. Division

**Use:** Table

**Rating:** 3

**Botanical name:** LIVISTONA chinensis

**Common name:** Chinese Fan Palm

**Origin:** China

**Description:** Palm with bright green, pleated, fanshaped leaves that are cut half way down into the center. The stems have hooked brown spines.

**Requirements:** Filtered light. heavy soil with good drainage kept evenly wet. Good humid air circulation and cool night temperatures.

**Propagation:** Seeds

**Use:** Floor, Table

**Rating:** 3

*MAMMILLARIA species*

**Botanical name:** MAMMILLARIA species

**Common name:** Pincushion Cactus

**Origin:** Mexico, S.W. United States, Central America

**Description:** A squat spherical or

cylindrical plant with no-fooling spines. This looks like a cactus and is a cactus. It grows slowly and flowers well with crowns of bright-colored flowers. *MAM-MILLARIA* is an example of a conserved name, a name kept for the sake of convenience, since the name was first used in describing an algae.

**Requirements:** Happiest with heavy soil; in fact, it will do well in ground-up rocks to which a little soil has been added. It wants good drainage, dry air, cool nights — especially in wintertime — and good air circulation. Likes to be drenched and let dry between waterings. Mammilaria seeds are about the slowest cactus seeds to germinate, and the seedlings are slow growers afterwards.

**Propagation:** Seeds, Offsets
**Use:** Floor, Table
**Rating:** 3

**Botanical name:** MANGIFERA indica
**Common name:** Mango
**Origin:** North India, Burma, Malaya
**Description:** A tree with large, leathery, green leaves which grow up to ten inches in captivity although it grows in fits and starts. It belongs to the same family as poison ivy, so some people get a rash from the sap.
**Requirements:** Bright light, even

*MANGIFERA indica*

moisture, house temperatures (although established plants often can survive 28°F for short periods of time), good air circulation, and almost any kind of soil. It likes a well-defined dry season, but usually doesn't communicate this too well. The mango is susceptible to fungus if it gets too moist, but the leaves will dry out around the edges if it doesn't get enough water. Like an avocado, this is a fun plant to try and grow from a leftover seed. And like the avocado, a plant with which the doing is more appealing than the keeping.

**Propagation:** Seeds
**Use:** Floor, Table
**Rating:** 2

*MARANTA
leuconeura kerchoveana*

**Botanical name:** MARANTA leuconeura kerchoveana
**Common name:** Prayer Plant, Rabbit Tracks
**Origin:** Brazil
**Description:** Low growing plant with oval, pale green leaves (about six inches long) that usually have five pairs of darker green spots on them (ten commandments). The leaves fold up at night.
**Requirements:** Filtered light and evenly moist heavy soil with excellent drainage. House temperatures (doesn't like temperatures above 75°F) and humid air. To multiply, gently

wash all the soil from the roots to see where the divisions of the plant should be made. Make the cuts with a sharp knife. The cuttings must be potted immediately, giving the roots plenty of room (not over-potting but do not crush, bruise or break them).

**Propagation:** Division
**Use:** Table, Hanging Basket
**Rating:** 3

**Botanical name:** MIMOSA pudica
**Common name:** Sensitive Plant
**Origin:** Brazil, naturalized in tropics
**Description:** A spiny plant with finely divided leaves that will collapse when touched. The younger plants are shyer and more sensitive. The flowers are small pink-lavender puffs. This plant doesn't last too long inside because it's hard to keep from testing its reflexes all the time.
**Requirements:** Filtered light, heavy soil kept evenly moist, house temperatures, good air circulation, and high humidity. It grows easily from seeds providing you pour boiling water on them before the seeds are planted. Remember, pour the boiling water *over* the seeds. Don't boil the seeds!

**Propagation:** Seeds
**Use:** Table
**Rating:** 1

*MIMOSA pudica*

**Botanical name:** MONSTERA deliciosa (juvenile stage known as PHILODENDRON pertusum)

**Common names:** Hurricane Plant, Swiss Cheese Plant, Split Leaf Philodendron

**Origin:** South Mexico, Guatemala

**Description:** A climbing plant with large leathery leaves that grow to three feet. The leaves are perforated with holes to let the rain and light through in the jungle. The flower is similar to the calla lily, and the fruit which appears occasionally on greenhouse plants tastes like a banana-flavored pineapple.

**Requirements:** Filtered light and heavy soil kept evenly moist. It will tolerate dry air and any temperature except freezing. A mature plant will exist in very low light. Air roots grow down from the stem, and if these are given something to grow into, like a totem pole, the plant will grow even larger.

**Propagation:** Cuttings

**Use:** Table, Floor

**Rating:** 5

*MONSTERA deliciosa*

**Botanical name:** MUSA nana (MUSA cavendishii)

**Common names:** Dwarf Banana, Dwarf Jamaica

**Origin:** South China

**Description:** A cluster of large, long leaves that grow from five to six feet from a trunklike stem. The creamy, fingerlike flowers grow from a stalk protected by a number of large, deep maroon "petals." It produces small bananas which are edible.

**Requirements:** They love high temperatures, bright light, and the air should be as humid as possible. The heavy soil, which should be kept wet, must have good drainage and if possible be about one-fourth well-rotted cow manure. They have a tremendous appetite when growing and should be fed regularly — maybe even twice a week if your light is strong and the leaves are growing fast. The stem is underground, and what is visible is a leaf stalk which will die after it fruits. Another leaf stalk will come up from the stem.

**Propagation:** Offsets
**Use:** Floor, Table
**Rating:** 2

*MUSA nana*

**Botanical name:** NARCISSUS jonquilla
**Common name:** Jonquil
**Origin:** S. Europe, N. Africa
**Description:** A plant with long, narrow, dark green leaves. Two to six daffodil-like yellow flowers grow on the top of a stem.
**Requirements:** Bright light and even moisture when blooming. Prefers cold temperatures and good air circulation, but isn't too particular about its soil as long as it's well-drained. This is one of the spring flowering bulbs. If you're going to force them indoors, it's best to start with new bulbs each year.
**Propagation:** Bulbs
**Use:** Table
**Rating:** 1

**Botanical name:** NARCISSUS
pseudo-narcissus
**Common name:** Daffodil, Lent
Lily
**Origin:** Europe
**Description:** A plant with long,
narrow, dark green leaves and
with flowers on top of a long
stem. Although mostly yellow,
the flowers also appear in
white, cream, pink, and in combinations of these colors. The
flowers are both single and
double. Although very temporary — either cut or in pots —
they provide a very cheerful
promise of spring when the
days are cold and grey outside.
**Requirements:** Bright light and
even moisture when blooming.
Prefers cold temperatures and
good circulation, but is not too
particular as to soil as long as it
drains well. When forcing the
bulbs to bloom indoors, start
with new bulbs each year. It's
also a good idea to check and
see if the particular variety you
are interested in is a good
forcer. Some are not and it
can be very frustrating to go to
all the effort and get nothing.
**Propagation:** Bulbs, Buy in Bud
**Use:** Table
**Rating:** 1


**Botanical name:** NARCISSUS
tazetta
**Common name:** Paper White Narcissus
**Origin:** Canary Islands

**Description:** Long, narrow, dark green leaves with fragrant white flowers in a cluster at the top of a long stem. This bulb plant makes everyone feel a master gardener. It's about as close to being fool-proof as any plant there is. It's low rating is due to it's disappointingly short life, especially at house temperatures.

**Requirements:** Bright light, even moisture, and cold temperatures. It will grow on an office desk with only artificial light during the day and none on weekends. It likes heavy soil, but it can also be grown in water, with or without the support of marbles, paperclips, rocks or soil. Put the bulb in a waterproof container, add water and light, and it's ready to grow. This is a great project for the kids. Like kleenex, the bulb should be discarded after it has been used.

**Propagation:** Bulbs
**Use:** Table
**Rating:** 1

*NARCISSUS tazetta*

**Botanical name:** NEPHROLEPIS exaltata
**Common name:** Sword Fern
**Origin:** Florida to Brazil, Africa, South Asia, Australia
**Description:** A fern with long, sword-shaped, bright green, stiffish fronds, which are usually two to four feet long, but can keep on growing almost

indefinitely. The plant sends out green woollike runners which produce new plants.

**Requirements:** Filtered light, evenly moist, heavy soil, good air circulation, and cool night temperatures. Poor drainage can cause the leaves to turn yellow, and not enough moisture or humidity can cause them to turn brown. It needs enough room so it isn't hit by people passing by because if the end of a frond is broken off, growth stops.

**Propagation:** Runners, Division
**Use:** Table, Hanging Basket
**Rating:** 3

**Botanical name:** NEPHROLEPIS exaltata 'Bostoniensis'
**Common name:** Boston Fern
**Description:** A fern with sword-shaped, graceful, green fronds that aren't as stiff as those of *NEPHROLEPIS exaltata*. It sends out green wooly runners which produce new plants.
**Requirements:** Filtered light, evenly moist, heavy soil, good air circulation, and cool night temperatures. Poor drainage can cause the fronds to turn yellow, and too little moisture or humidity can cause them to turn brown. They need enough room to grow without being brushed or hit.

**Propagation:** Runners
**Use:** Table, Hanging Basket
**Rating:** 3

*NEPHROLEPIS exaltata 'Bostoniensis'*

**Botanical name:** NEPHROLEPIS exaltata 'Fluffy Ruffles'

**Common name:** Fluffy Ruffles

**Description:** A dwarf variety of fern with rather stiff. upright. finely divided fronds. It is a very dense lacy-looking plant.

**Requirements:** Filtered light. evenly moist heavy soil, good air circulation, and cool night temperatures. Poor drainage and too much water can cause the fronds to turn yellow while too little water or too low humidity can cause them to turn brown.

**Propagation:** Runners. Division

**Use:** Table. Terrarium

**Rating:** 2

*NERIUM oleander*

**Botanical name:** NERIUM ole-ander

**Common name:** Oleander

**Origin:** Mediterranean

**Description:** A large shrub with willowy branches and leathery leaves that are arranged in pairs or in groups. Bunches of rosy-red flowers are at the ends of the branches. Some varieties have cream or white flowers. A good tub plant, it will grow six or seven feet high. Some people are allergic to it. and others find it poisonous, so proceed with caution.

**Requirements:** Bright light and even moisture during active growing period. Prefers heavy soil with good drainage, cool night temperatures. and good air circulation. It's easy to train and grow inside, and the flowers add a cheerful touch of color. The oleander is very attractive to mealybug and scale which are controlled by frequent baths.

**Propagation:** Cuttings
**Use:** Floor, Table
**Rating:** 4

**Botanical name:** NOTOCACTUS leninghausii
**Common names:** Golden Ball Cactus, Ball Cactus
**Origin:** South Brazil
**Description:** A small spherical to cylindrical cactus. The hairy golden spines really make it look like a cactus. It has many large, yellow flowers that are often one-fourth the size of the plant.
**Requirements:** Drench it and then let it dry between waterings. It likes heavy soil with good drainage, cold night temperatures, and good air circulation. It's easy to grow if you don't get it too wet.
**Propagation:** Seeds, Offsets
**Use:** Table
**Rating:** 3

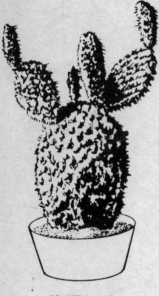

*OPUNTIA species*

**Botanical name:** OPUNTIA species
**Common names:** Prickly Pears, Bunny Ears, Beaver Tails
**Origin:** Alaska, Patagonia (South America)

**Description:** Succulent plants
with cylindrical or flat padlike
stems that grow from a few
inches above the ground to over
20 feet. They have large spines,
often with tufts of fish-
hook prickles (called glochides) that break off and stay
in the fingers. The beautiful
flowers are followed in several
species by delicious fruit.

**Requirements:** Generally, they
like bright light, to be drenched
and let dry, heavy soil with good
drainage, and good air circulation. But some are found in
areas of heavy rainfall and
others happily winter outside in
the Lake Michigan sand dunes.
These are very tough, tolerant,
and adaptable plants, and a
single species will vary under
different soils and climates.
Their only drawback is their
glochides — but you're only
getting what you deserve if you
get that forward with a cactus.

**Propagation:** Seeds, Cuttings,
Pads

**Use:** Floor, Table

**Rating:** 5

ORCHID

**Botanical name:** ORCHIDACEAE
genus and species

**Common name:** Orchids

**Origin:** Worldwide

**Description:** Tremendous variety
in size: a whole plant in bloom
no larger than a nickle, others
have flowers with 30-inch long
whiskery petals, or sprays of

smaller flowers 12-14 feet long. They grow in the ground, on trees and telegraph wires — from the jungles to the Arctic. Orchids have almost every color and combination of colors except dark blue and black; with the exception of the Vanilla orchid (vanilla flavoring) they are grown for the beauty of their flowers and not use.

**Requirements:** Their requirements are extremely varied. However, most of those grown inside need filtered light, a very light porous potting mix which can be drenched and allowed to dry out a bit, cold nights and a humid atmosphere. Although the requirements vary with the genus the biggest trick is to keep the humidity up and the temperature down.

**Propagation:** Seeds. Division
**Use:** Table, Hanging Basket
**Rating:** 2

**Botanical name:** OXALIS hedysaroides rubra
**Common name:** Firefern
**Origin:** Colombia, Venezuela, Ecuador
**Description:** A small, shrubby, erect plant with wiry stems and thin, three-part, wine-red leaves that are sensitive to the touch. The flowers are bright yellow.
**Requirements:** Bright or filtered light. Normally, they like to be

drenched and let dry a bit between waterings, but when actively growing often need more water. They like heavy soil with good drainage, good air circulation, and either cool or house temperatures.

**Propagation:** Seeds, Division
**Use:** Table
**Rating:** 3

**Botanical name:** OXALIS rubra
**Common name:** Grandmother's Shamrock
**Origin:** Brazil
**Description:** A plant with shamrocklike leaves on six- to eight-inch long stems. It has pink flowers with reddish veins and makes a very gay hanging basket. It often goes dormant after flowering and has the habit of closing its flowers during dull weather.
**Requirements:** Bright light and heavy soil with good drainage. Prefers cool or cold night temperatures and good air circulation. It normally likes to be drenched and let dry, but needs more water during its active growing period. Also, there are more flowers if the plant is regularly fertilized at this time. When dormant, they can be stored in a cellar, if you have one.
**Propagation:** Seeds, Tubers
**Use:** Table, Hanging Basket
**Rating:** 2

*OXALIS rubra*

**Botanical name:** PANDANUS veitchii

**Common name:** Screw Pine

**Origin:** Polynesia

**Description:** A large plant with saw-toothed, white-edged leaves that are arranged in a perfect spiral. It looks a bit like the top of a huge overgrown pineapple.

**Requirements:** Filtered light, house temperatures, and dry air. Normally likes its heavy soil to be drenched and then let dry, but while growing in the summer it needs more water.

**Propagation:** Offsets

**Use:** Floor, Table

**Rating:** 5

*PANDANUS veitchii*

**Botanical name:** PASSIFLORA caerulea

**Common name:** Passion Flower

**Origin:** Brazil

**Desciption:** A climbing plant with tendrils that curl around any support, including itself. It has a complex blue flower that the Spaniards were convinced was designed to assist in the conversion of the native Americans to Christianity. The fruit is edible but not as tasty as that of *PASSIFLORA coccinea*.

**Requirements:** Bright light, heavy soil, and even moisture. It prefers a cool temperature with good circulation in the winter and warmer (house) temperatures with humid air in the summer when it's actively growing. Keep cutting the vines back to make them branch, and don't let them get wrapped up in the rest of the plants since they are very difficult to separate without having to cut through one or the other.

**Propagation:** Seeds, Cuttings
**Use:** Table, Hanging Basket
**Rating:** 2

**Botanical name:** PASSIFLORA coccinea
**Common name:** Red Passion Flower
**Origin:** Tropical South America
**Description:** A climbing plant with tendrils that curl about any support, including itself. Not as vigorous as *PASSIFLORA caerulea*, it is also much simpler in the arrangement of its red flowers. The fruit is edible. Inside the gourdlike shell there is a very refreshing pulpy mass that tastes like frog's eggs in lemonade — with a dash of grenadine.
**Requirements:** Bright light and heavy soil with even moisture. A cool temperature with good circulation in winter and warm temperature with humid air in the summer when it is actively growing. It should be kept under control since it hugs any support it comes upon very tightly and is very difficult to separate.
**Propagation:** Seeds, Cuttings
**Use:** Table, Hanging Basket
**Rating:** 2

*PASSIFLORA caerulea*

**Botanical name:** PEDILANTHUS tithymaloides variegatus

**Common name:** Devil's Backbone

**Origin:** West Indies

**Description:** A succulent bush with zig-zag. fleshy. dark green stems. It has pale green leaves that are marked with white and tinged with red. The flowers are red.

**Requirements:** Filtered light and heavy soil kept evenly moist. However. it needs less water in the wintertime. It likes house temperatures. good air circulation. and a humid atmosphere although it will tolerate rather dry air.

**Propagation:** Cuttings

**Use:** Floor. Table

**Rating:** 4

*PELARGONIUM hortorum*

**Botanical name:** PELARGONIUM hortorum

**Common name:** Geranium

**Origin:** South Africa

**Description:** Erect shrubby plants with thick succulent branches and fragrant roundish leaves that are sometimes marked with colored zones. The flowers come in all shades of red. pink. lavender. white. and purple.

**Requirements:** They like their heavy soil to be drenched and let dry. Most geranium problems come from too much moisture and too much fertilizer. Firmly potted plants are usually bushier than those that are planted in loose soil. They also tend to bloom more. Good air circulation is important with cool to cold night temperatures. Misting ruins the flowers and too much moisture on the leaves or roots causes the droops. But if they are kept cool and on the dry side, they are cheerful additions to any plant family.

**Propagation:** Cuttings, Seeds
**Use:** Floor, Table
**Rating:** 3

**Botanical name:** PELARGONIUM peltatum
**Common name:** Ivy Geranium
**Origin:** South Africa
**Description:** A plant with trailing branches and ivy-shaped, waxy, sometimes multicolored leaves. Flowers range through the pinks, reds, and purples, to white. This is a very good hanging basket plant.
**Requirements:** Bright light, good air circulation, and cool to cold night temperatures. Prefers heavy soil with good drainage and usually likes to be drenched and then let dry out a bit between waterings. But when actively growing, it prefers to be kept moister than *PELARGONIUM hortorum*. Avoid overfertilizing, which can encourage leaves at the expense of flowers. Europeans have been playing with

*PELARGONIUM peltatum*

geraniums for over 250 years, so they come in all kinds of fascinating shapes, sizes, and fragrances.

**Propagation:** Cuttings
**Use:** Table, Hanging Basket
**Rating:** 3

**Botanical name:** PEPEROMIA caperata
**Common name:** Emerald Ripple
**Origin:** Brazil
**Description:** Dense clusters of heart - shaped, waxy, dark green, puckered leaves. The puckered leaves seem to have brownish valleys and silvery-grey hills. The stems are pinkish-red, and the flowers are greenish-white and grow on slender spires.
**Requirements:** Filtered light and heavy soil with good drainage. It likes to be drenched and then let dry. It does well in house temperatures and dry air. This is a nice plant for dish gardens or in open terrariums.
**Propagation:** Cuttings
**Use:** Table
**Rating:** 5

*PEPEROMIA caperata*

**Botanical name:** PEPEROMIA metallica
**Origin:** Peru
**Description:** A small plant with erect stems and narrow, waxy leaves that have a metallic copper luster and a silvery green

band down the middle.

**Requirements:** Filtered light and heavy soil with good drainage. It likes to be drenched and then let dry. It's a good house plant that does well in house temperatures and average house humidity.

**Propagation:** Cuttings

**Use:** Table

**Rating:** 5

**Botanical name:** PEPEROMIA obtusifolia

**Origin:** Venezuela

**Description:** A fleshy plant with fat brown stems and waxy, green, roundish leaves that have a notch on the end. Very small whitish flowers grow on the end of a spike.

**Requirements:** Filtered light and heavy soil with good drainage. It normally likes to be drenched and then let dry and prefers house temperatures and dry air. But in the winter, it likes lower temperatures and less water.

**Propagation:** Cuttings, Division

**Use:** Table

**Rating:** 5

*PEPEROMIA obtusifolia*

**Botanical name:** PEPEROMIA sandersii 'Argyreia'

**Common names:** Watermelon Peperomia, Watermelon Begonia

**Origin:** Brazil

**Description:** A small bushy plant with short, red-stemmed, pointed, oval, shiny, bright green leaves. The leaf is silver-striped; thus its common name. The flowers are whitish and very small and are carried on the end of a spike.

**Requirements:** Filtered light, heavy soil with good drainage, house temperatures and dry air. It normally likes to be drenched and then allowed to dry, but in the winter it prefers lower temperatures and less water.

**Propagation:** Cuttings, Division

**Use:** Table

**Rating:** 5

*PEPEROMIA sandersii 'Argyreia'*

**Botanical name:** PERSEA americana

**Common names:** Avocado, Alligator Pear

**Origin:** West Indies, Mexico

**Description:** A tree with large, green, leathery leaves when growing outdoors. The leaves are much thinner when grown indoors. Indoors, unless the stems are severely cut back, the leaves grow at the top of a long, thin, naked trunk.

**Requirements:** Bright light, even moisture, and heavy soil. Cool night temperatures in the winter and house temperatures in the summer, but likes good air circulation all the time. The leaf edges often brown if the air is very dry. After the challenge of growing it from a seed, one's interest often wanes unless there is an accident and the stem is broken off. Then there is the excitement to see if it comes back.

**Propagation:** Seeds (See "Fun With Plants")
**Use:** Floor, Table
**Rating:** 2

**Botanical name:** PHILODENDRON bipinnatifidum
**Origin:** Rio de Janeiro to Mato Grosso
**Description:** A large plant with stiff, waxy, large heart-shaped, much-cut leaves that grow to three feet long. It looks a lot like *PHILODENDRON selloum* except it's larger.
**Requirements:** Filtered light, even moisture, and heavy soil with good drainage. It is very tolerant of house conditions, liking house temperatures and being happy with dry air.
**Propagation:** Cuttings
**Use:** Floor, Table
**Rating:** 5

**Botanical name:** PHILODENDRON oxycardium (formerly PHILODENDRON cordatum)
**Common name:** Heart Leaf Philodendron
**Origin:** Puerto Rico to Jamaica, Central America
**Description:** A tall climbing vine

*PERSEA americana*

with fat, heart-shaped, dark green leaves. A philodendron's philodendron.

**Requirements:** Filtered light and evenly moist, heavy soil. This plant will tolerate almost everything but a hard freeze. It is very comfortable at house temperatures and in dry air.

**Propagation:** Cuttings

**Use:** Floor, Table, Hanging Basket

**Rating:** 5

*PHILODENDRON oxycardium*

**Botanical name:** PHILODENDRON panduraeforme

**Origin:** Southern Brazil

**Description:** A large vining plant with leathery, olive-green, horse-face-shaped leaves. Like most other philodendrons, this one will climb a support if given the chance.

**Requirements:** Filtered light, heavy soil kept evenly moist, house temperatures, and dry air. This is a very tolerant plant that will make the beginner feel like a pro.

**Propagation:** Cuttings

**Use:** Floor, Table, Hanging Basket

**Rating:** 5

**Botanical name:** PHILODENDRON radiatum

**Origin:** Southern Mexico, Guatemala

**Description:** A lush climbing

plant with deeply lobed green leaves. The immature form has smaller, less-lobed leaves and is often known as *PHILODENDRON dubia*.

**Requirements:** Filtered light and evenly moist, heavy soil, house temperatures and dry air. Like the other philodendrons, this is a very tolerant plant, perfect for the person too busy to really mother it.

**Propagation:** Cuttings
**Use:** Floor, Table
**Rating:** 5

**Botanical name:** PHILODENDRON selloum
**Common name:** Saddle Leaf Philodendron
**Origin:** S.W. Brazil
**Description:** A large plant with large, much-divided, heart-shaped, waxy, bright green leaves. This is one of the philodendrons that grows out rather than up, so give it plenty of room.
**Requirements:** Filtered light and evenly moist heavy soil. It will tolerate almost any temperature above freezing; it even does very well in spaces with fluctuating temperatures and is tolerant of dry air. This is a lush tropical-looking plant that's tough.
**Propagation:** Cuttings
**Use:** Floor, Table
**Rating:** 5

*PHILODENDRON*
*selloum*

**Botanical name:** PHILODEN-
DRON squamiferum
**Origin:** Guiana
**Description:** A twisting vine with
five-lobed. bright green leaves.
The leaves have olive-green
stems that are covered with red
and green hairs.
**Requirements:** Filtered light.
even moisture. good drainage
in heavy soil. house tem-
peratures. and a dry at-
mosphere.
**Propagation:** Cuttings
**Use:** Floor. Table
**Rating:** 5

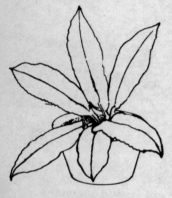

*PHILODENDRON wendlandii*

**Botanical name:** PHILODEN-
DRON wendlandii
**Origin:** Costa Rica. Panama
**Description:** A large rosette of
long. ovalish. waxy green
leaves. This looks a lot like a
birdnest fern.
**Requirements:** Filtered light,
even moisture. heavy soil with
good drainage. house tem-
peratures. and dry air. A
tolerant plant which will put up
with a beginner's fumblings.
**Propagation:** Division
**Use:** Floor. Table
**Rating:** 5

**Botanical name:** PHOENIX dac-
tylifera
**Common name:** Date Palm
**Origin:** Arabia. North Africa
**Description:** A palm with stiff

fronds that are rather spiny at the bottom. This is a tough plant that eventually will — after years and years — overgrow any indoor situation. It's a good plant for people who are trying to recapture the Twenties look.

**Requirements:** Filtered light, heavy soil kept evenly wet, cool to house temperatures, dry air, and good circulation. It will eventually need a lot of room, but it has a long childhood and adolescence.

**Propagation:** Seeds
**Use:** Floor, Table
**Rating:** 4

*PHOENIX roebelenii*

**Botanical name:** PHOENIX roebelenii
**Common name:** Miniature Date Palm
**Origin:** Assam to Viet Nam
**Description:** A small palm similar to the date palm but grows only two or three feet tall and has softer leaves. This slow grower was discovered in Laos by Mr. Roebelin who went there every year to collect palm seeds.
**Requirements:** Filtered light, heavy soil kept evenly wet, house temperature, dry air, and good circulation.
**Propagation:** Offshoots
**Use:** Table
**Rating:** 4

**Botanical name:** PILEA cadierei
**Common names:** Aluminum Plant, Watermelon Plant
**Origin:** Viet Nam, Annam
**Description:** A fast-growing plant with oval, bright green leaves that are striped with silvery-colored markings.
**Requirements:** Filtered light and evenly moist, heavy soil with good drainage. It likes house temperatures with dry air in the winter, but it prefers humid air in the summer. It should be pinched back occasionally to keep it bushy, or it will grow a floppy four feet tall and will have to be staked.
**Propagation:** Cuttings
**Use:** Table
**Rating:** 3

*PILEA cadierei*

**Botanical name:** PILEA involucrata
**Common names:** Pan-American Friendship Plant, Panamiga
**Origin:** Peru
**Description:** Plant with green to coppery-brown, quilted, oval, hairy leaves. Small pink flowers appear in the leaf joints.
**Requirements:** Filtered light, even moisture, heavy soil. Prefers to be dryer in the winter. House temperatures, humid air in summer, dry in winter.
**Propagation:** Cuttings
**Use:** Table, Terrarium
**Rating:** 3

**Botanical name:** PILEA microphylla

**Common name:** Artillery Plant

**Origin:** West Indies

**Description:** Small densely
branched plant with fleshy lettuce green stems and small
(1/4-inch) leaves. The name is
descriptive of the way the
pollen shoots off when the
plant is shaken.

**Requirements:** Prefers filtered
light and even moisture,
although it will grow in bright
light with high humidity. House
temperatures and good circulating air. A good terrarium
plant if it can get fresh air.

**Propagation:** Cuttings

**Use:** Table; Terrarium

**Rating:** 2

*PILEA microphylla*

**Botanical name:** PITTOSPORUM
tobira

**Origin:** China, Japan

**Description:** Bushy shrub with
shiny, dark green, ovalish,
thick, leathery leaves. The
small, creamy white flowers are
very fragrant and remind people
of orange blossoms.

**Requirements:** Bright light, heavy
soil, and good air circulation. It
prefers to be drenched and then
let dry out between waterings.
Cool to cold night temperatures
and humidity are important.
Sometimes it looks rather

peaked when kept too warm in dry air.

**Propagation:** Cuttings
**Use:** Floor, Table
**Rating:** 4

**Botanical name:** PITTOSPORUM tobira 'Variegatum'
**Description:** A bushy shrub with shiny, ovalish, leathery leaves that are greyish green with cream-colored margins. Some people think they look sick or sunburned; others feel they are rich and attractive. The flowers are small, creamy, and quite fragrant.
**Requirements:** Bright light, heavy soil, good air circulation, and cool to cold night temperatures. Likes to be drenched and then allowed to dry between waterings. If the air gets too dry, it is very attractive to red spider.
**Propagation:** Cuttings
**Use:** Floor, Table
**Rating:** 4

**Botanical name:** PLATYCERIUM bifurcatum
**Common name:** Staghorn Fern
**Origin:** E. Australia, New Guinea, New Caledonia, Sunda Island
**Description:** A fern with large grey-green fronds that are deeply lobed and look like a trophy of the hunt. The immature leaves are kidney-shaped and flat against the ground.

*PITTOSPORUM tobira 'Variegatum'*

**Requirements:** Filtered light, even moisture, and light soil with excellent drainage. It is tolerant of house temperatures, but can take it down to 15°F and prefers good humid air circulation.
**Propagation:** Offshoots
**Use:** Table, Hanging Basket
**Rating:** 3

**Botanical name:** PLECTRAN-THUS australis
**Common name:** Swedish Ivy
**Origin:** Australia, Pacific Island
**Description:** A creeping, bushy plant with round, leathery, bright green leaves. The flowers are white. This is a good privacy plant because when hung in a window, it looks good and filters the view.
**Requirements:** Filtered light and heavy soil kept evenly moist. It's happy with dry air and either cool or house temperatures. It can get quite dry without dying. Although the plant will go limp, it won't drop its leaves, and it will perk up when watered again.
**Propagation:** Cuttings
**Use:** Table, Hanging Basket
**Rating:** 5

*PLECTRANTHUS australis*

**Botanical name:** PLECTRAN-THUS oertendahlii
**Common name:** Candle Plant, Swedish Ivy
**Origin:** Natal

**Description:** A fleshy creeping plant with square stems and opposite silver-veined leaves. Sometimes the leaves get purple underneath when they get older. This is a good hanging basket plant.

**Requirements:** Filtered light with evenly moist, heavy soil, cool to house temperatures, and dry air. An excellent house plant, it isn't messy when not watered. It just goes limp but revives nicely when given water again.

**Propagation:** Cuttings

**Use:** Table, Hanging Basket

**Rating:** 5

**Botanical name:** PLEOMELE reflexa

**Common name:** Song of India

**Description:** A bushy plant with thin, willowy branches. The branches are covered with green leaves that have wide margins of creamy yellow. It looks a lot like a dracaena.

**Requirements:** Filtered light, heavy soil with good drainage kept wet, house temperatures, and dry air. It likes its roots wet but its leaves dry.

**Propagation:** Cuttings

**Use:** Floor, Table

**Rating:** 4

*PLEOMELE reflexa*

**Botanical name:** PLUMBAGO capensis

**Origin:** South Africa

**Description:** A scraggly shrub with pale blue, phloxlike

flowers. The pale blue flowers in winter make it almost worth the space and bother necessary.

**Requirements:** Bright light, heavy soil, even moisture, and cool night temperatures with good air circulation. The young plants don't bloom too well even under ideal conditions and they tend to flabbiness if their nights are too warm. On the other hand, if the nights go under 45°F, they generally lose their leaves.

**Propagation:** Cuttings
**Use:** Floor, Table
**Rating:** 2

**Botanical name:** PLUMBAGO indica coccinea
**Origin:** East Indies
**Description:** A plant with wiry, zig-zag stems with red phlox-like flowers. Although grown as a pot plant that will bloom in the wintertime, it grows long and thin and very tall if not kept cut back.

**Requirements:** Bright light, even moisture, and house temperatures with good air circulation. Pot it in heavy soil, and keep it cut back — but not too much or you'll lose the bloom.

**Propagation:** Cuttings
**Use:** Floor, Table
**Rating:** 2

*PLUMBAGO capensis*

*PODOCARPUS macrophylla*

**Botanical name:** PLUMERIA rubra (PLUMERIA acuminata)
**Common name:** Frangipani Tree
**Origin:** Mexico to Ecuador
**Description:** A small tree with large, oval, dark green leaves that it sheds if it has a dry season. The thick grey branches have a milky sap, and the large, waxy, single, pink flowers that grow at the end of the branches are very fragrant. This is a favorite cemetery tree in the South Pacific.
**Requirements:** Filtered light and evenly moist heavy soil. It needs more water in the summer though. It often rests in the winter, and at that time it should be kept rather dry. It likes house temperatures, good air circulation, and humid summers.
**Propagation:** Cuttings
**Use:** Floor, Table
**Rating:** 2

**Botanical name:** PODOCARPUS macrophylla
**Origin:** China, Japan
**Description:** A cone-bearing tree with long, narrow, leathery, dark green, needlelike leaves on willowy branches that grow to 40-plus feet outside in its native haunts. However, it often does poorly inside because of the warm night temperatures.
**Requirements:** Filtered light, heavy soil with good drainage kept evenly moist, cool to cold night temperatures, and good

air circulation. The feeble,
peaked look it often has when
inside is due not to being too
cold but too warm. This is a
plant that really perks up with
cold fresh nights.
**Propagation:** Cuttings
**Use:** Floor, Table
**Rating:** 2


**Botanical name:** POLYPODIUM
aureum
**Common name:** Hare's Foot Fern
**Origin:** West Indies to Brazil,
Australia
**Description:** A fern with thin,
leathery, bright bluish-green
fronds that gets its name from
the creeping stems that are
covered with rusty brown
hairlike scales. If you look at
them cross-eyed in the dark,
they look a bit like dried rabbit's feet.
**Requirements:** Filtered light and
organic soil with even moisture.
They like cool night tem-
peratures and will tolerate dry
air. This is one of the easier-to-
live-with ferns.
**Propagation:** Division
**Use:** Table, Terrarium
**Rating:** 3


**Botanical name:** POLYSCIAS
balfouriana
**Common name:** Balfour Aralia
**Origin:** New Caledonia
**Description:** Tall leafy bushes with

*POLYSCIAS fruticosa*

rounded leaves that are generally carried near the top. Since they are so tall and thin, they are generally planted three to five in a pot. They tend to drop a lot of leaves when moved from one location to another. Just wait until they get over their sulk, then they usually come around.

**Requirements:** Bright light but will tolerate very low light intensity — looking like graceful sticks with a few leaves on top. They also like even moisture, house temperatures, heavy soil with good drainage, and humid, circulating air — and they'll drop leaves to indicate disapproval of even minor changes. Once established and left alone they are quite handsome.

**Propagation:** Cuttings
**Use:** Floor, Table
**Rating:** 3

**Botanical name:** POLYSCIAS fruticosa

**Common names:** Parsley Aralia, Ming Tree

**Origin:** Polynesia, Malaysia, India

**Description:** A tall, leafy bush that has an oriental air with parsley-like leaves that are generally at the ends of the branches. It is quite tough but tends to drop a lot of leaves with environmental change (for example, when you bring it home from the store).

**Requirements:** Bright light but,

will tolerate lower intensities, although not as low as will *POLYSCIAS balfouriana*. It likes heavy soil with even moisture and good drainage, house temperatures, humidity, and good air circulation.

**Propagation:** Cuttings
**Use:** Floor, Table
**Rating:** 3

**Botanical name:** POLYSCIAS guilfoylei
**Common names:** Victoria Aralia, Wild Coffee
**Description:** A tall, thin bush with rather large leaves that are divided into three to seven leaflets (like a rose) which are often blotched, shaded, or edged with white.
**Requirements:** It prefers bright light (take care that it doesn't sunburn), but will tolerate lower light intensities. This plant also likes heavy soil with even moisture and good drainage, an even house temperature, good air circulation, and high humidity. Although a leaf dropper, it's a great plant if happy with its environment.
**Propagation:** Cuttings
**Use:** Floor, Table
**Rating:** 3

*PORTULACARIA afra*

**Botanical name:** PORTULA-CARIA afra
**Common name:** Elephant Bush
**Origin:** South Africa
**Description:** Succulent bush with

thick, grey or brownish stems and fat, juicy, bright green leaves. It looks rather like a sparse, small-leafed jade plant. Although usually under two feet tall, it can grow to six feet.

**Requirements:** Bright light and heavy soil with excellent drainage. Drench and allow to dry between waterings. Prefers good air circulation and cool night temperatures. Actually, it's very tolerant to everything except overwatering. If your problem is underwatering, the leaves will shrivel, but if you water before they drop, the plant will stick with you.

**Propagation:** Cuttings
**Use:** Floor, Table
**Rating:** 4

*PRIMULA malacoides*

**Botanical name:** PRIMULA malacoides
**Common names:** Fairy Primrose, Baby Primrose
**Origin:** Yunnan, China
**Description:** A small bushy plant with many light green leaves that are hairy underneath. It has a number of stems that carry the small pink, lavender, or white flowers. The flowers open in successive tiers. Some people have an allergic reaction to touching these primroses.
**Requirements:** Filtered light, heavy soil with good drainage kept evenly moist, a humid atmosphere, and cool night tem-

peratures. It's a pretty plant, but it doesn't last very long.

**Propagation:** Seeds
**Use:** Table
**Rating:** 1

**Botanical name:** PTERIS species
**Common names:** Brake Fern, Table Fern
**Description:** A fern with deeply cut fronds, sometimes crested and sometimes marked with white. The word *pteris* comes from the Greek and means "winged." The name refers to the plant's featherlike appearance.
**Requirements:** Shade; heavy or organic soil with excellent drainage kept evenly moist, and cool nights. It likes dry air in the winter but humid in the summer. It is not as tough as the holly fern, but it will live better inside than many of the other ferns. Small ones do well in terrariums.
**Propagation:** Division
**Use:** Table, Terrarium
**Rating:** 2

*PTERIS ensiformis 'Victoriae*

**Botanical name:** PTERIS ensiformis 'Victoriae'
**Common name:** Sword Brake
**Description:** A small fern with erect slender fronds banded with white and bordered with a wavy margin of bright green.
**Requirements:** Shade, heavy or

organic soil with excellent drainage kept evenly moist, and cool nights. It prefers dry air in the winter but humid air in summer. It does well in terrariums.

**Propagation:** Division
**Use:** Table, Terrarium
**Rating:** 2

**Botanical name:** PUNICA granatum
**Common name:** Pomegranate
**Origin:** S. E. Europe to Himalayas
**Description:** A small bushy tree with twiggy, brittle branches and narrow, shiny, green leaves with red veins. The orange-red flowers look a bit like a wad of crumpled tissue paper. The flowers are followed by fruit that has a leathery shell around the seeds, which are each packed in a juicy red capsule. Double flowered plants don't bear fruit.
**Requirements:** Bright light, cool air, good circulation, and even moisture. These are unforgiving plants, so if they dry out they're gone — usually forever. Although a real beauty, this plant either grows well or not at all. It's not a plant for forgetful people.
**Propagation:** Seeds (right out of the fruit salad), Cuttings
**Use:** Floor, Table
**Rating:** 3

*PUNICA granatum*

**Botanical name:** PUNICA granatum 'Nana'
**Common name:** Dwarf Pomegranate
**Origin:** Iran to Himalayas

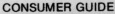

**Description:** A miniature version of *PUNICA granatum*, with twiggy, brittle branches that generally stay under three feet high when grown inside.

**Requirements:** Bright light and even moisture. If they dry out and their leaves wilt, they don't revive. Sometimes a second set of leaves will appear but more often they won't. It needs cool night temperatures and good circulation to do well. It also needs heavy soil with good drainage. Be careful when watering because the branches are brittle and won't take much pushing and shoving.

**Propagation:** Seeds, Cuttings

**Use:** Table

**Rating:** 3

**Botanical name:** REBUTIA species

**Description:** Very small globular cactuses (do you prefer cacti) many of them under 2 inches in diameter, with spines arranged in a variety of patterns. The flowers come in a variety of colors and sometimes are larger than the plant.

**Requirements:** Bright light, heavy soil with excellent drainage, good air circulation, and cool to cold night temperatures. It likes to be drenched and let dry. This is not a plant for compulsive waterers, but is rather good for those who practice benign neglect.

**Propagation:** Offsets

**Use:** Table

**Rating:** 3

*REBUTIA species*

**Botanical name:** RHAPIS excelsa

**Common name:** Lady Palm

**Origin:** South China

**Description:** A miniature fan palm with dark green, many-fingered leaves. It grows in thick clumps with leaves coming out all the way down the reedy stems.

**Requirements:** Filtered light and heavy soil with good drainage. If the soil is one-third sand, it will have the drainage it needs. It likes its roots to be kept wet and prefers good air circulation and cool night temperatures. Once established, this plant does very well.

**Propagation:** Division

**Use:** Floor, Table

**Rating:** 5

**Botanical name:** RHIPSALIS species

**Common name:** Mistletoe Cactus

**Description:** Tree growing cactuses contain the only un-American cactus species, *RHIPSALIS baccifera*, all others being American (from Canada to Patagonia) natives. Also knows as chain cactus. Their stems are either cylindrical or flat. Many with white or whitish berries.

**Requirements:** Filtered light, organic soil, good drainage, kept evenly moist. House temperatures and good air circulation.

**Propagation:** Cuttings, Division

**Use:** Hanging Basket, Table

**Rating:** 5

**Botanical name:** RHODO-DENDRON species

**Common name:** Azalea

**Description:** A bushy plant with small, shiny, green leaves and a variety of flowers. The flowers come in shades of red, pink, rose, lavender, and white, either plain or with spots or stripes. A beautiful gift plant, but the length of bloom depends on the coolness at which they can be kept.

**Requirements:** Bright light, good air circulation, and cold night temperatures. It likes organic soil that is one-half to three-fourths acid peat. The azalea will survive in a warm dry atmosphere, but the flowers will go very quickly. It also will lose its sharp, bright, fresh look. It's a transient guest in most cases, but a cool area and a person with a green thumb can keep them beautifully.

**Propagation:** Cutting, Purchase in full bud

**Use:** Floor, Table

**Rating:** 2

*RHOEO spathacea*

**Botanical name:** RHOEO spathacea

**Common name:** Moses in the Cradle, Moses in the Bullrushes, Man in a Boat, Oyster Plant

**Origin:** Mexico

**Description:** Stiff, waxy, dark green leaves. Glossy purple underneath with the small white flowers appearing in a little boat.

**Requirements:** Filtered light, heavy soil kept evenly moist. Cool night temperatures and good air circulation. If the temperature goes up so should the humidity.
**Propagation:** Cuttings
**Use:** Table
**Rating:** 4

*SAINTPAULIA ionantha*

**Botanical name:** SAINTPAULIA ionantha
**Common name:** African Violet
**Origin:** Tanganyika
**Description:** A stemless plant made up of a rosette of dark green, hairy leaves and violet flowers. Many varieties exist with differently shaped leaves, some variegated with white and light yellow. Some have single flowers, and some have double flowers. The flowers appear in white, blues, purples, and shades of pink and magenta.
**Requirements:** Filtered light and organic soil kept evenly moist. It likes cold night temperatures and dry air while it is resting, but prefers house temperatures and humid air while growing. Many varieties can be kept growing almost continuously. African violets object to cold water, even if it hasn't been put on their leaves. If chilled with cold water, they take on a deformed and spotted look.
**Propagation:** Seeds, Cuttings
**Use:** Table, Terrarium
**Rating:** 2

**Botanical name:** SANSEVIERIA
trifasciata

**Common names:** Snake Plant,
Mother-in-Law's Tongue, Bow-
string Hemp

**Origin:** Transvaal. Natal. Africa

**Description:** An erect plant with
thick, leathery, dark green.
leaves that have lighter green
cross markings. A well-grown
plant will grow five feet tall inside and will often bloom with a
cloudlike bunch of fragrant
white flowers.

**Requirements:** It likes to be
drenched and let dry between
waterings and prefers heavy
soil and good drainage. dry air.
and house temperatures. Although snake plant prefers
bright light. it will tolerate a
wide range of light intensity
and will stand almost any conditions except overwatering.
The variety with the yellow
bands on the leaves ('Lauren-
tii') will not come true from cuttings but must be reproduced by
division.

**Propagation:** Leaf cuttings (2"
pieces of leaf put in moist
sand). Division

**Use:** Floor. Table

**Rating:** 5

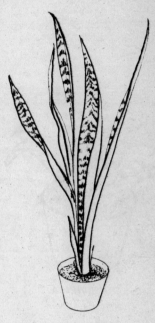

*SANSEVIERIA trifasciata*

**Botanical name:** SANSEVIERIA
trifasciata 'Hahnii'

**Common name:** Birdnest Sansevieria

**Origin:** New Orleans

**Description:** A low rosette of

wide, thick, leathery, dark green leaves. Although the dark green birdnest sansevieria is the common one, there are also yellow-branded (gold) and pale green (silver) variations.

**Requirements:** Although it prefers bright light and almost any condition except overwatering. Its choice is heavy soil with good drainage, house temperatures, and dry air. It produces a lot of offsets and is a very satisfying, easy-to-live-with plant.

**Propagation:** Offsets, Cuttings

**Use:** Table

**Rating:** 5

*SANSEVIERIA*
*trifasciata 'Hahnii'*

**Botanical name:** SAXIFRAGA sarmentosa

**Common names:** Strawberry Begonia, Mother of Thousands

**Origin:** China, Japan

**Description:** A low-spreading, round-leaved plant with bristly leaves that are olive-green splotched with silver-grey on top and spotted purple beneath. Small white flowers are carried loosely on top of a slender stem. It produces small plantlets on the end of slender threadlike stems.

**Requirements:** It likes bright light, heavy soil, and to be drenched and let dry. It also prefers cold night temperatures and circulating, humid air. However, it will tolerate less than these conditions. But if the

plant looks a bit off, it is usually
because its environment is too
warm and stuffy.
**Propagation:** Plantlets
**Use:** Table, Hanging Basket
**Rating:** 3

**Botanical name:** SCHLUMBER-
GERA bridgesii
**Common name:** Christmas Cactus
**Origin:** Bolivia
**Description:** A cactus with flat,
branching, leaflike stems. It has
a hanging flower which is bright
red touched with purple.
**Requirements:** Filtered light,
organic soil kept evenly moist,
house temperatures, and good
air circulation. It needs cooler
nights and shorter days to
bloom.
**Propagation:** Cuttings
**Use:** Table, Hanging Basket
**Rating:** 4

**Botanical name:** SCINDAPSUS
aureus (RAPHIDOPHORA au-
rea)
**Common names:** Pothos, Devil's
Ivy, Golden Pothos
**Origin:** Solomon Islands
**Description:** A climbing vine
with fleshy, shiny, sometimes
splotched leaves that look like
variegated philodendron. In the
mature plant, the leaves are
quite large and often become
lobed. This is a plant whose
common name is a bit more sta-

*SEDUM morganianum*

ble than its botanical name. The florists keep calling it pothos and the scientists keep looking for a better place to classify it.

**Requirements:** It prefers filtered light, dry air, and house temperatures and should be drenched and permitted to dry out. Its soil should be high in organic matter although it will grow for some time in just plain water. Easy to grow, this tolerant plant will last for a long time under almost any conditions — but without a lot of leaves. Frankly, though, it looks a lot better with leaves than without them.

**Propagation:** Cuttings

**Use:** Floor, Table, Hanging Basket

**Rating:** 5

*SCINDAPSUS aureus*

**Botanical name:** SEDUM morganianum

**Common names:** Burro Tail, Donkey's Tail

**Origin:** Mexico

**Description:** Hanging plant with long stems (sometimes five feet or more) covered with short, thick fleshy blue-green leaves. Small pink flowers. A very satisfying plant in a large basket. The only problem is trying to move plants with very long tails and not lose a tail or two.

**Requirements:** Bright light, drench and let dry. Heavy soil with good drainage. Prefers cool night temperatures with good circulation but will tolerate house temperatures. Leaves and stems root easily. If unwatered for six months, the leaves will shrivel up and start to drop. However, the plant will come back when watered again.

**Propagation:** Leaf, Stem Cuttings
**Use:** Table, Hanging Basket
**Rating:** 5

**Botanical name:** SEDUM rubrotinctum (SEDUM guatemalense)
**Common name:** Christmas Cheer
**Origin:** Mexico
**Description:** Short branching succulent with thick, fleshy green leaves tipped with red. Yellow flowers. Piles up nicely in a pot.
**Requirements:** Bright light (the red on the leaves grows with the brighter light), drench and let dry. Cool and cold night temperatures with good air circulation. Heavy soil with good drainage.
**Propagation:** Leaf Cuttings
**Use:** Table
**Rating:** 5

**Botanical name:** SELAGINELLA emmeliana
**Common name:** Sweat Plant
**Origin:** South America
**Description:** A small plant com-

prised of a rosette of lacy fern-like bright green fronds.

**Requirements:** It prefers shade, organic soil kept evenly moist, house temperatures, and high humidity.

**Propagation:** Cuttings
**Use:** Terrarium
**Rating:** 3

**Botanical name:** SELAGINELLA kraussiana
**Common name:** Spreading Club-moss
**Origin:** South Africa, Cameroons
**Description:** A mosslike plant with creeping stems that root as they go. The leaves are tiny and scalelike. This is a fast grower in terrariums.
**Requirements:** Shade, organic soil kept evenly moist, cool air, house temperatures, and high humidity.
**Propagation:** Cuttings
**Use:** Terrarium
**Rating:** 3

*SELAGINELLA uncinata*

**Botanical name:** SELAGINELLA uncinata
**Origin:** South China
**Description:** A scraggly, low, ir-ridescent blue-green creeping plant with scalelike leaves. The stems can reach 25 inches. Because of its love for high humidity, it is a good terrarium plant.
**Requirements:** It prefers shade,

organic soil kept evenly moist, cool and house temperatures with high humidity.

**Propagation:** Cuttings
**Use:** Terrarium
**Rating:** 3

**Botanical name:** SELAGINELLA willdenovii
**Origin:** East Himalayas, Burma, Malay Peninsula, Philippines, Malay Archipelago, New Guinea
**Description:** A strong-growing, climbing plant with fernlike blue-green fronds, brown stems, and stiltlike aerial roots. Its stems can grow as long as 20 feet.
**Requirements:** It likes shade, organic soil kept evenly moist, house temperatures, and high humidity.
**Propagation:** Cuttings
**Use:** Terrarium
**Rating:** 3

**Botanical name:** SEMPERVIVUM tectorum
**Common names:** Hens and Chickens, Roof-Houseleek
**Origin:** Europe
**Description:** Flat 3 to 4 inch rosettes of grey-green leaves tipped with brown. Pink flowers appear on top of a longish flower stalk. Charlemagne ordered every roof planted with them as a protection against

*SEMPERVIVUM tectorum*

lightning. Since the rosette died after blooming it was considered unlucky to let them flower.

**Requirements:** Bright light, drench and let dry. Heavy soil with good drainage. Prefers cold night temperature and good air circulation. Plants will exist for a long time with very little moisture, and can be used decoratively in wreaths of dried materials very effectively.

**Propagation:** Offsets
**Use:** Table
**Rating:** 2

**Botanical name:** SENECIO articulatus

**Common name:** Candle Plant

**Origin:** Cape Province

**Description:** Succulent with fat blue-green semitranslucent stems marked with darker lines. Deeply notched leaves appear at the ends of the stems. Creamish flowers. A leaf dropper.

**Requirements:** Bright light, drench let dry, heavy soil with good drainage. During period of active growth it prefers more moisture. Dry air with good circulation, cold nights in winter and house temperatures in the summer. An easy to remember plant, there aren't many that look like thin green sausages wearing leaves.

**Propagation:** Cuttings
**Use:** Table
**Rating:** 2

*SENECIO cruentus*

**Botanical name:** SENECIO cruentus

**Common name:** Cineraria of Florists

**Origin:** Canary Islands

**Description:** Flowering plant about a foot tall with bright green leaves and many daisy-like flowers in white and strong bright colors. It is a beautiful plant, well proportioned between flowers and leaves, and often a heartbreaker since it goes to pieces so quickly in most homes.

**Requirements:** Bright light, drench let dry a bit, give more water while actively growing. Heavy soil with good drainage. The temperature should be about 50°F and not dry, with good air circulation. This plant appears to be a real softy but only looks well if kept cold. As a temporary guest, it can add gaiety and charm to any setting providing you give it plenty of room to show-off.

**Propagation:** Seeds. Cuttings (but the best method is by purchase)

**Use:** Table

**Rating:** 1

**Botanical name:** SENECIO mikanioides

**Common names:** Parlor or German Ivy

**Origin:** South Africa

**Description:** A vining plant with fleshy, ivy-shaped bright green leaves. Small yellow flowers.

**Requirements:** Bright light, drench and let dry. Heavy soil with good drainage, cool to house night temperatures. Stands up well under dry air. A good filler plant for a window garden.

**Propagation:** Cuttings
**Use:** Table, Hanging Basket
**Rating:** 3

**Botanical name:** SETCREASEA purpurea
**Common name:** Purple Heart
**Origin:** Mexico
**Description:** Looks like a huge leafed, not too well-organized inch plant or wandering Jew with a small triangular lavender flower. The purple leaves turn quite green in weak light.
**Requirements:** Bright light, heavy soil, drench and let dry. To get bright colors this plant must have light. It prefers circulating air but is not too particular about temperature. Can sometimes get weedy looking, especially if the light is weak, but if given enough space for full growth can be a very satisfying plant to have around. It roots so easily you can be a very generous plant giver.
**Propagation:** Cuttings
**Use:** Table, Hanging Basket
**Rating:** 3

*SETCREASEA purpurea*

**Botanical name:** SINNINGIA pusilla

**Origin:** Brazil

**Description:** A tiny rosette of little oval leaves that is about 1 1/2 inches tall and looks a bit like an African violet. The tube-shaped lavender flowers grow on slender stems.

**Requirements:** Filtered light, organic soil with good drainage, even moisture, house temperatures, and high humidity. This is a small plant, so the pot and everything else should be kept in scale. Water it with a medicine dropper.

**Propagation:** Seeds, Leaf Cuttings

**Use:** Table, Terrarium

**Rating:** 2

*SINNINGIA speciosa*

**Botanical name:** SINNINGIA speciosa

**Common name:** Gloxinia

**Description:** A plant with large African violet-like hairy leaves growing on a very short stem. Originally the plant was stemless. It has large, deep, velvety, bell-shaped flowers which in modern varieties come in white, purple, red, and all shades and combinations.

**Requirements:** Filtered light, organic soil kept evenly moist, house temperatures, and a humid atmosphere. When growing from tubers, hold back on

the water until the roots really
start growing.
**Propagation:** Seeds. Cuttings
**Use:** Table
**Ratings:** 2

**Botanical name:** SPATHIPHYL-
LUM floribundum
**Common name:** Spathe Flower
**Origin:** Colombia
**Description:** Large. oblong. leathery. dark.green leaves about a
foot long with very short stems.
The "flower" (which is really
the sheath around the flower
stalk) is very white. This makes
an excellent filler in loca-
tions with low light intensity.
**Requirements:** Shade and evenly
moist to wet. Will tolerate low
light intensity and likes living in
a house or apartment with dry
air. Use a heavy soil that is half
peat moss.
**Propagation:** Division
**Use:** Table
**Rating:** 5

*SPATHIPHYLLUM floribundum*

**Botanical name:** STAPELIA grandiflora
**Common names:** Starfish Flower,
Carrion Flower
**Origin:** Cape Province. Transvaal
**Description:** A cactuslike plant
with grey-green, velvety stems 6
to 8 inches high. Large starfish-
like purple-brown flower has a
hairy lavender fringe. Usually

blooms in summer and fall. Some people aren't mad about their fragrance.

**Requirements:** Drench, let dry between waterings. Heavy soil with a good loading of broken brick bats and excellent drainage. Good air circulation, but not too particular as to temperatures. Should be left alone and permitted to sleep during the winter.

**Propagation:** Cuttings
**Use:** Table, Hanging Basket
**Rating:** 5

*STEPHANOTIS floribunda*

**Botanical name:** STEPHANOTIS floribunda
**Common names:** Madagascar Jasmine, Bridal Flower
**Origin:** Madagascar
**Description:** A climbing plant with shiny green opposite leaves and clusters of fragrant flowers. Can be trained on strings or around windows and will stay in the same pot for many years. A real favorite of brides, mealybug, and scale. Mealybug and scale can be controlled with regular washing of the plant.
**Requirements:** Bright light and even moisture during the summer. Reduce watering in the winter, giving it just enough to keep the leaves from withering. Prefers a heavy soil with good drainage, humid air, and house temperatures in the summer,

55°F at night in winter. Bathe regularly.

**Propagation:** Cuttings
**Use:** Table, Hanging Basket
**Rating:** 2

**Botanical name:** STRELITZIA reginae
**Common name:** Bird of Paradise
**Origin:** Transkei, South Africa
**Description:** A large pot plant that looks something like a deformed banana or palm tree. The flowers are spectacular — they look a bit like an orange bird's head with a blue bill. The genus was named in honor of George III's wife Charlotte Sophia of Mecklinburg-Strelitz. Had a few things turned out differently, this might have become our national flower.
**Requirements:** Bright light, drench and let dry although this bird drinks a lot of water in the summer. Heavy soil with good drainage (no brick or hard lumps please). Good air circulation and cool night temperatures. It needs a lot of room and can endure a good deal of neglect, graciously deigning to bloom only when good and ready and probably after good attentive care.
**Propagation:** Division (seeds if you have ages of time)
**Use:** Floor, Table
**Rating:** 4

*STRELITZIA reginae*

**Botanical name:** STREPTOCAR-
PUS hybridus

**Description:** A small bushy plant
— usually under a foot high —
with fat, light green, puckery
leaves. Its large trumpetlike
flowers come in white with purple netting, rose, blue, lavender
and purple.

**Requirements:** Filtered light,
heavy soil with good drainage
kept evenly moist, cool to cold
night temperatures, and humid
air. It does best in a huge cool
terrarium.

**Propagation:** Seeds

**Use:** Table

**Rating:** 1

*STREPTOCARPUS hybridus*

**Botanical name:** SYNADENIUM
grantii rubra

**Origin:** Tanganyika

**Description:** This succulent
shrub, a relative of the poinsettia, has thick stems and a milky
sap. The roundish leaves are a
dark maroon-red and they fall
off when neglect of the plant
has gone too far. Flowers are
red but are just incidental to the
strong maroon bush.

**Requirements:** Bright light, heavy
soil, drench and let dry between
waterings. Can go for a long
time without water but will drop
its leaves. Circulating air,
house temperatures and dry air.
This is a great inside plant for
forgetful people.

**Propagation:** Cuttings

**Use:** Floor, Table

**Rating:** 5

**Botanical name:** SYNGONIUM podophyllum

**Origin:** Mexico to Costa Rica

**Description:** A plant that changes appearance with maturity. It starts out as a small plant with arrow-shaped, thin, green leaves. As the plant gets more mature and starts creeping, the leaves first start growing "ears" and eventually become many-lobed.

**Requirements:** Filtered light, heavy soil with good drainage kept evenly moist, house temperatures, and dry air. If you keep a chicken wire pillar filled with sphagnum for them to climb on, the leaves will grow larger and the plant will mature earlier.

**Propagation:** Cuttings

**Use:** Floor, Table, Hanging Basket

**Rating:** 5

**Botanical name:** THUNBERGIA alata

**Common name:** Black-Eyed Susan

**Origin:** South Africa

**Description:** A climbing plant with opposite, triangular hairy leaves and generally a bright orange flower with a dark center.

**Requirements:** Bright light and even moisture, cool, humid air. Needs plenty of root room and feedings to flower and dislikes being cramped or cut back.

*SYNGONIUM podophyllum*

*THUNBERGIA alata*

Although perennials, they're grown as annuals since the larger they get the more unhappy they become.

**Propagation:** Seeds, Cuttings
**Use:** Table, Hanging Basket
**Rating:** 2

**Botanical name:** TILLANDSIA cyanea
**Origin:** Ecuador
**Description:** Bromeliad with a rosette of narrow leaves marked with a red-brown ''vase'' for holding water. Large lavender-blue flowers come out of the large, flat, pink flower stalk. This plant produces a lot of pups (the name for bromeliad offshoots).
**Requirements:** Filtered light, organic soil, drench and let dry, house temperature and humid atmosphere. Not as easy as some of the other bromeliads — but there are many that are harder.
**Propagation:** Offsets
**Use:** House, Table
**Rating:** 3

**Botanical name:** TILLANDSIA usneoides
**Common name:** Spanish Moss
**Origin:** S.E. United States to Argentina and Chile
**Description:** Silvery-grey string-like masses that hang from trees, telephone lines or anything that holds still in places

*TILLANDSIA cyanea*

where the climate is agreeable to them. Not a parasite, all the nourishment is taken from the air.

**Requirements:** Filtered light, organic soil, drench and let dry. Cool and dry during the winter, warm and humid during the summer. If you keep it on a branch you can dunk it in a bucket of warm water each day. Except when in bloom it is sometimes difficult to tell whether it's alive or dead. If you get bored with it, you can use it to stuff a pillow.

**Propagation:** Go to Florida or further South

**Use:** Hanging Basket

**Rating:** 3

*TOLMIEA menziesii*

**Botanical name:** TOLMIEA menziesii

**Common names:** Piggy-back Plant, Mother of Thousands

**Origin:** Alaska to California Coast

**Description:** A full plant with hairy, bright green, maple-shaped leaves. Small plants grow at the base of the mature leaves. There is a bunch of greenish flowers on the end of a long stem.

**Requirements:** Filtered light, heavy soil with good drainage kept evenly moist, cold night temperatures, and good air circulation. It sometimes misses that fresh Alaskan air when cooped up in a terrarium. A too warm and stuffy atmosphere is

what does it in.
**Propagation:** Plantlets
**Use:** Table, Hanging Basket, Terrarium
**Rating:** 3

**Botanical name:** TRADESCANTIA blossfeldiana
**Origin:** Brazil
**Description:** A branching plant with oval leaves that are shiny olive on top and purplish and hairy underneath. The flowers are lavender and white.
**Requirements:** Filtered light, cool night temperatures, and good air circulation. It likes its heavy soil to be drenched and then let dry. An occasional pruning back is necessary to keep the plant from being top heavy.
**Propagation:** Cuttings
**Use:** Table, Hanging Basket
**Rating:** 4

*TRADESCANTIA blossfeldiana*

**Botanical name:** TRADESCANTIA sillamontana
**Common name:** White Velvet
**Origin:** N.E. Mexico
**Description:** A creeping, hanging plant with dark green oval leaves that are completely covered with felty white hair. The flowers are a rosy lavender.
**Requirements:** Filtered light, cool night temperatures, and good air circulation. Prefers to have

its heavy soil drenched and then allowed to dry out.

**Propagation:** Cuttings
**Use:** Table, Hanging Basket
**Rating:** 4

**Botanical name:** TRIPOGANDRA multiflora
**Common name:** Tahitian Bridal Veil
**Origin:** Jamaica
**Description:** Full growing, slender-stemmed, creeping plant with small ovalish leaves that are dark olive on top and purple underneath. The plant is usually dotted with tiny white flowers.
**Requirements:** Filtered light, house temperatures, and good air circulation. It likes its heavy soil to be drenched and then let dry. This makes a good-looking hanging basket, especially where you want to screen out a view.
**Propagation:** Cuttings
**Use:** Table, Hanging Basket
**Rating:** 5

**Botanical name:** TULIPA hybrids
**Common name:** Tulip
**Origin:** Turkey
**Description:** Spring flowering plants with broad green leaves. Flowers, in almost every color except clear blue, on top of straight stems. Most tulips look like tulips although some look

*TULIPS*

a bit like peonies and others are very fringed and floppy. Forced for winter bloom inside.

**Requirements:** Bright light, cool temperatures, circulating air and heavy soil evenly moist are best for tulips inside. Force like most other spring bulbs or buy when the bud is still low in the leaves and enjoy the fruit of another person's labor. They are harder to force well than hyacinths or daffodils. Tulips that have been forced can be planted in the garden where they can be grown for cutting flowers although it is better to plant fresh bulbs if you want to be sure of what will come up next year.

**Propagation:** Bulbs
**Use:** Table
**Rating:** 1

**Botanical name:** VRIESEA carinata
**Common name:** Lobster Claws
**Origin:** S.E. Brazil
**Description:** This bromeliad has a rosette of pale green stiff leaves. The yellow flowers are carried on a flower stalk that is deep yellow fading to green with red at the base.
**Requirements:** Filtered light and organic soil that is drenched and then let dry. It prefers a cool temperature in the winter and house temperature in the summer. Like most bromeliads com-

monly found inside, it tolerates dry air.
**Propagation:** Offsets
**Use:** Table, Hanging Basket
**Rating:** 4

**Botanical name:** VRIESEA splendens
**Common name:** Painted Feather
**Origin:** Guiana
**Description:** A bromeliad with a rosette of stiffish, slender, blue-green leaves that have purplish cross bands. The bands are darker on the underside of the leaf. It gets its common name from a long feather-shaped, bright red flower stalk out of which the yellow flowers grow.
**Requirements:** Prefers filtered light and tolerates dry air. It likes its organic soil to be drenched and let dry, but it also likes its "vase" kept filled with water all the time. In the winter, likes cool night temperatures, but during the growing season in the summer it likes it warm. Tolerant of dry air.
**Propagation:** Offsets
**Use:** Table, Hanging Basket
**Rating:** 4

*VRIESEA splendens*

**Botanical name:** YUCCA elephantipes
**Common name:** Spineless Yucca
**Origin:** Mexico, Guatemala
**Description:** Large rosettes of sword shaped, grass-green

*VRIESEA splendens*

leaves that develop a trunk with age. The plant looks a bit like a fat dracaena with ivory white flowers.

**Requirements:** Bright light, drench and let dry. Heavy soil with good drainage. Prefers cool nights but is quite tolerant. Good circulation of dry air. Can set seeds if fresh pollen is transferred from one flower to another with a soft brush (preferably one on the main stem where the food supply is better).

**Propagation:** Cuttings, Offsets
**Use:** Floor, Table
**Rating:** 4

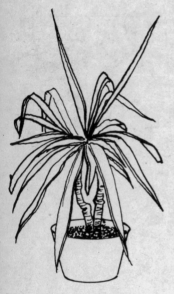

*YUCCA elephantipes*

**Botanical name:** ZANTEDESCHIA elliottiana
**Common name:** Calla
**Origin:** South Africa, Transkei
**Description:** Plant with large, arrow shaped bright green leaves marked with white spots. The flowers are bright yellow calla lilies.

**Requirements:** Filtered light, heavy soil kept evenly wet, but the bulbs must be kept rather dry until the roots develop. The pots fill up with roots before anything shows on top. Cool temperatures while resting and house temperatures while actively growing, and always good air circulation. Much happier outside than growing in a pot, but if you have one potted

keep it. Start fertilizing when
the flower stems appear.
**Propagation:** Bulbs, Seeds
**Use:** Table
**Rating:** 1


**Botanical name:** ZEBRINA pendula
**Common name:** Wandering Jew
**Origin:** Mexico
**Description:** A trailing semi-suc-
culent plant with pointed oval
leaves that range from deep
green to purple. They have two
silvery stripes on top and are
purple underneath. The flowers
are rosy lavender.
**Requirements:** Prefers filtered
light, heavy soil kept evenly
moist, humid air, good air circulation, and cool night temperatures. But it does very well
under most house conditions.
This can be a magnificent
hanging plant if given good
care.
**Propagation:** Cuttings
**Use:** Table, Hanging Basket, Terrarium
**Rating:** 5 •

*ZEBRINA pendula*

**Botanical name:** ZINGIBER offi-
cinale
**Common name:** Common Ginger
**Origin:** India to Pacific Islands
**Description:** A reedlike plant
about two feet high. It has
oblong, bright green leaves
whose swollen underground

stems (rhizomes) are used in cooking.

**Requirements:** Filtered light and heavy soil kept evenly moist. The water should be held back a bit until the roots have formed. When the plants are dormant they should be kept almost dry. Prefers house temperatures. humid air, and good circulation and will grow from stems bought in the grocery store.

**Propagation:** Rhizomes
**Use:** Table
**Rating:** 3

*ZYGOCACTUS truncatus*

**Botanical name:** ZYGOCACTUS truncatus
**Common name:** Thanksgiving Cactus
**Origin:** Organ Mountains near Rio de Janeiro
**Description:** A branching, flat-stemmed, jointed cactus without spines. It has a hanging bright red flower that blooms in late fall. This is a good plant for a hanging basket.
**Requirements:** Filtered light, organic soil with good drainage kept evenly moist, house temperature, and good air circulation.
**Propagation:** Cuttings
**Use:** Table, Hanging Basket
**Rating:** 4

# Rating the Plants

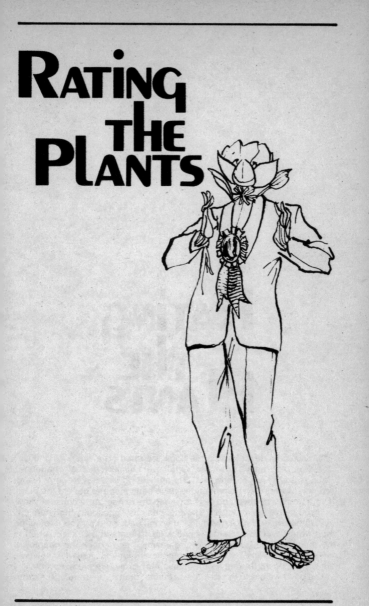

# Rating the Plants

The plants described in this book are rated on a scale from "Five" (tolerant, easy) down to "One" (very finicky, a real challenge). Ratings are based on how well a plant will do in an average house or apartment where no modifications have been made to benefit the plant. If your house isn't average — if you keep the temperature unusually low, or if you live in the middle of a swamp and have unusually high humidity in your house, or if you're home all day and have nothing you'd rather do than watch over your plants — check the "Plants at a Glance" chart in the chapter "Plants are Living Organisms," and check the chapter of "Plant Descriptions" to find the perfect plant for you. A plant that would die a slow death in an average house may grow like crazy for you.

The point we are trying to make is that all plants are great — the problem is with people. Therefore, the ratings are simply a reflection of house and habits.

Five stars go to those plants that are tolerant of indoor conditions and quite forgiving of forgetful people. These plants may flop over from thirst, but they do not die dead or drop a lot of leaves in recrimination if you forget to water them. And a "five" who has already had its fill will even take another drink just to be good company. Top-rated plants respond enthusiastically and honestly to good care and hang in there while new plant people learn what it's all about. "Fives" don't mind being moved or turned about and are resistant to pests and diseases. What's more, if you do kill one, it isn't messy — so you can clean it up easily and dispose of the evidence.

Four star plants are almost as accommodating as "fives." In fact, they would be "fives" if it weren't for their little peculiarities. For example, the *AGAVE americana* is easy to grow, but it has sharp hooks at the ends of the leaves that make them unpopular with panty-hose and knits. Another easy-grower is the *ASPARAGUS*. It can tolerate almost any conditions — providing you can tolerate the little thingies that drop off the plant onto your floor.

Plants rate lower if they require special treatment or environments, careful cutting back, dormant periods at certain times of the year, high humidity, or cold night temperatures. The more "specials," the fewer stars.

## ***** 5 STARS *****

| Botanical Name | Common Name |
|---|---|
| AECHME fasciata (BILLBERGIA rhodocyanea) | Urn Plant, Vase Plant |
| AGAVE victoriae-reginae | Queen Victoria Century Plant |
| AGLAONEMA commutatum | |
| AGLAONEMA modestum | Chinese Evergreen |
| ARAUCARIA bidwillii | Monkey-Puzzle Tree |
| ARAUCARIA heterophylla (ARAUCARIA excelsa) | Norfolk Island Pine |
| ASPIDISTRA elatior | Cast Iron Plant, Parlor Palm |
| BEAUCARNEA recurvata | Bottle Palm, Elephant Foot, Pony Tail |
| CARYOTA mitis | Fishtail Palm |
| CEPHALOCEREUS senilis | Old Man Cactus |
| CEROPEGIA woodii | Chinese Lantern Plant, Rosary Vine, String of Hearts |
| CHAMAEDOREA elegans 'Bella' (Neanthe bella) | Parlor Palm |
| CHAMAEDOREA erumpens | Bamboo Palm |

| Botanical Name | Common Name |
| --- | --- |
| CHLOROPHYTUM capense (CHLOROPHYTUM elatum) | Spider Plant |
| CHLOROPHYTUM comosum | Airplane Plant, Ribbon Plant, Spider Plant |
| CRYPTANTHUS zonatus 'Zebrinus' | Zebra Plant |
| CYCAS revoluta | Sago Palm |
| DIEFFENBACHIA amoena | Charming Dieffenbachia, Dumb Cane, Mother-in-Law Plant, Tuftroot |
| DIEFFENBACHIA exotica | Exotic Dieffenbachia |
| DIEFFENBACHIA picta (DIEFFENBACHIA brasiliensis) | Variable Dieffenbachia |
| DIEFFENBACHIA seguina | |
| DRACAENA deremensis | |
| DRACAENA draco | Dragon Tree |
| DRACAENA fragrans massangeana | Corn Plant |
| DRACAENA marginata | Red Margined Dracaena |
| DRACAENA sanderiana | |
| ECHEVERIA derenbergii | Painted Lady |
| ECHEVERIA elegans | Mexican Snowball |
| ECHINOCACTUS grusonii | Golden Barrel |
| EUPHORBIA splendens (EUPHORBIA milii splendens) | Crown of Thorns |
| EUPHORBIA tirucalli | Milk Bush, Pencil Cactus |
| FAUCARIA tigrina | Tiger Jaw |
| FICUS elastica | India Rubber Plant, Rubber Plant |
| FICUS elastica variegata | Variegated Rubber Plant |
| FICUS lyrata | Fiddle-Leaf Fig |
| GASTERIA hybrids | |
| GASTERIA verrucosa | Oxtongue Gasteria |
| HAWORTHIA species | |
| HOWEIA forsteriana | Kentia Palm, Paradise Palm, Thatch Leaf Palm |
| HOYA carnosa | Wax Plant |
| HOYA carnosa variegata | Variegated Wax Plant |
| MONSTERA deliciosa (juvenile stage known as PHILODENDRON pertusum) | Hurricane Plant, Swiss Cheese Plant, Split Leaf Philodendron |
| OPUNTIA species | Beavertail Cactus, Prickly Pears, Bunny Ears |
| PANDANUS veitchii | Screw Pine |
| PEPEROMIA caperata | Emerald Ripple |
| PEPEROMIA metallica | |
| PEPEROMIA obtusifolia | |
| PEPEROMIA sandersii 'Argyreia' | Watermelon Peperomia, Watermelon Begonia |

| Botanical Name | Common Name |
|---|---|
| PHILODENDRON bipinnatifidum | |
| PHILODENDRON oxycardium (formerly P. cordatum) | Heart Leaf Philodendron |
| PHILODENDRON panduraeforme | |
| PHILODENDRON radiatum | |
| PHILODENDRON selloum | Saddle Leaf Philodendron |
| PHILODENDRON squamiferum | |
| PHILODENDRON wendlandii | |
| PLECTRANTHUS australis | Swedish Ivy |
| PLECTRANTHUS oertendahlii | Candle Plant. Swedish Ivy |
| RHAPIS excelsa | Lady Palm |
| RHIPSALIS species | Mistletoe Cactus |
| SANSEVIERIA trifasciata | Bowstring Hemp. Mother-in-Law's Tongue. Snake Plant |
| SANSEVIERIA trifasciata 'Hahnii' | Birdnest Sansevieria |
| SCINDAPSUS aureus | Devil's Ivy. Golden Pothos. Pothos |
| SEDUM morganianum | Burro Tail. Donkey's Tail |
| SEDUM rubrotinctum (SEDUM guatemalense) | Christmas Cheer |
| SPATHIPHYLLUM floribundum | Spathe Flower |
| STAPELIA grandiflora | Carrion Flower. Starfish Flower |
| SYNADENIUM grantii rubra | |
| SYNGONIUM podophyllum | |
| TRIPOGANDRA multiflora | Tahitian Bridal Veil |
| ZEBRINA pendula | Wandering Jew |

## **** 4 STARS ****

| Botanical Name | Common Name |
|---|---|
| AGAVE americana | Century Plant |
| ALOE arborescens | Candelabra Aloe |
| ALOE variegata | Partridge Breast. Tiger Aloe |
| ALOE vera | Burn Plant. Lily of the Desert, Medicine Plant |
| ASPARAGUS meyeri | Asparagus Fern, Foxtail |
| ASPARAGUS plumosus | Asparagus Fern |
| ASPARAGUS sprengeri | Asparagus Fern |
| BRASSAIA actinophylla (SCHEFFLERA anctinophylla) | Australian Palm. Australian Umbrella Tree, Octopus Tree, Schefflera |
| CALLISIA elegans (SETCREASEA striata) | Wandering Jew, Striped Inch Plant |
| CALLISIA fragrans | |
| CEROPEGIA radicans | |

| Botanical Name | Common Name |
|---|---|
| CHAMAEROPS humilis | European Fan Palm |
| CIBOTIUM schiedei | Mexican Tree Fern |
| CISSUS antarctica | African Tree Grape, Kangaroo Ivy, Kangaroo Vine, Treebine |
| CISSUS rhombifolia | Grape Ivy, Treebine |
| CRASSULA arborescens | Silver Dollar |
| CRASSULA argentea | Chinese Rubber Plant, Jade Plant |
| CRASSULA pyramidalis | |
| CYPERUS alternifolius | Umbrella Plant |
| CYPERUS papyrus | Egyptian Paper Plant |
| DRACAENA godseffiana | Gold Dust Dracaena |
| EUPHORBIA grandicornis | Big Horned Euphorbia |
| EUPHORBIA lactea | Dragon Bones, Milk Striped Euphorbia |
| EUPHORBIA mammillaris | Corn Cob Cactus |
| EUPHORBIA mauritanica | Milk Bush, Pencil Cactus |
| FICUS benjamina | Weeping Fig |
| FICUS carica | Common Edible Fig |
| FICUS retusa nitida | Indian Laurel |
| GREVILLEA robusta (GREVILLEA banksii) | Silk Oak |
| GUZMANIA lingulata | |
| HOYA bella | Wax Plant |
| HOYA imperialis | Imperial Wax Plant |
| IMPATIENS walleriana sultanii | Busy Lizzie, Patient Lucy |
| KALANCHOE blossfeldiana | |
| KALANCHOE daigremontiana (BRYOPHYLLUM daigremontianum) | Air Plant |
| KALANCHOE pinnata | Air Plant |
| KALANCHOE tomentosa | Panda Plant, Pussy Ears |
| NERIUM oleander | Oleander |
| PEDILANTHUS tithymaloides variegatus | Devil's Backbone |
| PHOENIX dactylifera | Date Palm |
| PHOENIX roebelenii | Miniature Date Palm |
| PITTOSPORUM tobira | |
| PITTOSPORUM tobira 'Variegatum' | |
| PLEOMELE reflexa | Song of India |
| PORTULACARIA afra | Elephant Bush |
| RHOEO spathacea | Man in a Boat, Moses in the Bullrushes, Moses in the Cradle, Oyster Plant |
| SCHLUMBERGERA bridgesii | Christmas Cactus |
| STRELITZIA reginae | Bird of Paradise |
| TRADESCANTIA blossfeldiana | |
| TRADESCANTIA sillamontana | White Velvet |

| Botanical Name | Common Name |
|---|---|
| VRIESEA carinata | |
| VRIESEA splendens | Painted Feather |
| YUCCA elephantipes | Spineless Yucca |
| ZYGOCACTUS truncatus | Thanksgiving Cactus |

### *** 3 STARS ***

| Botanical Name | Common Name |
|---|---|
| AEONIUM arboreum | Saucer Plant |
| AEONIUM canariense | Giant Velvet Rose |
| ANANAS comosus (ANANAS sativus) | Pineapple |
| ANANAS comosus variegatus | Variegated Pineapple |
| ANTHURIUM andraeanum | Flamingo Flower. Flamingo Plant |
| ANTHURIUM crystallinum | |
| ARDISIA crispa (ARDISIA crenulata) | Coral Berry |
| ARECASTRUM romanzoffianum (COCOS plumosa) | Queen Palm |
| BEGONIA species | |
| CALATHEA insignis | |
| CALATHEA makoyana | Peacock Plant |
| CALATHEA ornata 'Sanderiana' | |
| CARISSA grandiflora | Natal Plum |
| CEROPEGIA debilis | |
| CITRUS limon 'Ponderosa' | American Wonderlemon |
| CITRUS mitis 'Calamondin' | Calamondin Orange |
| COFFEA arabica | Coffee |
| COLEUS blumei | Coleus |
| CORDYLINE australis (DRACAENA indivisa of florists) | Grass Palm |
| CORDYLINE terminalis | Red Dracaena. Ti Plant |
| CYANOTIS somaliensis | Pussy Ears |
| CYATHEA arborea | Tree Fern |
| CYRTOMIUM falcatum (ASPIDIUM falcatum) | Hollyfern |
| DIZYGOTHECA elegantissima | False Aralia. Finger Aralia. Threadleaf |
| EPIPHYLLUM oxypetalum | Queen of Night |
| ERIOBOTRYA japonica | Japan Plum. Loquat |
| GYNURA aurantiaca | Purple Passion Plant. Velvet Plant |
| HELICONIA humilis | Lobster Claw |
| HELXINE soleirolii | Baby Tears. Irish Moss |
| HIBISCUS rosa-sinensis | Chinese Rose. Shoeflower |
| HIBISCUS schizopetalus | Hibiscus |
| IRESINE herbstii | Bloodleaf |
| LITHOPS species | Living Stones |

| Botanical Name | Common Name |
|---|---|
| LIVISTONA chinensis | Chinese Fan Palm |
| MAMMILLARIA species | Pincushion Cactus |
| MARANTA leuconeura kerchoveana | Prayer Plant. Rabbit Tracks |
| NEPHROLEPIS exaltata | Sword Fern |
| NEPHROLEPIS exaltata 'Bostoniensis' | Boston Fern |
| NOTOCACTUS leninghausii | Ball Cactus. Golden Ball Cactus |
| OXALIS hedysaroides rubra | Firefern |
| PELARGONIUM hortorum | Geranium |
| PELARGONIUM peltatum | Ivy Geranium |
| PILEA cadierei | Aluminum Plant. Watermelon Plant |
| PILEA involucrata | Pan-American Friendship Plant. Panamiga |
| PLATYCERIUM bifurcatum | Staghorn Fern |
| POLYPODIUM aureum | Hare's Foot Fern |
| POLYSCIAS balfouriana | Balfour Aralia |
| POLYSCIAS fruticosa | Ming Tree, Parsley Aralia |
| POLYSCIAS guilfoylei | Victoria Aralia. Wild Coffee |
| PUNICA granatum | Pomegranate |
| PUNICA granatum 'Nana' | Dwarf Pomegranate |
| REBUTIA species | |
| SAXIFRAGA sarmentosa | Mother of Thousands, Strawberry Begonia |
| SELAGINELLA emmeliana | Sweat Plant |
| SELAGINELLA kraussiana | Spreading Clubmoss |
| SELAGINELLA uncinata | |
| SELAGINELLA willdenovii | |
| SENECIO mikanioides | German Ivy, Parlor Ivy |
| SETCREASEA purpurea | Purple Heart |
| TILLANDSIA cyanea | |
| TILLANDSIA usneoides | Spanish Moss |
| TOLMIEA menziesii | Mother of Thousands, Piggy-back Plant |
| ZINGIBER officinale | Common Ginger |

## ** 2 STARS **

| Botanical Name | Common Name |
|---|---|
| ABUTILON hybridum | Chinese Bellflower, Flowering Maple, Parlor Maple |
| ACORUS gramineus variegatus | Calamus Root, Dwarf Japanese Sweet Flag, Sweet Flag |
| AGAPANTHUS africanus | Blue African Lily, Lily of the Nile, Love Flower |
| ASPLENIUM nidus | Birdnest Fern, Spleenwort, Shuttlecock |

| Botanical Name | Common Name |
|---|---|
| ASPLENIUM viviparum | Mother Fern |
| BOUGAINVILLEA glabra | |
| CITRUS paradisi | Grapefruit |
| CITRUS sinensis | Sweet Orange |
| CLIVIA miniata | Kafir Lily |
| COLUMNEA gloriosa | |
| COLUMNEA hirta | |
| DAVALLIA species | Rabbit Foot Ferns |
| EPISCIA cupreata | Flame Violet |
| EPISCIA lilacina | |
| EPISCIA reptans | |
| EUPHORBIA pulcherrima | Lobster Flower, Mexican Flame Leaf, Poinsettia |
| FATSHEDERA lizei | Fat Lizzie, Tree Ivy |
| FATSIA japonica | Japanese Aralia |
| FICUS pumila (FICUS repens) | Creeping Fig |
| HEDERA helix | English Ivy |
| HYDROSME rivieri (Amorphophallus) | Devil's Tongue, Voodoo Plant |
| LAMPRANTHUS emarginatus | Ice Plant |
| LANTANA camara | |
| MANGIFERA indica | Mango |
| MUSA nana (MUSA cavendishii) | Dwarf Banana, Dwarf Jamaica Banana |
| NEPHROLEPIS exaltata 'Fluffy Ruffles' | Fluffy Ruffles |
| OXALIS rubra | Grandmother's Shamrock |
| PASSIFLORA caerulea | Passion Flower |
| PASSIFLORA coccinea | Red Passion Flower |
| PERSEA americana | Alligator Pear, Avocado |
| PILEA microphylla | Artillery Plant |
| PLUMBAGO capensis | |
| PLUMBAGO indica coccinea | |
| PLUMERIA rubra (PLUMERIA acuminata) | Frangipani Tree |
| PODOCARPUS macrophylla | |
| PTERIS species | Brake Fern, Table Fern |
| PTERIS ensiformis 'Victoriae' | Sword Brake |
| RHODODENDRON species | Azalea |
| SAINTPAULIA ionantha | African Violet |
| SEMPERVIVUM tectorum | Hens and Chickens, Roof-Houseleek |
| SENECIO articulatus | Candle Plant |
| SINNINGIA pusilla | |
| SINNINGIA speciosa | Gloxinia |

| Botanical Name | Common Name |
| --- | --- |
| STEPHANOTIS floribunda | Bridal Flower, Madagascar Jasmine |
| THUNBERGIA alata | Black-Eyed Susan |

## * 1 STAR *

| Botanical Name | Common Name |
| --- | --- |
| ACER palmatum | Japanese Maple |
| ADIANTUM species and varieties | Maidenhair Fern |
| APHELANDRA squarrosa Louisae | Zebra Plant |
| BELOPERONE guttata | Shrimp Plant |
| CALADIUM hortulanum | Fancy Leaved Caladium |
| CALCEOLARIA herbeohybrida | Pocketbook Plant |
| CAMELLIA japonica | |
| CAPSICUM annuum 'Conoides' | Christmas Pepper |
| CHRYSANTHEMUM morifolium (CHRYSANTHEMUM hortorum) | Mum |
| CODIAEUM (CROTON) 'Variegatum' | Croton |
| CROCUS species | |
| CYCLAMEN persicum | Alpine Violet, Florist's Cyclamen |
| FITTONIA argyroneura | Silver-nerved Fittonia |
| FITTONIA verschaffeltii | Red-nerved Fittonia |
| FUCHSIA hybrids | Lady's Eardrops |
| GARDENIA jasminoides | |
| HIPPEASTRUM (AMARYLLIS) hybrids | Amaryllis |
| HYACINTHUS orientalis | Hyacinth |
| MIMOSA pudica | Sensitive Plant |
| NARCISSUS jonquilla | Jonquil |
| NARCISSUS pseudo-narcissus | Daffodil, Lent Lily |
| NARCISSUS tazetta | Paper White Narcissus |
| PRIMULA malacoides | Baby Primrose, Fairy Primrose |
| SENECIO cruentus | Cineraria of florists |
| STREPTOCARPUS hybridus | |
| TULIPA hybrids | Tulip |
| ZANTEDESCHIA elliottiana | Calla |

# Plants Are Living Organisms

**P**lants are living organisms, and like people, they come in many sizes and with a great variety of preferences. Some plants are more accommodating than others and will adapt to almost any situation. Others are much less tolerant and will just give up and quit if their every desire isn't met. Perhaps these plants have a greater sense of self-worth and always want to look their best. Generally speaking, a plant will respond to the kind of treatment it gets.

In the typical house or apartment, the temperature is set for the comfort of the human inhabitants. The condition that is different from house to house is the amount of light that is available. For this reason, the plants in the following charts are arranged according to the amount of light they prefer. To find a plant that will grow perfectly in that empty spot in your living room, first determine if the light in that spot is bright, filtered, or shady. Then turn to the page of the charts that lists the plants that like that light condition. Keep in mind however, that plants and people share the ability to exist under many situations, although they can bloom splendidly under better ones. An example of this is the rarity in which one sees a really well-grown sansevieria. This plant will exist under the poorest conditions, but given half the chance, will grow over six feet tall and be an asset to any decorating scheme. Another frequently mistreated plant is the schefflera, which also can exist in the grungiest corner of the room, but can be really magnificent in sufficient bright light.

## Light

**Bright.** This means bright light or full sun with no curtains or blinds between the plant and the window. On the other side of the window, there is no tree, sign, or building to obstruct the light from the outside. In bright light, when you hold your hand a foot over a sheet of paper, you get a clear, sharp shadow.

**Filtered.** This means sunlight which is diffused by a glass curtain in the window. In filtered light, your hand makes a fuzzy, but distinguishable shadow when held a foot above a sheet of typing paper.

**Shady.** This means no direct sun or other light, and your hand held a foot over a sheet of paper will produce nothing more than a blob. All plants that tolerate shade need high humidity.

## Watering

The plants are also organized according to how wet they like to be. If you don't have time to check your plants daily, you'd probably be happiest with those that like to dry out between watering.

**Drench and Let Dry.** Soak the plant thoroughly by submerging the pot in a bucket or sink filled with tepid water until all the bubbles have stopped coming out. The plant can then dry out until its next soaking, which should take place when the surface of the soil is dry to the touch. Most of the plants that prefer drenching and drying have thick white roots.

**Moist.** These plants should be watered so that the soil is kept evenly moist and never gets soaked or too dry. These plants have delicate hairlike roots that rot if they are too wet; or if the soil gets too dry, they up and die.

**Wet.** These like to be kept wet at all times, and a few of them even like to sit in water all the time.

## Temperature

When trying to match your house temperature to a plant's favorite climate, the important point of comparison is night temperature. The night temperature is most important in a plant's growth, and most plants prefer a distinct difference between their night and day temperatures.

**Cold.** This indicates a night temperature of 40 - 45°F.

**Cool.** These plants like a night temperature of 50 - 55°F.
A good many of the old-fashioned favorites are in this category. When these plants look listless and not quite bright, they probably had a bad night.

**House.** This indicates night temperatures of 60 - 65°F. These are what the old timers used to call stovehouse or hothouse plants. In the old days, these temperatures were reserved for picky exotic plants and finicky invalid humans.

### Air

Some plants tolerate dry air, and others insist on it being humid. Some can't stand drafts and love a stagnant corner, while others prefer good circulation and plenty of fresh air.

**Dry.** This means a typical modern house, apartment, or office — which contains half the percentage of moisture that's found in the Sahara.

**Circulating.** These plants need fresh air and good ventilation. They appreciate getting out of the house into the fresh air in the summer, although when they go outside, they should always be protected from full sun.

**Humid.** These plants prefer a humidity of 70 percent, which generally means a terrarium or a clear cleaner's bag. For special occasions, you can take the plastic bags off the plants just as you take the plastic covers off the furniture.

### Soil

Plants will usually grow in what they get — especially if they're growing indoors and are going to be fed. But they do have certain preferences, so if you have a choice, give them what they want. See the chapter on Potting and Repotting to find your plant's favorite soil recipe.

**Heavy.** This is made of good garden soil, clay, or loam with about one-third humus. When good drainage is required, it should contain about one-third washed builder's sand or perlite. Perlite is very light, so if you use it, be sure to put a few rocks in the bottom of your pot to keep your plant from tipping over.

**Organic.** This is soil that is rich in humus, leaf mold (disintegrated leaves), or some other organic soil. Coarse builder's sand or perlite will improve the drainage.

**Light.** This means open-textured material with excellent drainage that can be kept moist but never wet. It is good for plants that in nature spend their time in trees, such as bromeliads, orchids, and some ferns. These materials include fern root fiber (osmunda), shredded fir bark, and sometimes sphagnum moss (sheet not milled). Broken clay pots can be added to increase drainage.

# PLANTS AT A GLANCE

Light Requirement: Bright

Watering Requirement: Drench, Let Dry

| RATING | BOTANICAL NAME | COMMON NAME | SIZE | TEMP. | AIR | SOIL |
|---|---|---|---|---|---|---|
| * | ACER palmatum | Japanese Maple | F,T | Cold | Circulating | Heavy |
| **** | AGAVE americana | Century Plant | F,T | Cool | Dry | Heavy |
| ***** | AGAVE victoriae-reginae | Queen Victoria Century Plant | T | Cool | Dry | Heavy |
| **** | ALOE arborescens | Candelabra Aloe | F | Cool | Dry | Heavy |
| **** | ALOE variegata | Partridge Breast, Tiger Aloe | T | Cool | Dry | Heavy |
| **** | ALOE vera | Medicine Plant, Lily of the Desert, Burn Plant | T | Cool | Dry | Heavy |
| ***** | BEAUCARNEA recurvata | Bottle Palm, Elephant Foot, Pony Tail | F,T | Cool | Dry | Heavy |
| * | BELOPERONE guttata | Shrimp Plant | H,T | Cool | Circulating | Heavy |
| ** | BOUGAINVILLEA glabra | | H,T | House | Circulating | Heavy |
| **** | BRASSAIA actinophylla (SCHEFFLERA actinophylla) | Australian Palm, Australian Umbrella Tree, Octopus Tree, Schefflera | F,T | House | Dry | Heavy |
| *** | CEPHALOCEREUS senilis | Old Man Cactus | T | House | Dry | Heavy |
| *** | CITRUS limon 'Ponderosa' | American Wonderlemon | F,T | Cool | Circulating | Heavy |
| *** | CITRUS mitis 'Calamondin' | Calamondin Orange | T | Cool | Circulating | Heavy |
| *** | CITRUS paradisi | Grapefruit | F,T | Cool | Circulating | Heavy |
| *** | CITRUS sinensis | Sweet Orange | F,T | Cool | Circulating | Heavy |
| *** | CYANOTIS somaliensis | Pussy Ears | H,T | Cool | Circulating | Heavy |
| ***** | ECHEVERIA derenbergii | Painted Lady | T | Cool | Circulating | Heavy |
| ***** | ECHEVERIA elegans | Mexican Snowball | T | Cool | Circulating | Heavy |
| ***** | ECHINOCACTUS grusonii | Golden Barrel | T | Cool, house | Circulating | Heavy |

| | Scientific Name | Common Name | Placement | Temperature | Air | Watering |
|---|---|---|---|---|---|---|
| **** | EUPHORBIA grandicornis | Big Horned Euphorbia | F,T | Cool house | Circulating | Heavy |
| **** | EUPHORBIA lactea | Milk Striped Euphorbia. Dragon Bones | F,T | Cool house | Circulating | Heavy |
| **** | EUPHORBIA mammillaris | Corn Cob Cactus | T | Cool house | Circulating | Heavy |
| **** | EUPHORBIA mauritanica | Milk Bush. Pencil Cactus | F,T | Cool house | Circulating | Heavy |
| ** | EUPHORBIA pulcherrima | Lobster Flower, Mexican Flame Leaf, Poinsettia | F,T | Cool house | Circulating | Heavy |
| ***** | EUPHORBIA splendens (Euphorbia milii splendens) | Crown of Thorns | F,H,T | Cool house | Circulating | Heavy |
| **** | EUPHORBIA tirucalli | Indian Tree Spurge. Milk Bush. Pencil Cactus | F,T | Cool house | Circulating | Heavy |
| **** | FAUCARIA tigrina | Tiger Jaw | T | Cool | Circulating | Heavy |
| **** | GREVILLEA robusta | Silk Oak | F,T | Cool | Circulating | Heavy |
| **** | HOYA bella | Wax Plant | H,T | Cool house | Circulating | Heavy |
| **** | HOYA carnosa | Wax Plant | H,T | Cool | Circulating | Heavy |
| **** | HOYA carnosa variegata | Variegated Wax Plant | H,T | Cool | Circulating | Heavy |
| **** | HOYA imperialis | Imperial Wax Plant | H,T | Cool | Circulating | Heavy |
| **** | KALANCHOE blossfeldiana | | T | Cool | Circulating | Heavy |
| **** | KALANCHOE daigremontiana (BRYOPHYLLUM daigremontianum) | Air Plant | T | Cool | Circulating | Heavy |
| **** | KALANCHOE pinnata | Air Plant | T | Cool | Circulating | Heavy |
| **** | KALANCHOE tomentosa | Panda Plant, Pussy Ears | T | Cool | Circulating | Heavy |
| ** | LAMPRANTHUS emarginatus | Ice Plant | H,T | Cool | Circulating | Heavy |
| ** | LANTANA camara | | F,H,T | Cold cool | Circulating | Heavy |
| *** | LITHOPS species | Living Stones | T | Cool | Circulating | Heavy |

F=floor; H=hanging; T=table; Tr=terrarium

Light Requirement: Bright          Watering Requirement: Drench, Let Dry

| RATING | BOTANICAL NAME | COMMON NAME | SIZE | TEMP. | AIR | SOIL |
|---|---|---|---|---|---|---|
| * * * | MAMMILLARIA species | Pincushion Cactus | F,T | Cool | Circulating | Heavy |
| * * * | NOTOCACTUS leninghausii | Golden Ball Cactus, Ball Cactus | T | Cold | Circulating | Heavy |
| * * * * * | OPUNTIA species | Bunny Ears, Beaver-tail Cactus, Prickly Pears | F,T | Cool, house | Circulating, Dry | Heavy |
| * * * | OXALIS hedysaroides rubra | Firefern | T | Cool house | Circulating | Heavy |
| * * | OXALIS rubra | Grandmother's Shamrock | H,T | Cold, cool | Circulating | Heavy |
| * * * | PELARGONIUM hortorum | Geranium | F,T | Cold, cool | Circulating | Heavy |
| * * * | PELARGONIUM peltatum | Ivy Geranium | H,T | Cold, Cool | Circulating | Heavy |
| * * * * | PITTOSPORUM tobira | | F,T | Cold, cool | Circulating | Heavy |
| * * * * | PITTOSPORUM tobira 'Variegatum' | | F,T | Cool | Circulating | Heavy |
| * * * | PORTULACARIA afra | Elephant Bush | F,T | Cold, cool | Circulating | Heavy |
| * * * | REBUTIA species | | T | | Circulating | Heavy |
| * * * * * | SANSEVIERIA trifasciata | Snake Plant, Mother-in-Law's Tongue. Bowstring Hemp | F,T | House | Dry | Heavy |
| * * * * * | SANSEVIERIA trifasciata 'Hahnii' | Birdnest Sansevieria | T | House | Dry | Heavy |
| * * * | SAXIFRAGA sarmentosa | Strawberry Begonia. Mother of Thousands | H,T | Cold | Circulating, humid | Heavy |
| * * * * * | SEDUM morganianum | Burro Tail, Donkey's Tail | H,T | Cool | Circulating | Heavy |
| * * * * * | SEDUM rubrotinctum (SEDUM guatemalense) | Christmas Cheer | T | Cool, cold | Circulating | Heavy |

| RATING | BOTANICAL NAME | COMMON NAME | SIZE | TEMP. | AIR | SOIL |
|---|---|---|---|---|---|---|
| ** | SEMPERVIVUM tectorum | Hens and Chickens, Roof-Houseleek | T | Cold | Circulating | Heavy |
| ** | SENECIO articulatus | Candle Plant | T | Cold, house | Circulating, dry | Heavy |
| * | SENECIO cruentus | Cineraria of florists | T, H | Cold | Circulating, humid | Heavy |
| *** | SENECIO mikanioides | Parlor Ivy, German Ivy | T | Cool, house | Dry | Heavy |
| *** | SETCREASEA purpurea | Purple Heart | H, T | Cool, house | Circulating | Heavy |
| ***** | STAPELIA grandiflora | Starfish Flower, Carrion Flower | H, T | Cool, house | Circulating | Heavy |
| **** | STRELITZIA reginae | Bird of Paradise | F, T | Cool | Circulating | Heavy |
| **** | SYNADENIUM grantii rubra | | F, T | House | Circulating | Heavy |
| **** | YUCCA elephantipes | Spineless Yucca | F, T | Cool | Circulating | Heavy |

## Light Requirement: Bright

### Watering Requirement: Moist

| RATING | BOTANICAL NAME | COMMON NAME | SIZE | TEMP. | AIR | SOIL |
|---|---|---|---|---|---|---|
| ** | ABUTILON hybridum | Chinese Bellflower, Flowering Maple, Parlor Maple | F, T | Cool | Circulating | Heavy |
| ** | AGAPANTHUS africanus | Blue African Lily, Lily of the Nile, Love Flower | F, T | Cool | Dry | Heavy |
| *** | ANANAS comosus (ANANAS sativus) | Pineapple | F, T | House | Humid | Organic |
| *** | ANANAS comosus variegatus | Variegated Pineapple | F, T | House | Humid | Organic |
| *** | CAPSICUM annuum Conoides | Christmas Pepper | T | House | Circulating | Heavy |
| *** | CARISSA grandiflora | Natal Plum | T | Cool | Circulating | Heavy |
| | CHRYSANTHEMUM morifolium (CHRYSANTHEMUM hortorum) | Mum | T | Cold | Circulating | Heavy |
| | CODIAEUM (CROTON) variegatum | Croton | F, T | House | Circulating, humid | Heavy |

F=floor, H=hanging, T=table, Tr=terrarium

Light Requirement: Bright   Watering Requirement: Moist

| RATING | BOTANICAL NAME | COMMON NAME | SIZE | TEMP. | AIR | SOIL |
|---|---|---|---|---|---|---|
| *** | COLEUS blumei | Coleus | T,H | House | Circulating | Heavy |
| * | CROCUS species | | T | Cold | Circulating | Heavy |
| *** | ERIOBOTRYA japonica | Loquat, Japan Plum | F,T | Cool | Circulating | Heavy |
| ** | FATSHEDERA lizei | Fat Lizzie, Tree Ivy | F,T | Cold, Cool | Circulating | Heavy |
| * | GARDENIA jasminoides | Velvet Plant, | F,T | House | Circulating | Organic |
| ** | GYNURA aurantiaca | Purple Passion Plant, | H,T | House | Circulating | Heavy |
| ** | HEDERA helix | English Ivy | H,T | Cold | Circulating | Heavy |
| ** | HIBISCUS rosa-sinensis | Chinese Rose, Shoe Flower | F,T | House | Circulating | Heavy |
| ** | HIBISCUS schizopetalus | Hibiscus | F,T | House | Circulating | Heavy |
| * | HIPPEASTRUM (AMARYLLIS) hybrids | Amaryllis | T | Cool, house | Circulating | Heavy |
| **** | IMPATIENS walleriana sultanii | Patient Lucy, Busy Lizzie | H,T | Cool | Circulating | Organic |
| ** | IRESINE herbstii | Bloodleaf | T | Cool | Circulating | Heavy |
| ** | MANGIFERA indica | Mango | F,T | House | Circulating | Heavy |
| * | NARCISSUS jonquilla | Jonquil | T | Cold | Circulating | Heavy |
| * | NARCISSUS pseudo-narcissus | Daffodil, Lent Lily | T | Cold | Circulating | Heavy |
| * | NARCISSUS tazetta | Paper White Narcissus | T | Cold | Circulating | Heavy |
| **** | NERIUM oleander | Oleander | F,T | Cool | Circulating | Heavy |
| ** | PASSIFLORA caerulea | Passion Flower | H,T | Cool, house | Circulating, humid | Heavy |
| ** | PASSIFLORA coccinea | Red Passion Flower | H,T | Cool, house | Circulating, humid | Heavy |
| ** | PERSEA americana | Avocado, Alligator Pear | F,T | Cool, house | Circulating | Heavy |
| ** | PLUMBAGO capensis | | F,T | Cool | Circulating | Heavy |
| ** | PLUMBAGO indica coccinea | | F,T | House | Circulating | Heavy |

| RATING | BOTANICAL NAME | COMMON NAME | SIZE | TEMP. | AIR | SOIL |
|---|---|---|---|---|---|---|
| *** | POLYSCIAS balfouriana | Balfour Aralia | F,T | House | Circulating, Humid | Heavy |
| *** | POLYSCIAS fruticosa | Parsley Aralia, Ming Tree | F,T | House | Circulating, humid | Heavy |
| *** | POLYSCIAS guilfoylei | Victoria Aralia / Wild Coffee | F,T | House | Circulating, humid | Heavy |
| *** | PUNICA granatum | Pomegranate | F,T | Cool | Circulating | Heavy |
| *** | PUNICA granatum 'nana' | Dwarf Pomegranate | T | Cool | Circulating | Heavy |
| *** | STEPHANOTIS floribunda | Bridal Flower; Madagascar Jasmine | H,T | House | Humid | Heavy |
| ** | THUNBERGIA alata | Black-Eyed Susan | H,T | Cool | Humid | Heavy |
| ** | TULIPA hybrids | Tulip | T | Cool | Circulating | Heavy |

## Light Requirement: Bright    Watering Requirement: Wet

| RATING | BOTANICAL NAME | COMMON NAME | SIZE | TEMP. | AIR | SOIL |
|---|---|---|---|---|---|---|
| **** | CHAMAEROPS humilis | European Fan Palm | F,T | Cool | Circulating | Heavy |
| ** | HYACINTHUS orientalis | Hyacinth | T | Cold | Circulating | Heavy |
| ** | HYDROSME rivieri* (Amorphophallus) | Devil's Tongue, Voodoo Plant | F, T | House | Circulating, humid | Heavy |
| ** | MUSA nana (MUSA cavendishii) | Dwarf Banana, Dwarf Jamaica | F,T | House | Circulating, humid | Heavy. |
| ** | RHODODENDRON species | Azalea | F,T | Cold | Circulating | Organic |

*Keep wet April-September, Drench thoroughly and let dry between waterings during November-February.

## Light Requirement: Filtered    Watering Requirement: Drench, Let Dry

| RATING | BOTANICAL NAME | COMMON NAME | SIZE | TEMP. | AIR | SOIL |
|---|---|---|---|---|---|---|
| *** | AEONIUM arboreum | Saucer Plant | F,T | Cool | Circulating | Heavy |
| *** | AEONIUM canariense | Giant Velvet Rose | T | Cool | Circulating | Heavy |
| *** | CEROPEGIA debilis | | H,T | Cool | Dry | Organic |
| **** | CEROPEGIA radicans | | H,T | Cool | Dry | Organic |

F=floor; H=hanging; T=table; Tr=terrarium

| | | Light Requirement: Filtered | | Watering Requirement: Drench, Let Dry | | |
| --- | --- | --- | --- | --- | --- | --- |
| RATING | BOTANICAL NAME | COMMON NAME | SIZE | TEMP. | AIR | SOIL |
| ***** | CEROPEGIA woodii | String of Hearts, Rosary Vine, Chinese Lantern Plant | H,T | Cool | Dry | Organic |
| **** | CISSUS antarctica | Kangaroo Vine, Kangaroo Ivy, Treebine, African Tree Grape | H,T | Cool | Dry | Heavy |
| **** | CISSUS rhombifolia | Grape Ivy, Treebine | H,T | Cool, house | Circulating | Heavy |
| ** | CLIVIA miniata | Kafir Lily | F,T | Cool | Circulating | Heavy |
| *** | CRASSULA arborescens | Silver Dollar | F,T | Cool | Circulating | Heavy |
| *** | CRASSULA argentea | Jade Plant, Chinese Rubber Plant | F,T | Cool | Circulating | Heavy |
| *** | CRASSULA pyramidalis | | T | Cool | Circulating | Heavy |
| *** | CRYPTANTHUS zonatus 'Zebrinus' | Zebra Plant | T | House | Dry | Organic |
| *** | CYCAS revoluta | Sago Palm | F,T | Cool | Dry | Heavy |
| *** | DIEFFENBACHIA amoena | Dumb Cane, Tuftroot, Charming Dieffenbachia, Mother-in-law Plant | F,T | House | Dry | Heavy |
| ***** | DIEFFENBACHIA exotica | Exotic Dieffenbachia | F,T | House | Dry | Heavy |
| ***** | DIEFFENBACHIA picta (DIEFFENBACHIA brasiliensis) | Variable Dieffenbachia | F,T | House | Dry | Heavy |
| ***** | DIEFFENBACHIA sequina | | F,T | House | Dry | Heavy |
| ***** | GASTERIA hybrids | | T | Cool | Circulating | Heavy |
| ***** | GASTERIA verrucosa | Oxtongue Gasteria | T | Cool | Circulating | Heavy |
| ** | HAWORTHIA species | | T | Cool | Dry | Heavy |
| ** | ORCHIDACEAE genus and species | | H,T | Cold | Humid | Light |
| ***** | PANDANUS veitchii | Screw Pine | F,T | House | Dry | Heavy |
| ***** | PEPEROMIA caperata | Emerald Ripple | F,T | House | Dry | Heavy |
| ***** | PEPEROMIA metallica | | T | House | Dry | Heavy |
| ***** | PEPEROMIA obtusifolia | | T | House | Dry | Heavy |

| RATING | BOTANICAL NAME | COMMON NAME | SIZE | TEMP. | AIR | SOIL |
|---|---|---|---|---|---|---|
| ***** | PEPEROMIA sandersii Argyreia | Watermelon Peperomia. Watermelon Begonia | T | House | Dry | Heavy |
| ****** | SCINDAPSUS aureus | Pothos, Devil's Ivy, Golden Pothos | F,H,T | House | Dry | Organic |
| *** | TILLANDSIA cyanea | | H,T | House | Humid | Organic |
| *** | TILLANDSIA usneoides | Spanish Moss | H | Cool. house | Dry. humid | Organic |
| ***** | TRADESCANTIA blossfeldiana | White Velvet | H,T | Cool | Circulating | Heavy |
| *** | TRADESCANTIA sillamontana | | H,T | Cool | Circulating | Heavy |
| ***** | TRIPOGANDRA multiflora | Tahitian Bridal Veil | H,T | House | Circulating | Heavy |
| | VRIESEA carinata | | H,T | Cool. house | Dry | Organic |
| ***** | VRIESEA splendens | Painted Feather | H,T | Cool. house | Dry | Organic |

## Light Requirement: Filtered
## Watering Requirement: Moist

| RATING | BOTANICAL NAME | COMMON NAME | SIZE | TEMP. | AIR | SOIL |
|---|---|---|---|---|---|---|
| ***** | AECHMEA fasciata (BILLBERGIA rhodocyanea) | Vase Plant, Urn Plant | H,T | House | Dry | Light |
| * | APHELANDRA squarrosa 'Louisae' | Zebra Plant | T | House | Dry | Organic |
| ***** | ARAUCARIA bidwillii | Monkey-Puzzle Tree | F,T | Cool | Dry | Organic |
| ***** | ARAUCARIA heterophylla (ARAUCARIA excelsa) | Norfolk Island Pine | F,T | Cool | Dry | Organic |
| *** | ARDISIA crispa (ARDISIA crenulata) | Coral Berry | T | Cool | Circulating | Heavy |
| **** | ASPARAGUS meyeri | Foxtail. Asparagus Fern | H,T | Cool | Circulating | Heavy |
| *** | ASPARAGUS plumosus | Asparagus Fern | H,T | Cool | Circulating | Heavy |
| *** | ASPARAGUS sprengeri | Aspargus Fern | H,T | Cool | Circulating | Heavy |
| *** | BEGONIA species | | H,T | House | Circulating. humid | Organic |

F=floor; H=hanging; T=table. Tr=terrarium

Light Requirement: Filtered    Watering Requirement: Moist

| RATING | BOTANICAL NAME | COMMON NAME | SIZE | TEMP. | AIR | SOIL |
|---|---|---|---|---|---|---|
| **** | BROMELIACEAE genus and species | Bromeliads | H,T | House | Circulating | Heavy |
| * | CALADIUM hortulanum | Fancy Leaved Caladium | T | House | Circulating, dry, humid | Organic |
| *** | CALATHEA insignis | | T | House | Humid | Organic |
| *** | CALATHEA makoyana | Peacock Plant | T | House | Humid | Organic |
| *** | CALATHEA ornata 'Sanderiana' | | T | House | Humid | Organic |
| *** | CALLISIA elegans (SETCREASEA striata) | Wandering Jew. Striped Inch Plant | H,T | Cool | Circulating | Heavy |
| **** | CALLISIA fragrans | | H,T | Cool | Circulating | Heavy |
| **** | CHLOROPHYTUM capense (CHLOROPHYTUM elatum) | Spider Plant | H,T | Cool | Circulating | Heavy |
| ***** | CHLOROPHYTUM comosum | Spider Plant. Airplane Plant. Ribbon Plant | H,T | Cool | Circulating | Heavy |
| *** | CIBOTIUM schiedei | Mexican Tree Fern | F,T | House | Dry | Organic |
| *** | COFFEA arabica | Coffee | F,T | House | Circulating | Heavy |
| *** | COLUMNEA gloriosa | | H,T,Tr, | House | Humid | Organic |
| *** | COLUMNEA hirta | | H,T,Tr, | House | Humid | Organic |
| *** | CORDYLINE australis (DRACAENA indivisa of florists) | Grass Palm | F,T | House | Circulating | Heavy |
| *** | CORDYLINE terminalis | Red Dracaena. Ti Plant | F,T | House | Circulating | Heavy |
| * | CYCLAMEN persicum | Florist's Cyclamen. Alpine Violet | T | Cold | Humid | Organic |
| *** | DIZYGOTHECA elegantissima | False Aralia. Threadleaf. Finger Aralia | F,T | House | Circulating | Heavy |
| ** | EPISCIA cupreata | Flame Violet | H,T,Tr, | House | Humid | Organic |
| ** | EPISCIA lilacina | | H,T,Tr, | House | Humid | Organic |
| ** | EPISCIA reptans | | H,T,Tr, | House | Humid | Organic |

| | | | | | | |
|---|---|---|---|---|---|---|
| ** | FATSIA japonica | Japanese Aralia | F,T | Cold | Circulating | Heavy |
| ** | FICUS benjamina | Weeping Fig | F,T | House | Circulating, dry | Heavy |
| ** | FICUS carica | Common Edible Fig | F,T | Cool | Circulating, dry | Heavy |
| ** | FICUS elastica | India Rubber Plant | F,T | House | Dry | Heavy |
| ***** | FICUS elastica variegata | Variegated Rubber Plant | F,T | House | Circulating, dry | Heavy |
| ***** | FICUS lyrata | Fiddle-Leaf Fig | F,T | House | Circulating, dry | Heavy |
| ** | FICUS pumila (FICUS repens) | Creeping Fig | H,T | House | Circulating, humid | Heavy |
| ** | FICUS retusa nitida | Indian Laurel | F,T | House | Circulating, dry | Heavy |
| *** | FITTONIA argyroneura | Silver-nerved Fittonia | T,Tr, | House | Humid | Heavy |
| * | FITTONIA verschaffeltii | Red-nerved Fittonia | T,Tr, | House | Humid | Heavy |
| ** | FUCHSIA (hybrids) | Lady's Eardrops | H,T | Cold, cool | Circulating | Heavy |
| *** | GEOGENANTHUS undatus | Seersucker Plant | T | House | Dry | Organic |
| *** | GUZMANIA lingulata | | H,T | House | Dry | Organic |
| *** | HELICONIA humilis | Lobster Claw | F,T | House | Circulating | Heavy |
| *** | HELXINE soleirolii | Baby Tears, Irish Moss | T,Tr, | Cool | Circulating, humid | Organic |
| ***** | HOWEIA forsteriana | Kentia Palm, Paradise Palm, Thatch Leaf Palm | F,T | Cool | Dry | Heavy |
| *** | MARANTA leuconeura kerchoveana | Prayer Plant, Rabbit Tracks | H,T | House | Humid | Heavy |
| * | MIMOSA pudica | Sensitive Plant | T | House | Circulating, humid | Heavy |
| ***** | MONSTERA deliciosa (juvenile stage known as PHILODENDRON pertusum) | Hurricane Plant, Swiss Cheese Plant, Split Leaf Philodendron | F,T | House | Dry | Heavy |
| ** | NEPHROLEPIS exaltata | Sword Fern | H,T | Cool | Circulating | Heavy |
| ** | NEPHROLEPIS exaltata 'Bostoniensis' | Boston Fern | H,T | Cool | Circulating | Heavy |

F=floor. H=hanging; T=table. Tr=terrarium

Light Requirement: Filtered     Watering Requirement: Moist

| RATING | BOTANICAL NAME | COMMON NAME | SIZE | TEMP. | AIR | SOIL |
|---|---|---|---|---|---|---|
| ** | NEPHROLEPIS exaltata 'Fluffy Ruffles' | Fluffy Ruffles | T,Tr. | Cool | Circulating | Heavy |
| **** | PEDILANTHUS tithymaloides variegatus | Devil's Backbone | F,T | House | Circulating, humid | Heavy |
| ***** | PHILODENDRON bipinnatifidum | Heart Leaf | F,T | House | Dry | Heavy |
| ***** | PHILODENDRON oxycardium (formerly P. cordatum) | Philodendron | F,H,T | House | Dry | Heavy |
| ***** | PHILODENDRON panduraeforme | | F,H,T | House | Dry | Heavy |
| ***** | PHILODENDRON radiatum | | F,T | House | Dry | Heavy |
| ***** | PHILODENDRON selloum | Saddle Leaf Philodendron | F,T | Cool, house | Circulating, dry | Heavy |
| ***** | PHILODENDRON squamiferum | | F,T | House | Dry | Heavy |
| ***** | PHILODENDRON wendlandii | | F,T | House | Dry | Heavy |
| **** | PILEA cadierei | Aluminum Plant, Watermelon Plant | T | House | Dry, humid | Heavy |
| *** | PILEA involucrata | Pan-American Friend-ship Plant, Panamiga | T,Tr. | House | Dry, humid | Heavy |
| ** | PILEA microphylla | Artillery Plant | T,Tr. | House | Circulating | Heavy |
| *** | PLATYCERIUM bifurcatum | Staghorn Fern | H,T | Cool, house | Circulating, humid | Light |
| ***** | PLECTRANTHUS australis | Swedish Ivy | H,T | Cool, house | Dry | Heavy |
| ** | PLECTRANTHUS oertendahlii | Candle Plant, Swedish Ivy | H,T | Cool, house | Dry | Heavy |
| ** | PLUMERIA rubra (PLUMERIA acuminata) | Frangipani Tree | F,T | House | Circulating, humid | Heavy |
| ** | PODOCARPUS macrophylla | | F,T | Cold, cool | Circulating | Heavy |
| ** | POLYPODIUM aureum | Hare's Foot Fern | T,Tr. | Cool | Circulating, humid | Organic |
| ** | PRIMULA malacoides | Fairy Primrose, Baby Primrose | T | Cool | Humid | Heavy |

| RATING | BOTANICAL NAME | COMMON NAME | SIZE | TEMP. | AIR | SOIL |
|---|---|---|---|---|---|---|
| ***** | RHIPSALIS species | Mistletoe Cactus | H.T | House | Circulating | Organic |
| **** | RHOEO spathacea | Moses in the Cradle. Moses in the Bull-rushes. Man in a Boat. Oyster Plant | T | Cool | Circulating | Heavy |
| ** | SAINTPAULIA ionantha | African Violet | T.Tr. | Cold. house | Dry, humid | Organic |
| **** | SCHLUMBERGERA bridgesii | Christmas Cactus | H.T | House | Circulating | Organic |
| * | SINNINGIA pusilla | | T.Tr. | House | Humid | Organic |
| * | SINNINGIA speciosa | Gloxinia | T | House | Humid | Organic |
| * | STREPTOCARPUS hybridus | | T | Cold. cool | Humid | Heavy |
| ***** | SYNGONIUM podophyllum | | F.H.T | House | Dry | Heavy |
| *** | TOLMIEA menziesii | Piggy-back Plant. Mother of Thousands | H.T.Tr. | Cold. cool | Circulating | Heavy |
| ***** | ZEBRINA pendula | Wandering Jew | H.T.Tr. | Cool. house | Circulating, humid | Heavy |
| *** | ZINGIBER officinale | Common Ginger | T | House | Circulating, humid | Heavy |
| **** | ZYGOCACTUS truncatus | Thanksgiving Cactus | H.T | House | Circulating | Organic |

## Light Requirement: Filtered     Watering Requirement: Wet

| RATING | BOTANICAL NAME | COMMON NAME | SIZE | TEMP. | AIR | SOIL |
|---|---|---|---|---|---|---|
| ** | ACORUS gramineus varigatus | Calamus Root, Dwarf Japanese Sweet Flag. Sweet Flag | T.Tr. | Cold | Circulating | Heavy. |
| *** | ARECASTRUM romanzoffianum (COCOS plumosa) | Queen Palm | F.T | House | Humid | Heavy |
| * | CAMELLIA japonica | | F.T | Cold | Circulating | Organic |
| ***** | CARYOTA mitis | Fishtail Palm | F.T | House | Dry | Heavy |

F=floor H=hanging T=table. Tr=terrarium

## Light Requirement: Filtered      Watering Requirement: Wet

| RATING | BOTANICAL NAME | COMMON NAME | SIZE | TEMP. | AIR | SOIL |
|---|---|---|---|---|---|---|
| *** | CYATHEA arborea | Tree Fern | F,T | House | Circulating, humid | Organic |
| **** | CYPERUS alternifolius | Umbrella Plant | F,T | Cool | Dry | Heavy |
| **** | CYPERUS papyrus | Egyptian Paper Plant | F,T | Cool | Dry | Heavy |
| **** | DRACAENA deremensis | | F,T | House | Dry | Heavy |
| **** | DRACAENA draco | Dragon Tree | F,T | House | Dry | Heavy |
| **** | DRACAENA fragrans massangeana | Corn Plant | F,T | House | Dry | Heavy |
| **** | DRACAENA godseffiana | Gold Dust Dracaena | T | House | Dry | Heavy |
| **** | DRACAENA marginata | Red Margined Dracaena | F,T | House | Dry | Heavy |
| ***** | DRACAENA sanderiana | | F,T | House | Dry | Heavy |
| ** | LIVISTONA chinensis | Chinese Fan Palm | F,T | Cool, house | Circulating, humid | Heavy |
| **** | PHOENIX dactylifera | Date Palm | F,T | Cool, house | Circulating, dry | Heavy |
| **** | PHOENIX roebelenii | Miniature Date Palm | T | House | Circulating, dry | Heavy |
| **** | PLEOMELE reflexa | Song of India | F,T | House | Dry | Heavy |
| ***** | RHAPSIS excelsa | Lady Palm | F,T | Cool | Circulating | Heavy |
| * | ZANTEDESCHIA elliottiana | Calla | T | Cool, house | Circulating | Heavy |

## Light Requirement: Shade      Watering Requirement; Drench, Let Dry

| RATING | BOTANICAL NAME | COMMON NAME | SIZE | TEMP. | AIR | SOIL |
|---|---|---|---|---|---|---|
| * | CALCEOLARIA herbeohybrida | Pocketbook Plant | T | Cold | Circulating | Organic |

## Light Requirement: Shade      Watering Requirement: Moist

| RATING | BOTANICAL NAME | COMMON NAME | SIZE | TEMP. | AIR | SOIL |
|---|---|---|---|---|---|---|
| ***** | AGLAONEMA commutatum | | T | House | Dry | Heavy |

| RATING | BOTANICAL NAME | COMMON NAME | SIZE | TEMP. | AIR | SOIL |
|---|---|---|---|---|---|---|
| ***** | AGLAONEMA modestum | Chinese Evergreen | T | House | Dry | Heavy |
| ***** | ASPIDISTRA elatior | Cast Iron Plant, Parlor Palm | T | Cool | Dry | Heavy |
| ***** | CHAMAEDOREA elegans 'Bella' (Neanthe bella) | Parlor Palm | F.T | House | Dry | Heavy |
| ***** | CHAMAEDOREA erumpens | Bamboo Palm | F.T | House | Dry | Heavy |
| | CYRTOMIUM falcatum (ASPIDIUM falcatum) | Hollyfern | T.Tr. | Cool | Dry | Heavy |
| ** | DAVALLIA species | Rabbit Foot Ferns | T.Tr. | Cool, house | Dry | Organic |
| ** | PTERIS species | Brake Fern, Table Fern | T, Tr. | Cool | Dry, humid | Heavy, organic |
| ** | PTERIS ensiformis 'Victoriae' | Sword Brake | T, Tr. | Cool, house | Dry, humid | Heavy, organic |
| *** | SELAGINELLA emmeliana | Sweat Plant | Tr. | House | Humid | Organic |
| *** | SELAGINELLA kraussiana | Spreading Clubmoss | Tr. | Cool, house | Humid | Organic |
| *** | SELAGINELLA uncinata | | Tr. | Cool, house | Humid | Organic |
| *** | SELAGINELLA willdenovii | | Tr. | House | Humid | Organic |
| ***** | SPATHIPHYLLUM floribundum | Spathe Flower | T | House | Dry | Heavy |

## Light Requirement: Shade    Watering Requirement: Wet

| RATING | BOTANICAL NAME | COMMON NAME | SIZE | TEMP. | AIR | SOIL |
|---|---|---|---|---|---|---|
| * | ADIANTUM species and varieties | Maidenhair Fern | T.Tr. | House | Humid | Organic |
| *** | ANTHURIUM andraeanum | Flamingo Flower, Flamingo Plant | T | House | Humid | Organic |
| * | ANTHURIUM crystallinum | | T | House | Humid | Organic |
| *** | ASPLENIUM nidus | Birdnest-Fern, Spleenwort, Shuttlecock | T.Tr. | Cool | Humid | Organic |
| ** | ASPLENIUM viviparum | Mother Fern | T, Tr. | Cool | Humid | Organic |

F=floor: H=hanging: T=table: Tr=terrarium

# How Do You Acquire Plants?

# Inherit Them, Have Them, Do it Yourself

**H**ow do you acquire a plant? Some people inherit them quite unintentionally. There are certain heirloom plants, such as some aspidistras and Chinese evergreens, that have been with families for generations. These faithful plants with their patient endurance have supported, encouraged, and developed confidence in their people. Some plants become so much a part of a place — like a piece of built-in furniture — that no one can visualize their being moved. If a plant has been in the same spot since the administration of President McKinley, it sometimes happens that it becomes invisible to all that go by it. This means that sometimes plants just come with the house or apartment you move into, having been left or abandoned by the previous occupants.

Plants aren't necessarily abandoned out of negligence; sometimes it's necessity. At times large plants are left behind because the movers won't move them and a car can't carry them. Sometimes at auctions or house sales, they are thrown in with a box of contents or are part of the purchase such as a plant in a plant stand or jardiniere.

You may also inherit a plant by receiving it as a gift. At certain seasons and on certain occasions the giving of plants is considered appropriate, and if there is a giver then it follows that there is also a givee.

If you unexpectedly are given custody of a plant, you have two choices. You can keep the plant and learn how to live with it, or you can immediately give it away. If the plant was purchased, there is usually a three day grace period, but if you wait beyond that period, you're going to be stuck with it since there are very few used plant dealers around. Besides that, after three days the plant will have you feeling either guilty or parental.

### Vegetative Reproduction

When you become a compulsive plant person you will take anyone's rejects and try to make them well again, pinch other people's plants, or become adept at propagating them yourself.

Vegetative reproduction is an activity where less results in more. It is a means of duplicating the original plant exactly, producing a larger plant more quickly, and giving the illusion of having created something out of nothing.

**Multiplication by division.** One way to get more plants is to separate or divide a large one into several small ones. In separation of large clumps with many stems, the plant is taken out of the pot and gently pulled or broken apart into the obvious parts. Sometimes soaking the plant in a bucket will soften the soil and make separation easier. This works well with ferns, orchids and papyrus, and most many-stemmed plants that aren't too old.

*Gently separate clumps of stems.*

With older plants that have tightly interwoven root balls or tough roots, *root division* is more satisfactory. A large mature asparagus fern, for example, needs a strong arm, plenty of room, and a sharp instrument. Root division is supposed to be surgery, not butchery, so the instrument should be sterile and the cutting neat. After the plant has been divided, the excess soil should be removed from the roots. Each part is potted separately and put where it can get intensive care for a couple of weeks.

**Addition by subtraction.** Some plants have offsets or offshoots that grow at their base. These can be removed gently with a sharp knife and potted up. Other plants, such as strawberry begonias and spider plants, send off runners with small plants at the ends. These can be rooted in small pots while the plantlet is still attached to the parent. Then when the plantlet is well rooted, the cord can be cut.

Other plants, such as ivy and philodendron, will produce a plant at almost every leaf joint. This procedure is called *layering*. You lay the stem attached to the plant across a pot, pin it down, and wait until it grows roots. If there's a long stem, you can sometimes pin it down three or four times.

*Air Layering* uses the same principle, except the rooting is done up in the air, and the rooting medium is attached to the stem rather than the stem to the soil. This is done by making a cut or small notch with a clean disinfected knife on one side of the stem you want to cut off. Keep the cut open with a small sliver of wood, and wrap the spot with sheet sphagnum moss that has been soaked in water and then had as much as possible squeezed out. Cover the sphagnum with clear plastic and tie it tightly above and below. Wait until the roots show through the moss; then cut the whole stem off just below the new roots. Treat the new roots gently when potting. It's often a good idea to keep the newly separated plant in an incubator made out of a large clear plastic bag for a week or so until it adjusts to life on its own.

Many plants are capable of reproducing themselves from a piece of stem, root, or leaf. Under favorable conditions they will

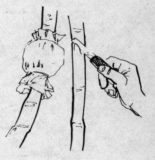

*Air Layering*

form new buds and reproduce the entire plant. A cutting or a piece cut or pinched off a plant can be rooted in a windowsill garden (described in "Fun With Plants") or in a well-drained mixture that can be kept warm and moist.

Many indoor plants can be produced from *stem cuttings:* coleus, wandering Jew, and many succulents. A stem cutting is a piece of stem, with or without leaves, that has some buds on it. If there are a lot of leaves, it's better to remove most of them or cut them way back so they don't keep on working and exhausting the rootless stem.

A good time to make a cutting is when you're *pinching* a plant back, that is cutting off long or straggly stems or training it by stopping its forward growth and diverting it to each side. A plant can be pinched with fingers or with a clean knife or razor blade. The cut should be made just above a joint.

To make a *root cutting,* you spread the cut roots on a nice soft bed of soil and then cover them with a bit more soil, which should be kept moist. Very few house plants are reproduced by root cutting although one can do it with dracaena.

On the other hand, many leaves can be rooted. The leaf can be put in either soil or water in either a vertical position or laid flat. A long sansevieria leaf can be made into almost any number of two- to three-inch chunks and stuck in sand, bottom down. African violet leaves root easily and produce new plants, and rex begonia leaves can be laid on soil, cut through the veins, and new plantlets will grow from those

*Stem Cutting*

points. Leaves for leaf cuttings have to be strong and healthy — you can't get new plants from a dead or dying leaf. With crotons. some succulents. and other plants. it's possible to get a leaf to root but still not produce a plant. The leaf cutting has to have a piece of the stem with it because the new plant comes from the tiny bud in the joint where the leaf connects to the stem.

Plants can also be produced from *seed*, and although this takes longer. it's the way most new plants get their start. To grow seeds. you need something to grow them in. something to hold the stuff they're growing in. and a place to grow (generally where it's nice and warm and humid). Some seeds germinate sprouts almost overnight. and some may take as long as two years. Until the seeds germinate they don't need light. but once they've sprouted they should be moved into a light they can grow in. and they should never be allowed to dry out.

*Pinching*

When the seedlings have their third pair of leaves. it's time to separate them and give each a small pot of its own. But don't over-pot a young plant. Placing it in too large a pot can scare it to death trying to live up to your expectations all at once. Too large a pot will also keep the roots too wet so the plant will rot.

# For The Record

## The Accession List

If you have more than one plant and are not gifted with total recall it often makes things much easier to keep some kind of record. The record can help by reminding you what contributed to success and what precipitated failure, where and when you got the plant, how fast or slow it grew — in fact everything to help one learn by doing. Don't forget to record the plant's "exit." Did you give it away? Did it die?

This record also provides a count of how many plant dependents you have at any one time. Reviewing the successes and failures gives you a better idea of the kinds of plants that will thrive under your care and conditions.

Many large plant conservatories give each newly acquired plant an accession number. The record for that plant is kept either on cards or in a notebook. Each plant is given a number in the order received, and when that plant leaves the collection that number is not reassigned to a new plant.

| Number | Name | Date added Where obtained Cost | Size, age and condition | Notes: location, light, fertilizing (when, what) Flowering Repotting, division & cuttings, other | Exit: gift died |
|--------|------|--------------------------------|-------------------------|-------------------------------------------------------------------------------------------------|-----------------|
|        |      |                                |                         |                                                                                                 |                 |
|        |      |                                |                         |                                                                                                 |                 |
|        |      |                                |                         |                                                                                                 |                 |

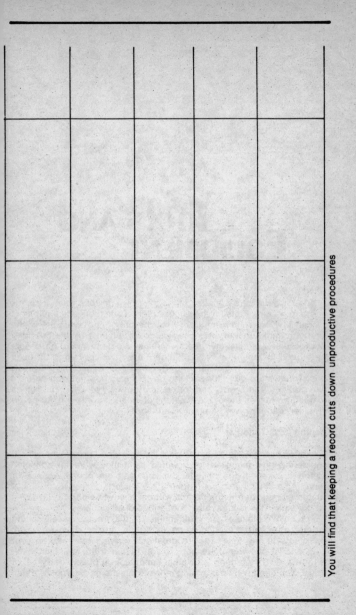

You will find that keeping a record cuts down unproductive procedures

# Tools and Equipment

Indoor gardeners are often left to their own devices when it comes to gardening tools for their house plants. The tools and equipment you can buy are rather limited. About the only thing available in the stores are miniatures of tools used outdoors, which are cute but don't work too well. Actually, the greatest tools available to indoor gardeners are fingers, thumbs, and hands. Fingers are good for taking off dead leaves, for sensing the moisture of the soil, and for picking off mealy bugs. Thumbs are good for packing down the soil, for making holes to plant cuttings and seeds, and for comparing with your friends. Hands are good for hefting the pot to see if the plant needs watering, for carrying water, and for giving a plant to a friend.

**Keeping It All Together**

We often use materials from all over the house and apartment without considering how much easier it would be if they were all collected together and kept in one place for the sole use of the plants. A place for everything and everything in its place. It's easier and less frustrating if you can do your gardening chores without always having to run about and get stuff. This is imperative for serious plant people.

If you have a place where you can keep it, it's great to have a rolling cart that you can put everything on so that you are ready to work with your plants at any time. They're great for carrying materials to your plants and for carrying plants back to the kitchen or the tub. If you can't manage a cart, try putting your plant supplies in a plastic carry-all, or bucket. You can keep your potting mix in a plastic garbage can, which will keep it clean and will keep it away from the cat. In addition to having a place for soil, pots, and equipment, you need a safe place for fertilizers, fungicides, and pesticides. It's imperative to keep all of these away from children and pets. In order to do the work they have to, some of this stuff is really potent.

Another essential item for plant people is an information box in which you can collect clippings from newspapers and store all those plant books you've been collecting. This would be a good place to keep a notebook listing the names and important facts about each of your plants and something you can grab when you hear a plant expert on radio or TV. If you jot down ideas that appeal to you when you hear them, you'll have them all together later on when you may have to use them. It's a good idea to keep a pencil or pen attached to your notebook at all times so you don't have to run around and look for one at the last minute. In your information box, you can keep plant labels and felt marking pens. (It makes your plants feel important if you keep their names and the date they became members of the family on a label in the pot.) If you don't have plant labels, masking tape can be used for making a name tag on the side of the pot.

## Tools for Grooming

There is need for grooming tools, such as toothbrushes, scissors, and clean rags, which should be reserved for the particular use of plants. Use the **toothbrushes** to clean off the leaves, scrub off the scale and mealy bugs, and brush the hair of your old man cactus. Although you may not want to share your toothbrush with anyone, plants aren't as finnicky. One brush is enough for all of them, unless some prefer a harder bristle.

A fat **watercolor brush** is great for cleaning off the furry leaves of African violets, and it can also be used to carry pollen from one flower to another — thereby doing your bit to increase the citrus and yucca populations.

A good pair of **scissors** or shears is important for cutting out dead branches or pruning a plant to shape. An old **razor blade** with one side protected with adhesive tape can be used for the close cuts inside.

Clean **rags** have a number of uses. They can tie a plant to the stake; they can be used to protect your hands when transplanting cactuses; or they can be used for giving your plants a bath. All plants love a good bath every once in a while, but especially the big ones. It gets the dust off their leaves so they can breathe better, and it gets rid of insects. A tiny, dusty plant may go unnoticed by your visitors, but a huge dirty rubber plant brings out the white glove syndrome in almost everyone.

You can make caring for large plants a lot simpler by putting each one on an individual platform with casters. This makes it much easier for hauling your biggies to the tub for their bath and also for moving them or turning them about so they get equal light on all sides.

Plants like to look their best, and sometimes they will need something more than moral support. **Popsicle sticks** are good for small plants. For larger plants, you can use green **bamboo stakes,** cut off and decoratively painted **broomsticks,** or old **umbrella spokes.** This will keep those tall, wobbly plants from falling on their sides.

You may have some choice bent or broken **coat hangers** lying on the floor of your closet. These are excellent for suspending small pots from the wall, for supporting weak plants or, if opened up with one end twisted around a wad of cotton, you have an instrument for cleaning up the inside of your bottle garden. But if wire coat hangers are going to be part of your indoor gardening equipment, you should also consider having a good pair of **pliers** and **wire cutters** to work with.

### . . . for light

A good **squeegee** is handy for cleaning windows. (What may look like a clean window to you may be filthy to a sun-loving plant.) If you catch your purple passion rubbing up against the window, you should take a hint.

If you are short on windows that get sun, and you would like to provide your plants with a little light refreshment, how about an indoor light fixture. **Fluorescent bulbs** (two 20-watt bulbs, at least) can be attached under a kitchen cabinet, under a shelf, or hung by chains from the ceiling. Eight or ten inches below the light you can suspend a shelf. On this shelf you can put your plants in a tray which has been covered with a layer of pebbles or vermiculite. And voila´ — you're an instant indoor light gardener.

Thinking about light and the lack of it, a luxurious item can be a **closet** that isn't opened between 4:00 p.m. and 6:00 a.m. This is a great thing to have in order to get short day flowering plants such as kalanchoes and poinsettias to rebloom. Of course, if you don't have a closet to spare, you can use opaque **black cloth** made into dunce caps or black plastic **garbage bags.** Slip either one over the plant and pot, and you will fool it into blooming.

### . . . for watering

**Plastic bags** are very useful. "Zip-lock" bags are great for rooting cuttings that you have cut off your other plants (see "Fun With Plants"). Large clear cleaner bags are good for putting over your plants when you are going on vacation and you want them to stay home and do their own watering. Large clear cleaner bags are also good for hospitalizing or isolating sick or infested plants so they don't share whatever is bothering them. The best way to handle large plastic bags, both black and clear, is to place the plant in its pot inside the bag, place a long bamboo stake or some other kind of pole in the pot and bring the bag carefully up around the plant and attach it to the stake with twistems, scotch tape, rubber bands, or old shoestrings. You can also use plastic wrap to cover new seedlings. This protects them until they're strong enough to breathe the polluted air, but its greatest advantage is in keeping the moisture content in the air high while the seedlings are germinating and need it most. When your seedlings get a few inches high, repot them in their own pot. (See Potting and Repotting.)

Water is very important to plants. Therefore, a **bucket** is a handy tool. Not only is it great for carrying water to your plants, but it is handy for storing water overnight. Most plants prefer their water at room temperature or a little warmer. If you have a place where you can keep a bucket filled overnight, this will not only allow the water to reach room temperature, but will let some of the chlorine evaporate out of the water before feeding it to your plants.

The type of watering tool you use depends on your and the plant's preferences. A **watering can** with a long spout is good for getting water onto the soil and not on the leaves. Just be sure to get yourself a good watering can that will hold water without dribbling it over the top and down your arm and onto the floor. Some people prefer to use a **pitcher** for larger plants. If you look for them you can find a long **water wand,** which you attach to a reservoir. This is good for watering plants at the back of an indoor light garden or in a crowded window. A dunking **bucket** is good for plants that like to be drenched. But then a large **dish-pan** will be needed also for the pots to drain in after their dunking. For watering terrarium plants or bottle gardens, there are small **misters** available, or you can reuse — after washing it out thoroughly — a bottle that contained spray window cleaner. For succulent seedlings and other small plants, an **eye dropper** prevents the catastrophe of overwatering. **Self-watering pots** work well for plants that like to be constantly moist, but they're not too satisfactory for those plants that have to dry out between waterings.

As part of the plant watering and humidifying equipment, you will need something to catch the water since it is very difficult to water a plant satisfactorily without having some of it drain out. **Saucers** should be glazed clay, metal, or plastic because the porous clay saucers will leave water marks on your sill or table. This is a good place to use the beautiful tea-leaf luster saucers whose cups were lost long ago; a small plant such as an African violet can feel quite dressed up sitting on an antique saucer. For a more modern look, you can use the aluminum pans from frozen pot pies; and for the larger plants, you can use the ones from frozen fruit pies. Here is a place to use those old TV table trays that have been collecting dust. Add pebbles and plants and you have an instant garden.

### . . . for gardening

For potting plants, for removing top soil, and for stirring things up in general, it's good for your plants to have their own forks and spoons. Don't use your spouse's favorite soup spoon; the plants deserve their own. A large plastic mixing spoon that feels comfortable in your hand is much easier to use than a garden trowel; and a fork or a pair of chopsticks is much easier for working up or removing the soil at the roots of plants than a rake. People who work with bonsai use chopsticks all the time to remove the excess soil from the rootball. These are the

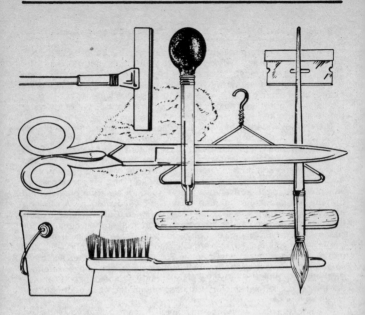

large kitchen chopsticks with pointed ends. One could probably use a large knitting needle to the same effect, but it wouldn't be as aesthetic.

### . . . for health

A plastic measuring cup and a set of plastic measuring spoons should be kept with your fertilizer, insecticides, and other materials you are using with your plants. It's not only handier, but it could be safer too. And a bag of cotton balls, a box of toothpicks, and a bottle of rubbing alcohol are essential for a well-equipped mealybug department.

### . . . etc.

Finally, you need newspapers and brown paper bags — the newspapers to put under your plants when you're working with them, so you can roll up the mess, and clean up quickly afterwards; and the brown paper bags for disposing of dead leaves (and plants). A neatly wrapped up dead plant is easier to dispose of than one that's just been thrown in the garbage loose. That way, when you hold the memorial services, no one will pull it out of the trash container and say, "mommy, make it well."

# Potting and Repotting

**D**irt is what you get from newspaper columns or the town gossip. Soil is the stuff in the backyard and what you put in pots or other containers so you can grow plants. It consists of bits and pieces of rocks or minerals, organic matter, moisture, and gases. Soil should provide two basic requirements of plants: physical support and mineral nutrition. But while soil should contain various nutrients, it can also contain disease-causing agents and weed seeds, so you have to be careful about what is in the soil you are going to use as well as what isn't in it.

### Growing Mediums

A good standard mix to start with for your potted plants contains:
- 1 part top soil (good loamy soil from a reasonably unpolluted area)
- 1 part rich humus or leaf-mold compost
- 1 part clear sand (don't use beach sand, which is usually dirty or salty, or extra fine sand, which cakes)

This, and all other mixtures, should be thoroughly stirred and blended. Careful mixing is especially important when your mix calls for a few tablespoons of this or that additive.

Succulents and cacti require quick and complete drainage. A good mix for them can be made from:
- 1 part sharp coarse builder's sand
- 1 part standard potting mix

Soil isn't absolutely essential in a potting mix. Most tropical plants, for instance, do well in a soil-free humus mix:

1 part coarse perlite
1 part rough sphagnum peat moss
2 parts leaf mold or rotted humus

This soil-free humus mix has good drainage and is hard to drown if you have the right type of container.

Another useful mix, particularly good for holding water longer, is made of:

1 part coarse sphagnum peat moss
1 part medium-grade vermiculite
1 part medium to coarse perlite

For plants that usually grow on trees or rocks *(epiphytes)* a light and airy mix is needed. Many bromeliads and orchids are in this upper class. Osmunda fiber (pieces of fern roots) forms the basis of this growing medium. These pieces should be tightly packed in small pots that have excellent drainage. An alternative to this consists of:

1 part builder's sand
1 part rough-chopped sphagnum moss
1 part medium-grade fir bark

Mixtures such as these underline the fact that the texture of a potting mix is more important than its nutrient richness. Air, which is almost as important as water, must be able to get into the mix. Since all of the soilless mixtures only provide support for the plant, food must be added to enrich all of these mixes, but keep in mind one of the basic rules of green thumb: it's much better to use too little plant food than too much.

Soilless growing mediums are useful because they are relatively sterile to begin with. Also, since they are light in weight, they're great for hanging baskets. A good mix contains:

1 part no. 2 grade vermiculite
1 part shredded peat moss

An aspect of growing medium that people often hear about, get confused by, and get scared off by is the rather scientific-sounding pH. You don't need a PhD though to understand what is really only a simple scale of proportions. Some plants like a mix with more alkaline material in it, while other plants prefer a higher proportion of acid material. The scale runs from 14 (highest proportion of alkaline) down to 0 (highest proportion of acid). The mid-point, 7, is called neutral. Most plants grow more happily at one spot on this scale than they do at others, although many plants can exist over a broad range.

### How to Pasteurize Your Soil

If you have a yard with lots of nice soil, you may think it wasteful to go out and buy soil for potting. Soil from the yard is fine for potting, but it ought to be treated before it's used. When you bring soil from the yard into your house or apartment, you will want to pasteurize it. One of the major advantages of pre-packaged mixes from the store is that they usually have already been pasteurized (or sterilized, as the writing on the package will usually put it). However, if you use your own mix, you will have to kill off the bugs, viruses, and weed seeds. This not only makes it healthy for the plants that will be growing in the soil, but it will also keep these nuisances from spreading to the rest of your plants.

After you have the soil inside the kitchen, add the other items needed to produce the mix you want, and then pasteurize the whole mixture. This can be done by heat or chemicals.

The simplest way to pasteurize your soil is to use your oven. Put the mix into a baking pan or roaster to a depth of four inches or less. As a check on the thoroughness of the pasteurization, bury a small potato (about an inch and a half across) in the middle of your mix. The potato should be nicely done when you are through. Cover the container tightly with heavy aluminum foil, stick a meat or candy thermometer through the foil into the middle of the mix, and put the container into the hot oven. When the thermometer reaches 180°, continue baking, keeping the thermometer at 180° - 200° (don't go over 200°), for half an hour or so. Then take the pan or roaster out of the oven, and let it cool off for 24 hours. This method of pasteurization will produce safe soil, but it will also produce some cooking odors you haven't had before — good air circulation through the kitchen during cooking will be helpful.

Chemical treatment can also be used, but this method is a bit trickier. Be sure to read the instructions on the chemical package carefully both before you start and again as you go through each step. Liquid fumigants and hand applicators are available at many plant supply places. Use a liquid that kills off the widest variety of pests so that you will only have to do the chore once. Be careful not to use the growing medium until the amount of time required by the instructions has passed. Pasteurization kills off the good as well as the bad bacteria, which means that your "clean soil" is very vulnerable to infection.

### Hydroponics

Growing plants in water enchants children of all ages, and actually seeing the roots gives you a total picture of a plant's structure. With soil-potted plants you've been missing half the story!

Plants have been grown experimentally in water since the 1690s, but only in the past 50 years has hydroponics been widely used to grow plants and vegetables. Because of the high initial costs and the fairly involved methods necessary to maintain an even nutrient concentration that will produce an even product, most water cultivation is done by commercial growers. However, it can be great fun to see indoor plants grow without any soil around the roots for a short period of time.

Growing plants without soil requires the same conditions of water, temperature and air as growing plants in soil. Some people have good luck in keeping the concentration of the nutrients balanced over a long period of time. Others find it difficult to judge how much of the nutrients have been slurped up by the plant and how much water has been lost through evaporation.

Seeds can be germinated between wet sheets of blotting paper or paper towels and then given a collar of plastic to hold them just above the solution. If you are starting with a plant, be sure the roots are washed clean. You have to be very careful not to drown the plant by submerging all the roots under the water. The easiest way to grow a plant in water is to suspend it above the nutrient solution so some of the roots get air and they can stretch down into the nutrient solution. The roots work best if they are kept in the dark. But, since the fun of hydroponics is seeing how they grow, they can be grown in a glass container that is wrapped with black construction paper. You can use a light-proof collar to support the plant. A basic solution used commercially for growing plants hydroponically consists of:

| | |
|---|---|
| calcium nitrate | 0.8 gram |
| potassium nitrate | 0.2 gram |
| potassium dihydrogen phosphate | 0.2 gram |
| magnesium sulfate | 0.2 gram |
| iron phosphate | trace |
| water | 1,000 cc |

This solution can be used either in a water culture or in a sand and gravel culture. Good results can also be achieved by using a diluted solution of all-purpose fertilizer — but the plant will last a short time only.

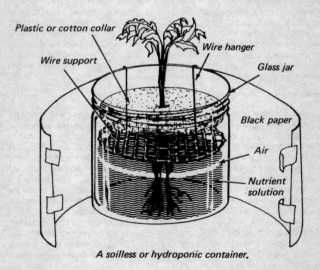

*A soilless or hydroponic container.*

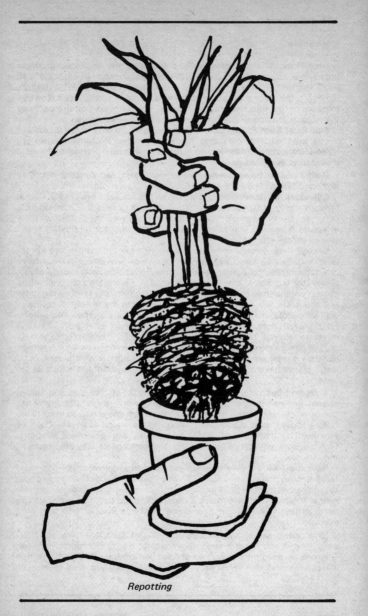

*Repotting*

## Containers

**Clay Pots.** The standard terra cotta pots are available in many handsome designs, and come in sizes from 1¼ inches (thumb pots) to 18 to 24 inches in diameter, and are as tall as they are wide at the top. However, the largest pots are often hard to get and are very expensive because of the high shipping costs. Clay pots are very popular because the natural clay color harmonizes with indoor furnishings.

**Azalea or Fern Pots.** These squat containers were once available in only a few sizes, but now range from 6 to 14 inches in diameter. They are three-fourths as high as they are wide and in better proportion to most plants than standard pots.

**Bulb Pans or Seed Bowls.** These look like deep saucers but have drainage holes. They are available in 6 to 12 inch diameters.

**Cylinders** are handsome and welcome departures from the traditional tapered design of pots. Glass cylinders and bottles are occasionally used as decorative plant containers. However, they do not have drainage holes, so you must put in a layer (about 2 inches) of small stones before you add soil.

**Glazed Pots.** Glazed pots come in many sizes and colors, are attractive, and can be used in many places. However, most do not have drainage holes, so plants potted in them must be watered carefully. Generally, it is better to slip a plant potted in a separate container into a glazed pot that has gravel at the bottom. Occasionally remove the inner pot and drain any excess water accumulated in the glazed container.

**Plastic Pots** are lightweight and come in many shapes and colors. Like glazed pots, they hold water longer than clay pots because moisture cannot evaporate through the walls. Therefore, plants in plastic pots require less frequent waterings, which can be an advantage to some gardeners. However, because of the lightness of plastic pots, large plants have a tendency to tip over unless weight is added at the base.

**Tubs and Such.** Japanese soy tubs (available at nurseries and basket shops) are handsome, and plants look good in them. But many are poorly made, and after a few months the bottom drops out, so think twice before you buy one. Wood and bamboo tubs are also available, but they too must be inspected carefully to be sure they are made properly. Galvanized washtubs or buckets painted dark colors may also be used indoors.

Sawed-off wine casks banded with galvanized iron make fine containers. They come in two sizes, 20- and 26-inch. Barrels and kegs come in many sizes from 12 to 24 inches; most are decorative, and plants grow well in them. If you want to use a cask or keg, be sure to have drainage holes drilled in it. However, remember that any wooden container will eventually rot.

**Urns, Jardinieres, and Cachepots.** Glazed Japanese urns are stunning, and if you have a special place that needs rich color, try one. Chinese ceramic pots in various shapes are ideal for foliage plants like caladiums and dieffenbachias. They are generally glazed in blue or green hues. Some are excessively ornate and others are simple. Perhaps not Chinese but with a Far East flavor, are brass pots and gold-leaf tubs. They make almost any common plant appear special. Cachepots are elegant decorative containers that come in handsome shapes and many sizes, and are made of various glazed materials. The porcelain ones, generally splashed with fruit and flower designs, are especially pleasing and always look good indoors.

**One-of-a-Kind Pottery Plant Containers.** Some of these are exceptionally lovely. You can choose from a wide range of sizes and shapes in a variety of colors. If the container is one you made yourself or one you received from a friend, your plant will have double the pleasure for you. Many of these containers have porous walls, so moisture evaporates more quickly than from glazed or plastic. Do not use a pot that overpowers the plant. But for that special plant or place where you want something unique, the one-of-a-kind piece of pottery is an excellent choice.

**Hanging Baskets.** Hanging baskets are decorative, give more plants their place in the sun, and can increase privacy. Some hanging planters have built-in saucers, but if yours doesn't, be sure to provide some kind of saucer or tray attached to the container or on the floor underneath to catch the excess water.

Most baskets come with wire, chain, or rope for hanging. Simply put a screweye or a clothesline hook into the ceiling, or attach a hook or bracket to the wall, and the plant is ready for hanging. Be sure that these will hold the weight of a filled and watered basket.

If you are a do-it-yourselfer, try making a hanging planter by cutting off the top of a used bleach or ammonia container (be sure it's washed out first). Hang it up with a chain of pop-can lids or macrame. If you use a natural fiber for the hanger, it's good to reinforce it with monofilament (a clear thread which you can buy in a sewing or fishing supply store). Then if the fibers rot away from moisture or wear, your plant won't end up on the floor.

Plants hung too far above eye level are not easily seen, and pots hung too high are difficult to water, unless you put them on a pulley or have a stepladder or stepstool. But they also cannot be hung so low that they are in the way of traffic through the room. A black eye caused by a hanging plant would be hard to explain.

**And Others.** Plants can also be planted in holes in rocks and driftwood, in old coffee pots or shoes, or in almost anything as long as their air, water, and light requirements are satisfied.

## Potting and Repotting

Generally plants that you buy will be in standard clay or plastic pots and can be left in their original containers. But often it is difficult to determine just how long the potted plant has been in the soil, how old the soil is, and whether or not the nutrients have been all used up. To make sure that the plant has the necessary nutrients for growth, repotting with fresh soil is a good idea. To pot a new plant from the nursery or florist use the following method:

Tap the bottom of the pot gently on concrete, wood, or other hard surface, and then grasp the trunk of the plant and wiggle it until the plant seems loose. If it will not come out of the pot, don't pull it; it's better to break the container than accidentally bruise the root system of the plant or break off its top. When removing a plant from any container, get out as much of the rootball as possible. Then crumble away some (not all) of the old soil from around the ball. If the rootball remains somewhat intact, the plant has a much better chance of surviving the shock of transplant.

Now take a new container a size or two larger than the old one. If you are using a clay pot, it should be soaked in water overnight before planting; otherwise it will pull the moisture out of the soil. Or you may use an old pot that has been thoroughly scoured. Boiling old clay pots for 20 minutes will usually kill any harmful bugs or viruses. Clean old plastic pots by soaking them in a clorox solution and rinsing thoroughly. Cover the pot's drain holes with mesh screen or pieces of broken pots to keep soil from sifting out. Then add a scant layer of gravel.

If you have a favorite decorative container that you want to plant and it doesn't have a drain-hole, the best thing to do is to double pot. That means potting your plant in a smaller pot that does have a drain hole and sitting that pot on gravel inside your favorite planter. If double potting isn't possible (maybe the neck of the planter is too small to insert a pot), fill the planter with about two inches of gravel before adding any soil. This is to provide adequate drainage. However, a plant potted in such a planter should not be fertilized because the fertilizer will never wash out of the pot, but will accumulate in the gravel.

On top of the gravel, fill one-third of the container with fresh soil. Then lift the plant gently, and place it on the mound of soil. If the plant is too high in the pot, remove some soil; if it is too low, add soil. You can spot the correct soil line on a plant because the color of the trunk or stem is lighter above the line and darker below it.

Hold the plant in the center of the pot with one hand, and add fresh soil around the old rootball with your other hand or with a spoon. Push the fresh soil down with your fingers, a piece of wood, or some other helper, and continue to add soil until it's within one inch of the rim of the pot. Pack the soil in place firmly. Water the plant thoroughly. Let it drain, and then move it to a place where you can watch it for a while before you move it to its permanent place. For the first few weeks, observe the plant closely since it has just undergone a major operation. Do not panic if it loses a few leaves or appears limp or peaked — this is normal.

If you've had a plant for some time, it's a good idea to replace the old, tired soil with fresh soil. To repot a plant you've had for some time, tap the container against a hard surface (but don't tap so hard that you break the pot, unless breaking the pot is necessary to avoid bruising the roots or breaking off the plant), and then jiggle the trunk of the plant several times. Again, do *not* pull. Work the trunk around in a wiggly or circular motion until it becomes loose in the pot. Now place the container and plant on its side and try to slide the plant from the container. Get as much of the rootball as possible. Crumble away the old soil. Always use a sharp pair of scissors or a sharp knife if you need to cut back any damaged or unneeded roots. Don't try to tear them off with your hands. Keep the roots moist while they are exposed to the air. You are now ready to repot the plant. Proceed in the same manner as previously described for potting new arrivals.

Occasionally you can avoid repotting plants that are in very large pots by simply digging out the top four or five inches of old soil and putting in fresh soil. But other times repotting is absolutely necessary, especially when the plant has outgrown its quarters. Then the plant must be moved to a larger pot, a process known as *potting on*. Usually this is done when a plant has become root-bound, which sometimes causes the lower leaves to yellow and the whole plant to wilt. You can tell that a plant is root-bound by lifting it out of the pot. A root-bound plant will lift out of the pot easily. The soil ball will be bound together with roots and will look like somebody's old string collection.

When you are putting the plant into its new pot spread the roots out carefully so they can take advantage of the new space. But this new pot shouldn't be too much larger than the old one, or else the plant may suffocate or become water-logged.

# How and
# Where To Buy

**Y**ou usually have one of two reasons for buying a plant. It may be the result of careful planning — a specific plant to fill a hole in your decor or your plant population — or it may be on impulse, just for the fun of buying something that grows. In any case be sure that the plant you buy will go with what you already have, that it will fit in happily — in short, that it is you. If you are the casual cactus type maybe you wouldn't be comfortable with fluffy ruffles and perhaps fluffy ruffles wouldn't be comfortable with you.

**Choosing a Plant**

Choose your plant as you would produce in a supermarket. Look for plants that are bright-eyed and bushy-tailed. Avoid the limp, leggy, or bored-looking ones. Tired-looking plants will be just as much party poopers as will the wilted lettuce and yellowed broccoli. And, unless you want to punish yourself, don't ever buy (or let yourself be given) plants showing evidence of insects or disease. Buying a sick plant to make it better is in the same unproductive category as trying to reform a drunk or a philanderer.

After you have chosen the perfect plant for you, remember: plants need special protection getting from the store to their new home just as a baby needs care on the trip from the hospital. Plants must be wrapped carefully to protect them from too much sun or from freezing temperatures. Plastic will not do, so forget about trying to use that old dry-cleaning bag. Use wrapping paper or newspaper, and be sure that there are no gaps to let drafts, cold, or bright sun through to your tender plant.

After you get your new plant home, keep it away from your other plants

# What Type of Person Are You?

*The Fluffy Ruffles Type*

*The Casual Cactus Type*

*The Perfectionist*

*The Optimist*

for awhile. Intelligent and well-disciplined plant people always keep their new plants in quarantine for two weeks after they bring them home. The end of the kitchen counter makes a good quarantine station. If the plant suddenly develops a disease or insects, you can treat it or even eliminate it without damage to your other plants. This period also gives the new plant a chance to be introduced to its new family and adjust to the light and temperature conditions of its new home.

## Where to Buy a Plant

With so many places to buy plants, you will have to take the responsibility upon yourself for deciding where to make your plant purchases. The most reliable advice is simply word-of-mouth recommendations of satisfied plant people. But if you do not have recommendations to rely on, there are some basic things to look for in a plant store.

A good plant place will not let you buy large unrooted material (and they know enough not to buy it either) that has just made the trip up from Florida. Their plants will have been in the store for a while and will have made part of the transition from the high humidity and light of the greenhouse to the shock of "real life" in the drier and darker confines of the typical apartment or house.

But how do you know if a particular plant store is a good place for buying large plants? A helpful rule of thumb is to look for a shop that has been in business at the same location for at least two years. A store that sells immature plants or ones that haven't been properly acclimated will not last even that long. Their customers will die off as quickly as their plants do.

However, don't treat the two-year residency as an absolute requirement. Newer shops can be treasure-troves run by enthusiastic earthpeople. While more established shops can be death traps, existing on the strength of their sales of small plants and cut flowers.

Basically, the how and where of buying plants at a local plant store comes down to two things: what the store looks like, and what the plants look like. The store should be run by successful plant people, businesslike plant lovers. The place should be clean and tidy (although some creative disorder is permitted), and it should smell green. The plants should have breathing room — they shouldn't be all jammed together. Each category of plants, or each plant, should be priced and labeled.

As your confidence in yourself grows, and you begin to know what you want, you can buy just about anywhere. Chain stores and groceries often use the same wholesaler as your local plant store and often offer terrific bargains. However, you should buy a plant from such a source within a few days of its arrival since, generally, no one takes care of it. The supermarket can offer a lower price because it relies on quick movement of large shipments, is not in the year-round plant business, does not deliver, and generally gives no advice or special handling.

## Mail Order Brides

Small plants can be bought long distance as well as locally. Try out mail order places with small initial orders to get the feel of their material and service. See how the plants themselves match the printed descriptions in the ads, lists, or catalogs. Some of the very good mail order houses don't use illustrations in their catalogs, so you will want to check the plant out in an illustrated book or in a plant store or conservatory to be sure you know what you're ordering. Latin names help to pinpoint specific plants, but some old names are still in use and there are lots of synonyms. Therefore, ordering by mail should be undertaken with a certain sense of adventure.

### Sources for Plants

Abbey Garden, P.O. Box 30331, Santa Barbara, California 93105.
   Catalog, $1.00. Cacti and other succulent plants.
Alberts and Merkel, P.O. Box 537, Boynton Beach, Florida 33435.
   Catalog, $1.00. Orchids, Bromeliads, and tropicals in general.
   Good shipper.
Antonelli Brothers, 2545 Capitola Road, Santa Cruz, California 95010.
   Tuberous begonias and gesneriads.
Buell's Greenhouses, Eastford, Connecticut 06242.
   Catalog, $1.00. Many cultivated gesneriads; miniatures.
W. Atlee Burpee, Philadelphia, Pennsylvaniia 19132; Clinton, Iowa, 52733; Riverside, California 92502.
   Free catalog. Seeds, bulbs, plants, and supplies.
de Jager and Sons, Inc., 188 Ashbury Street, South Hamilton, Massachusetts 01982.
   Free catalog. Bulbs and pips for forcing.
L. Esterbrook Greenhouses, 10 Craig Street, Butler, Ohio 44822.
   African violets, gesneriads, and other exotics.
   Good shipper.
Fennell Orchid Company, 26715 S.W. 157th Avenue, Homestead, Florida 33030.
   Catalog, $1.00. Free list. Orchids and supplies.
Fischer Greenhouses, Linwood, New Jersey 08221.
   Catalog, $.15. African violets and some other gesneriads; supplies.
Hausermann's Orchids, P.O. Box 363, Elmhurst, Illinois 60126.
   Send postage for free catalog. Species orchids; information on fluorescent light and meristem culture.
The House Plant Corner, P.O. Box 810, Oxford, Maryland 21654.
   Catalog, $.25. Equipment and supplies.
Logee's Greenhouse, 55 North Street, Danielson, Connecticut 06239.
   Catalog, $1.00. All kinds of tropical exotics.
Lyndon Lyon, 14 Mutchley Street, Dolgeville, New York 13329.
   Send postage for free list. African violets and other gesneriads.
   Good shipper.

Rod McLellan Co., 1450 El Camino Real South, San Francisco, California 94080.
Catalog, $1.00. Orchids and supplies.
Merry Gardens, Camden, Maine 04843.
Catalog, $1.00. Large collection of indoor plants (especially Begonias, Geraniums, and ivies) and herbs.
Good shipper.
Oakhurst Gardens, P.O. Box 444, Arcadia, California 91008.
Catalog, $.50. Tropicals, bulbous plants and carniverous plants.
George W. Park Seed Company, Inc., Greenwood, South Carolina 29647.
Free catalog. Seeds, bulbs, some plants, and supplies.
Roehrs Exotic Nurseries, P.O. Box 144, Farmingdale, New Jersey 07727.
Free list; booklet: *Decorative Plants for Interiors,* $1.50; tropical plants.
Fred A. Stewart, Inc., 1212 East Las Tunas Drive, San Gabriel, California 91778.
Free catalog. Orchids and supplies.
Tinari Greenhouses, 2325 Valley Road, Huntingdon Valley, Pennsylvania 19006.
Catalog $.25. African violets, other gesneriads, and supplies.
Wilson Brothers, Roachdale, Indiana 46172.
Free catalog. Geraniums and supplies.

# Sources of Information

# WHERE TO GO FOR HELP

What can you do when you have exhausted your own resources, need a definitive answer to a specific question, or are looking for a second opinion? There are many sources for help but the quality can vary tremendously and the information can sometimes be conflicting or unclear. The first step is to match your potential source as closely as possible to your need.

Helpful information may come from an individual, institution, or group. The final decision on what you do is your own responsibility but you are at least giving yourself much better odds when you seek out expert advice.

The managers of established plant stores and garden centers where you have bought plants are generally not only knowledgeable about the plants they sell but are also eager to keep their customers happy. They can often give you good information about the care and habits of your plant when you purchase it. However, the manager is often very busy, and the assistants can sometimes be more enthusiastic than informed. Whatever you do, don't seek advice over the phone from a plant store or garden center for a plant you bought at the gas station or the grocery store — this is a real no-no.

When you want general or long-term information about a particular plant ask around to see if there is a local society that specializes in this type of plant. Such groups are called "single plant societies" and they can provide you with a wealth of advice, information and materials. These organizations welcome every degree of expertise and are expecially generous in sharing their knowledge and enthusiasm with newcomers to their field. If there is no local chapter of the plant society you are interested in the national membership secretary can often give you the names of members in your area. One of the real advantages in joining a single-plant society, in addition to information, is that you will be able to take part in plant and seed sales and exchanges — and so obtain material that would not be available otherwise. The major benefit of membership in a single plant society is its people. No matter what the other members do for a living, where they live, or what their personal foibles may be, you all share one thing — the overwhelming interest in and curiosity about the same plant or group of plants. Single plant societies do not require exclusive loyalty, and as your interests vary and expand you might very well join several.

## Single Plant Societies

African Violet Society of America, Inc.
P.O. Box 1326
Knoxville, TN 37901
$6.00 yearly dues
Magazine, 5 times a year

American Begonia Society
Membership Secretary
6333 West 84th Place
Los Angeles, CA 90045
$4.00 yearly dues
Monthly publication

The American Bonsai Society
Herbert R. Brawner,
Membership Secretary
953 South Shore Drive - Lake Waukomis
Parkville, MO 64151
$10.00 yearly dues
Quarterly journal

The American Camellia Society
P.O. Box 212
Fort Valley, GA 31030
Yearly dues
Quarterly journal

American Daffodil Society
89 Chichester Rd.
New Canaan, Ct 06840
$7.50 yearly dues
Quarterly publication

The American Dahlia Society
c/o Mrs. Caroline Meyer
92-21 W. Delaware Dr.
Mystic Islands
Tuckerton, NJ 07087
Yearly dues
Quarterly bulletin

American Fern Society
c/o LeRoy K. Henry, Treasurer
Div. of Plants, Carnegie Museum
Pittsburgh, PA 15213
$5.00 yearly dues
Quarterly journal

The American Gesneria Society
Worldway Postal Center
Box 91192
Los Angeles, CA 90009
$4.00 yearly dues
Bi-monthly bulletin

The American Gloxinia
& Gesnerad Society, Inc.
c/o Mrs. Diantha Buell, Secretary
Dept. P.F.S.O.
Eastford, CT 06242
$4.00 yearly dues
Bi-monthly magazine

The American Orchid Society
Botanical Museum of Harvard University
Cambridge, MA 02138
$10.00 yearly dues
Monthly bulletin

The American Plant Life Society
and American Amarylis Society
c/o Dr. Thomas Whitaker,
Executive Secretary
P.O. Box 150
La Jolla, CA 92037
Yearly dues
Publication included

The American Primrose Society
c/o Mrs. L. Tait, Treasurer
14015 84th Ave., NE
Bothell, WA 98011
Yearly dues
Quarterly publication

American Rhododendron Society
c/o Mrs. W. Curtis,
Executive Secretary
24450 SW Grahams Ferry Rd.
Sherwood, OR 97140
Yearly dues
Quarterly publication

The American Rose Society
P.O. Box 30,000
Shreveport, LA 71130
$10.50 yearly dues
Monthly magazine

Bonsai Clubs International
2354 Lida Dr.
Mountain View, CA 94040
Yearly dues
Publication 10 times a year

The Bromeliad Society, Inc.
P.O. Box 3279
Santa Monica, CA 90403
$7.50 yearly dues
Bi-monthly magazine

Cactus and Succulent
Society of America, Inc.
Box 167
Reseda, CA 91335
$6.00 yearly dues
Bi-monthly journal

Garden Club of America
598 Madison Ave.
New York, NY 10022
Yearly dues
Bulletin 5 times a year

The Herb Society of America
300 Massachusetts Ave.
Boston, MA 02115
Yearly dues
Annual publication

Indoor Light Gardening
Society of America, Inc.
c/o The Horticultural
Society of New York, Inc.
128 West 58th St.
New York, NY 10019
Yearly dues

International Geranium Society
c/o Arthur Thiede,
Membership Secretary
11960 Pascal Ave.
Colton, CA 92324
Yearly dues
Quarterly publication

Los Angeles International
Fern Society
P.O. Box 448
Hawthorne, CA 90250
$4.50 yearly dues

Men's Garden Clubs of America
c/o Secretary
5560 Merle Hay Rd.
Des Moines, IA 50323
$5.00 yearly dues
Bi-monthly magazine

National Council of State Garden
Clubs, Inc.
Mrs. C.E. Fitzwater
4401 Magnolia Ave.
St. Louis, MO 63110

National Chrysanthemum Society
Mrs. Walter A. Christoffers,
   Secretary
394 Central Ave.
Mountainside, NJ 07092
$5.00 yearly dues
Quarterly publication


National Fuchsia Society
Mrs. Martha Rader,
   Membership Secretary
10934 E. Flory St.
Whittier, CA 90606
$5.00 yearly dues

North American Lily Society
c/o Fred Abbey,
   Executive Secretary
North Fernisburg, VT 05473
Yearly dues
Quarterly bulletin

The Palm Society
c/o Mrs. Lucita Wait
7229 SW 54th Ave.
Miami, FL 33143
$10.00 yearly dues
Quarterly journal

Saintpaulia International
P.O. Box 10604
Knoxville, TN 37919
$4.00 yearly dues
Bi-monthly magazine

## Where else?

In a large community you might have a park district, botanic garden, or horticultural society you can draw on for answers to specific questions. The responses from these groups depend first on their interest in "the public" and second on whether they are understaffed. They are well worth trying at least once, and you may be lucky and strike pay dirt both for the specific information you need and for their broad views of plants and local growing requirements and possibilities.

## Extension

Extension is a helping hand available to all individuals everywhere. Cooperative extension, the umbrella term for a wide variety of helpful services, is an organizational entity of the U.S. Department of Agriculture and the land-grant institutions created under the Smith-Lever Act in 1914. The overall purpose is to transmit information from researchers to the public through educational activities of an informal, non-resident, problem-oriented nature. These activities are carried out primarily through the extension staffs of your county and state councils and land-grant colleges and universities.

The local extension people have different names, such as extension agent, county agent or farm adviser. Finding their number in the phone book sometimes takes a bit of doing. A good place to start is under the name of your land-grant educational institution and then "Cooperative Extension" or "College of Agriculture." If you can't find them — they are not lost, they know where they are — write your state college or university. Extension people are well informed, know the various local situations, and have many additional resources. Remember your taxes help support both the state educational institutions and the extension services.

For information about cultural problems, availability, and recommended varieties of plants consult your *extension horticulturist*.

For bugs, insects, and other creepy things you can see (or even barely see) consult your *extension entomologist*.

For information about diseases get in touch with your *extension plant pathologist*.

These experts are often available at both the county and state levels. When dealing by mail, address your letter to the most appropriate of title in care of your state land-grant institution.

EXAMPLE:

Extension Entomologist
College of Agriculture
State Land Grant Institution
City, State ZIP

## Free Publications

For a list of free publications, write to the Bulletin Room, College of Agriculture, at your state university.

ALABAMA: Auburn University, Auburn 36830.

ALASKA: University of Alaska, College 99735 (or Experiment Station, Palmer 99645).

ARIZONA: University of Arizona, Tucson 85721.

ARKANSAS: University of Arkansas, Fayetteville 72701 (or Cooperative Extension Service, 1201 McAlmont Ave., P. O. Box 391, Little Rock 72203).

CALIFORNIA: University of California, Berkeley 94720; Riverside 92502; or Davis 95616.

COLORADO: Colorado State University, Fort Collins 80521.

CONNECTICUT: University of Connecticut, Storrs 06268 (or Connecticut Agricultural Experiment Station, New Haven 06504).

DELAWARE: University of Delaware, Newark 19711.

FLORIDA: University of Florida, Gainesville 32603.

GEORGIA: University of Georgia, Athens 30601 (or Agricultural Experiment Station (State)., Experiment 30212; Coastal Plain Station, Tifton 31794).

HAWAII: University of Hawaii, Honolulu 96822.

IDAHO: University of Idaho, Extension Service, Boise 83702; Agricultural Experiment Station, Moscow 83843.

ILLINOIS: University of Illinois, Urbana (or Illinois National History Survey, (Urbana) 61801.

INDIANA: Purdue University, W. Lafayette 47907.

IOWA: Iowa State University, Ames 50010.

KANSAS: Kansas State University, Manhattan 66502.

KENTUCKY: University of Kentucky, Lexington 40506.

LOUISIANA: Louisiana State University, University Station, Baton Rouge 70803.

MAINE: University of Maine, Orono 04473.
MARYLAND: University of Maryland, College Park 20742 (or Vegetable Research Farm, Quantico Road, Salisbury 21801).
MASSACHUSETTS: University of Massachusetts, Amherst 01002.
MICHIGAN: Michigan State University, East Lansing 48823.
MINNESOTA: Institute of Agriculture, University of Minnesota, St. Paul 55101.
MISSISSIPPI: Mississippi State University, State College 39762.
MISSOURI: University of Missouri, Columbia 65202.
MONTANA: Montana State University, Bozeman 59715.
NEBRASKA: College of Agriculture, University of Nebraska, Lincoln 68503 (or Scott's Bluff Experiment Station, Mitchell 69357).
NEVADA: University of Nevada, Reno 89507.
NEW HAMPSHIRE: University of New Hampshire, Durham 03824.
NEW JERSEY: State College of Agriculture, Rutgers, The State University, New Brunswick 08903.
NEW MEXICO: New Mexico State University, University Park 88070.
NEW YORK: New York State College of Agriculture, Cornell University, Ithasca 14850 (or Agricultural Experiment Station, Geneva 14456; Ornamentals Research Laboratory, Farmingdale 11735).
NORTH CAROLINA: North Carolina State University, State College Station, Raleigh 27607 (or A. & T. College of North Carolina, P. O. Box 1014, Greensboro 28053; Horticultural Crops Research Station, Rte. 1, Box 121A, Castle Hayne 28429).
NORTH DAKOTA: North Dakota State University, State University Station, Fargo 58103.
OHIO: The Ohio State University, Columbus 43210 (or Ohio Agricultural Research & Development Center, Wooster 44691).
OKLAHOMA: Oklahoma State University, Stillwater 74075.
OREGON: Oregon State University, Corvallis 97331.
PENNSYLVANIA: The Pennsylvania State University, University Park 16802.
PUERTO RICO: Agricultural Extension Service, University of Puerto Rico, Rio Piedras 00927.
RHODE ISLAND: University of Rhode Island, Kingston 02881.
SOUTH CAROLINA: Clemson University, Clemson 29631.
SOUTH DAKOTA: South Dakota State University, Brookings 57007.
TENNESSEE: University of Tennessee, P. O. Box 1071, Knoxville 37901.
TEXAS: Texas A & M University, College Station 77841 (or Box 746, Weslaco 78596; Tyler Experiment Station No. 2, R. 6, Tyler 75703; Texas Agricultural Experiment Station, Rte. 3, Lubbock 79414).
UTAH: Utah State University, Logan 84321.
VERMONT: University of Vermont, Burlington 05401.
VIRGIN ISLANDS: Virgin Islands Agriculture Project, Kingshill, St. Croix 00801 (officer in charge).
VIRGINIA: Virginia Polytechnic Institute, Blacksburg 24061 (or Virginia Truck Experiment Station (truck crops), Norfolk 28501; Piedmont Fruit Research Laboratory, Charlottesville 22903; Winchester Fruit Research Laboratory, Winchester 22601).

WASHINGTON: Washington State University, Pullman 99163 (or Western Washington Experiment Station, Puyallup 98371; Irrigation Experiment Station, Prosser 99350).
WEST VIRGINIA: West Virginia University, Morgantown 26506 (or Fruit Experiment Station, Kearneysville 25430).
WISCONSIN: University of Wisconsin, Madison 53706 (or Peninsular Branch Experiment Station, Sturgeon Bay 54235).
WYOMING: University of Wyoming, Laramie 82070.

## P. S.

If you want to send a specimen of a plant or pest by mail to extension or any other expert, here are a few suggestions that will make it worth the effort and the postage. Popping material naked into an envelope often results in stuff being squished beyond recognition when it goes through the Postal Services cancelling machine.

First gather together all the materials you are going to need:
1. A plastic bag, aluminum foil or wax paper to wrap the specimen in.
2. A crush-proof box or mailing tube large enough to hold wrapped specimen.
3. Write a letter to enclose (or attach) which gives the following information when applicable:
   a. Date collected
   b. Kind of plant (if you know)
   c. Description of problem giving severity and extent
   d. Recent watering and fertilizing schedule (what and when)
   e. Recent pest control measures
   f. YOUR NAME AND ADDRESS! People who don't include this item, often don't get an answer.

Then, collect fresh specimen showing range of symptoms (for plant identification, at least one whole leaf) and put in plastic bag, aluminum foil or wax paper and seal tightly. DO NOT ADD MOISTURE. Place sealed specimen and letter in crush proof box or mailing tube, seal and address it to the appropriate individual.

Finally, MAIL AT ONCE! For best results, plan for material to arrive early in the week rather than late Friday afternoon.

# The Written Word

**P**lants are such complex living things that we should always be slightly suspicious about believing everything we read or hear about them. Just because something is in print, doesn't mean it's the gospel truth or that there aren't one or more valid exceptions that can be taken to just about every positive statement. However, books and magazines can save time by taking a load off the mind, relieving it of the necessity of remembering a lot of important trivia and infrequently needed information. If printed materials are treated with the proper skepticism, you will often find they provide the clue to solving a pressing problem of the botanical name of that nifty office plant that everyone calls "George."

Use your local library, and visit book stores. You can browse at length in the library, but remember that stores exist to sell books and not to provide reading places out of the rain. Keep checking for other works by authors you like and in the library, check other books listed under the same subject heading as the ones you have already found useful.

When you are thinking of buying a book, check to see if you are getting a good buy. Does the book really contain useful information? Is it meat and potatoes or just cream puffs? Also take a moment to figure out the cost per page. This will often open your eyes to a real bargain that may originally have looked awfully expensive or to a bit of fluff that is way overpriced. Never buy a book by its cover — check it out.

If you are a serious plant person, take a bread box, a folding file box, or a banana box and label it in large letters: PLANT INFORMATION (or whatever suits your fancy). This will make it easy to find information when you want it because everything will be in one place. It also makes it less likely that your materials will be sent off by mistake to a rummage sale or to be recycled. Use the box to file the materials torn out of newspapers or magazines, and to store the Extension Bulletins and even the books on plants and plant care that you have been collecting.

The books and magazines listed below are some suggestions of the kind available and a starting place for your expedition to search out the written word.

## Reading Suggestions

Baines, Jocelyn, and Key, Katherine. *The ABC's of Indoor Plants*. New York: Alfred A. Knopf, 1973.

Benjamin, Lovell. *The Love of Indoor Plants.* London: Octopus Books, 1973.

*Better Homes and Gardens House Plants 2nd ed.* Des Moines: Meredith, 1971.

Boddy, Fredrick A. *Foliage Plants*. New York: Drake Publishers 1973.

Baumgardt, John Philip. *Hanging Plants for Home, Terrace, and Garden.* New York: Simon and Schuster, 1972.

Canaday, John. *The Artful Avocado*. Garden City, N.Y.: Doubleday, 1973.

Carleton, R. Milton, Guest Editor. *Gardening Under Artificial Light*. Brooklyn: Brooklyn Botanic Garden, 1970. *(Plants & Gardens, Vol. 26, no. 1).*

Compton, Joan. *House Plants*. New York: Grosset & Dunlap, 1972.

Crockett, James Underwood. *Foliage House Plants*. New York: Time-Life, 1972.

Elbert, George A. *The Indoor Light Gardening Book*. New York: Crown Publishers, 1973.

Elbert, Virginie, and Elbert, George A. *Fun With Terrarium Gardening*. New York: Crown Publishers, 1973.

Evans, Charles M. *Rx for Ailing House Plants*. New York: Random House, 1974.

Faust, Joan Lee. *The New York Times Book of House Plants*. New York: Quadrangle, 1973.

Fitch, Charles Marden. *The Complete Book of Houseplants*. New York: Hawthorn Books, 1972.

Graf, Alfred Byrd. *Exotic House Plants Illustrated; All the Best in Indoor Plants. 8th ed.* East Rutherford, N.J.: Roehrs, 1973. (Previous editions published under title: *Exotic Plants Illustrated.)*

Graf, Alfred Byrd. *Exotica 3.* Rutherford, N.J.: Roehrs, 1968.

Handelsman, Judith, and Baerwald, Sara. *Greenworks: Tender Loving Care for Plants*. New York: Macmillan, 1974.

Herwig, Rob. *128 Houseplants More You Can Grow,* New York: Collier, 1974.

Herwig, Rob. *128 Houseplants You Can Grow*. New York: Collier, 1972.

Kramer, Jack. *Flowering House Plants Month by Month*. New York: Cornerstone Library, 1973.

Laden, Nancy Roca. *House Plants: A Primer for a Dumb Thumb*. Ten Speed, 1973.

Loewer, Peter. *The Indoor Water Gardener's How To Handbook*. New York: Walker, 1973.

McDonald, Elvin. *The Complete Book of Gardening Under Lights*. New York: Popular Library, 1965.

McDonald, Elvin. *Little Plants for Small Spaces*. New York: Popular Library, 1974. (Revision of *Miniature Plants for Home and Greenhouse.*)

McDonald, Elvin. *The World Book of House Plants*. New York: Popular Library, 1963.

Muller-Idzerda, A. C. *100 Indoor Plants in Color*. New York: Hippocrene Books, 1973. (Translation of *100 Kamerplanten in Kleur*. First published in Great Britain in 1955.)

*Ortho Books House Plants Indoors/Outdoors*. San Francisco: Ortho Books, 1974.

Perkins, Harold O., Guest Editor. *House Plants*. Brooklyn: Brooklyn Botanic Garden, 1957. *(Plants & Gardens*, vol. 18, no. 3).

Perry, Frances. *Flowers of the World*. New York: Crown Publishers, 1972.

Pierot, Suzanne Warner. *The Ivy Book: The Growing and Care of Ivy and Ivy Topiary*. New York: Macmillan, 1974.

Shurtleff, Malcolm C. *How to Control Plant Diseases in House and Garden*. 2nd ed. Ames: Iowa State University Press, 1966.

Sunset Editors. *Terrariums and Miniature Gardens*. Menlo Park, California: Lane, 1973.

Taloumis, George. *House Plants for Five Exposures*. New York: Abelard-Schuman, 1973.

Tenenbaum, Frances. *Nothing Grows for You?* New York: Scribners, 1974.

Teuscher, Henry, Guest Editor. *Handbook on Succulent Plants*. Brooklyn: Brooklyn Botanic Garden, 1963. *(Plants & Gardens*, vol. 19, no. 3).

U. S. Department of Agriculture. *Selecting and Growing House Plants. Home and Garden Bulletin, No. 82*, 1962.

U. S. Department of Agriculture. *Indoor Gardens with Controlled Lighting*. Home and Garden Bulletin, *no.* 187, 1971.

Van Rooten, Luis d'Antin. *The Floriculturist's Vade-Mecum of Exotic and Recondite Plants, Shrubs, and Grasses and One Malignant Parasite*. New York: Doubleday, 1973.

Ward, Frank and Peskett, Peter. *Indoor Plants*. London: Triune, 1973.

Westcott, Cynthia. *The Gardener's Bug Book, 4th ed.* New York: Doubleday, 1973.

Wilson, Helen Van Pelt. *Houseplants Are for Pleasure; How to Grow Healthy Plants for Home Decoration*. Garden City, N.Y.: Doubleday, 1973.

Woodward, Carol H., Guest Editor. *Handbook on Orchids*. Brooklyn: Brooklyn Botanic Garden, 1967. *(Plants & Gardens*, vol. 23, no. 2).

## Magazine Suggestions

*Light Garden*. The Indoor Light Gardening Society of America, Inc., 423 Powell Drive, Bay Village, Ohio 44140. Bi-monthly. Comes with membership ($5.00/year).

*Plants Alive: Indoor Growing and Greenhouse Journal*. Plants, Inc., 319 NE 45th, Seattle, Washington 98105. Monthly, except July and August, $9.00/year.

*Under Glass: The Home Greenhouse Gardener's Magazine*. Lord & Burnham, P.O. Box 114, Irvington, New York 10533. Bi-monthly, $2.00/year.

# Why Be Formal?

You probably have pet names for members of your family and for close friends. When you tell people at home that you saw Uncle Joe at the store yesterday, everyone knows just who you mean. Some of your friends know who Uncle Joe is too. But if you casually mention Uncle Joe to the person in front of you at the supermarket check-out counter, the chances are you won't communicate. The person in front of you probably doesn't know your Uncle Joe, and, to make matters even more confusing, may have an Uncle Joe you don't know.

The same confusion occurs with the use of common names for plants. The use of the name certainly makes it easier to converse. With the name, you avoid the need to use descriptive phrases every time you refer to the plant, "I bought an elephant ear today" is much easier than saying, "I bought a lush plant with fresh green, fleshy, arrow-shaped leaves." Of course, using common names can give you a bit of trouble too. Is your elephant ear a *PHILODENDRON hastatum, COLOCASIA esculenta, ENTEROLOBIUM cyclocarpum,* or one of the *CALADIUMS?*

If you had said, "I bought a *PHILODENDRON hastatum* today," there would have been absolutely no confusion about what you had bought — just as you would have saved confusion if you had used the name *Joe Smith* instead of *Uncle Joe* at the supermarket. Formal names make communication clear and reliable. When two plant people are communicating with each other, they want to be sure they are referring to the same thing. This is especially important when the plant is not in front of both people at the same time, as when describing a great find or ordering a new plant through the mail. Unless the name is unambiguous, there can be trouble.

## The Naming of Plants

Knowledge of the plant kingdom is still quite incomplete. For one thing, of the 350,000 known species of plants, only a small minority have been thoroughly studied. For another thing, many species known to science have been classified from one or only a few specimens which may not have given the full picture of their natural variation. This is why some stores carry a plant labeled, *PHILODENDRON pertusum,* which is really an immature form of MONSTERA deliciosa, the Swiss cheese plant.

The scientific naming of plants is based on classification of the plants according to species. A species is the smallest natural group of plants which shares inherited physical features that distinguish it from other related plants. Since the presence of the features can be confirmed or denied, membership in a species is not a matter of judgement or conjecture. If you try to mate members of two different species, the offspring will be infertile, for example, the mule, whose parents are the horse and the ass. However, you can mate members of the same species, even though they may appear quite different. For example, cauliflower, Brussels sprouts, broccoli, kohlrabi, and kale are all varieties of *BRASSICA oleracea.* Nurserymen raising seed must be very careful to keep them apart.

The name of a species is made up of two parts: the name of the genus to which it belongs, and a second word called the *specific epithet.* These epithets (Joe) are only meaningful in combination with a generic name (Smith), as in Smith, Joe. This two-name (binomial) system of naming plants was worked out about 250 years ago by a Swede, Linne (Linnaeus was the Latinized form of his name). Latin was chosen as the language for the system for two reasons: first, it was the international language of scholars in the time the system was developed, and second, it was conveniently dead so it avoided all the problems of jealousy and bias that might have resulted had a modern language been used.

The great strength of the binomial system is that it makes it possible to make inferences about unfamiliar plants. Generally, you can assume that they will resemble each other in *some* respects (as will the Smiths) and you can predict with *some* degree of certainty their care and other requirements. The weakness of the system lies in that the name of the species depends on the name of the genus, and if it is found that the plant has been placed in the wrong genus, the name will invariably change when it is moved. This can be a real pain, for it seems that just as one learns the names of a number of plants, they are changed by some busybody botanist.

Scientific nomenclature is still a live subject. The Americans went their own way in 1892 with the Rochester Code and in 1907 with the American Code. The world botanists really didn't get together until 1930, when international harmony was on its way. Today, the International Code of Botanical Nomenclature (1966) and the International Code of Nomenclature for Cultivated Plants (1969) help keep everyone playing the same game.

### Rules for Botanical Names

1. Plant names are separate from animal names, although a plant may have the same scientific name as some animal and often does. For example, *RICINUS*, the name of the genus that the castor oil plant belongs to, is also the name of certain bird lice.
2. The name of the species consists of two words in Latin, the genus and its specific epithet (Smith, Joe).
3. The purpose of giving the name is to provide a means of identifying the plant and not to indicate its character or history.
4. Plant names are based on the principle of priority (barring certain exceptions). The first Latin name given a flowering plant after May 1, 1753, is the valid name of the plant.
5. However, names of certain genera long in common use, but not necessarily the oldest, are sometimes kept.
6. In order to be valid, the scientific name must be published in a recognized botanical book or magazine and must include, for a species described for the first time, a description in Latin. Descriptions that are photocopies or appear in newspapers are illegitimate.

### Rules Covering Cultivar Names (since January 1, 1959)

Cultivated varieties known as *cultivars* are indicated with an initial capital letter preceded by the abbreviation "cv," or appear in single quotes. These may be used after generic, specific, or common names.

1. New cultivar names must be names of one or two words but not more than three words, in modern languages.
2. If the botanical name of the plant is changed, the cultivar name must remain unchanged, i.e. *SCHEFFLERA 'Variegata'* retains its name

regardless of whether the species is called *SCHEFFLERA actinophylla* or *BRASSAIA actinophylla.*

3. Two or more cultivars of the same genus may not bear the same name, even if they belong to different species. An exception is made in the case where there are distinct crops involved and there is no danger of confusion. One could have a cabbage, broccoli, and cauliflower with the name 'Supreme', though they all belong to the genus *BRASSICA.*

4. New cultivar names must not be the same as a botanical or common name. Names like geranium 'Pansy' or *PELARGONIUM* 'Poinsettia' are no longer permitted.

5. Cultivar names must be published by the distribution of printed or duplicated matter dated at least as to the year. A description, which can be in any language, is also required.

6. The name must then be registered with the appropriate international registration authority (an organization, institute or society — never an individual). This serves to provide accuracy and uniformity in the naming of cultivated plants.

# What's in a Name?

**A**nyone who has tried to pronouce the tongue-twisting botanical names may wonder if the names were chosen as some cruel hoax on the lay public. But actually there is a meaning behind the madness of the species names. Those scientific-sounding names describe certain characteristics of the particular plants. And when they're translated — lo and behold! — there's no great mystery about them after all. You can understand why a *DRACAENA draco* is called a dragon tree when you know that *draco* means "dragon." If you're in love with your *DIEFFENBACHIA amoena*, you'll appreciate the fact that *amoena* means "beautiful."

Here is a list of the species names and their translations. Now you can understand how your plant got it's name. You can dazzle your friends with this bit of knowledge.

| Species Name | English Equivalent |
|---|---|
| actinophylla | starlike leaf |
| acuminata | tapering down into a narrow point |
| afra | African |
| Africanus | African |
| alata | winged |
| alternifolius | one leaf right after another |
| americana | American |
| amoena | beautiful |
| andreanum | manly |
| annuum | annual |
| antarctica | likes cool temperature, but not freezing |
| arabica | Arabian |
| arborea | treelike |
| arborescens | becoming treelike |

| Species Name | English Equivalent |
|---|---|
| argentea | silvery |
| argyreia | silver |
| argyroneura | silver-veined |
| articulatus | jointed |
| aurantiaca | orange |
| aureum (aureus) | golden |
| australis | southern |
| balfouriana | of Balfour |
| bella | pretty |
| benjamina | of Benjamin |
| bidwillii | of Bidwill |
| bifurcatum | having two prongs |
| bipinnatifidum | shaped like a feather with smaller feathers attached |
| blossfeldiana | of Blossfeld |
| blumei | of Blum |
| bridgesii | of Bridges |
| cadierei | of Cadier |
| caerulea | deep blue |
| camara | vaulted |
| canariense | from the Canary Islands |
| capensis (capense) | from the Cape |
| caperata | wrinkled |
| carica | from Caria |
| carinata | keeled |
| carnosa | fleshy |
| cavendishii | of Cavendish |
| chinensis | Chinese |
| coccinea | deep red |
| commutatum | changed |
| comosus (comosum) | bearing a tuft of hairs or leaves |
| cordatum | with two, equal, rounded lobes at the base |
| crenulata | with small, rounded teeth |
| crispa | wavy |
| cruentus | blood-stained |
| crystallinum | crystalline |
| cupreata | copper-colored |
| cyanea | dark blue |
| dactylifera | bearing fingers |
| daigremontiana | of Daigremont |
| debilis | weak |
| deliciosa | delightful |
| derenbergii | of Derenberg |
| draco | dragon |
| elastica | elastic |
| elatior | taller |
| elatum | tall |
| elegans | elegant |

| Species Name | English Equivalent |
|---|---|
| elephantipes | ivory-petaled |
| elliottiana | of Elliott |
| emarginatus | shallowly notched |
| ensiformis | sword-shaped |
| erumpens | breaking through |
| exaltata | raised high |
| excelsa | lofty |
| exotica | exotic |
| fasciata | bandage-shaped |
| falcatum | sickle-shaped |
| floribunda (floribundum) | bearing many flowers |
| fosteriana | of Foster |
| fragrans | fragrant |
| fruticosa | like a shrub |
| gausonii | of Gauson |
| glabra | without hair |
| glorioso | glorious |
| godseffiana | of Godseff |
| gramineus | grasslike |
| granatum | granular |
| grandicornis | with large horn |
| grandiflora | with large flowers |
| grantii | of Grant |
| guatemalense | from Guatemala |
| guilfoylei | of Guilfoyle |
| guttata | spotted |
| hedysaroides | vetchlike |
| helix | spiral |
| herbeohybrida | herby hybrid |
| herbstii | of Herbst |
| heterophylla | having leaves of more than one form |
| hirta | hairy |
| hortorum | of gardens |
| hortulanum | of a gardener |
| humilis | low |
| hybridum | hybrid |
| imperialis | imperial |
| indica | from India |
| insignis | outstanding |
| involucrata | ringed |
| ionantha | with violet flowers |
| japonica | Japanese |
| jasminoides | jasminelike |
| jonquilla | jonquil |
| kraussiana | of Krauss |
| lactea | milky |
| leninghausii | of Leninghaus |
| leuconeura | white-nerved |

| Species Name | English Equivalent |
|---|---|
| limon | lemon |
| lingulata | tongue-shaped |
| macrophylla | large-leaved |
| makoyana | of Makoy |
| malacoides | mollusclike |
| mammillaris | breastlike |
| marginata | margined |
| massangeana | of Massange |
| mauritanica | Mauritanian |
| menziesii | of Menzies |
| merallica | metallic |
| meyeri | of Meyer |
| microphylla | small-leaved |
| millii | of millet |
| miliioid | |
| miniata | flame-scarlet |
| mitis | soft |
| modestum | moderate |
| morganianum | of Morgan |
| morifolium | mulberry-leaved |
| multiflora | many flowers |
| nana | dwarf |
| nidus | nest |
| obtusifolia | blunt leafed |
| oertendahlii | of Oertendahlii |
| officinale | official |
| oleander | latin name of bush |
| orientalis | Oriental, eastern |
| ornata | ornate |
| oxycardium | sharp-hearted |
| oxypeatllum | sharp-petaled |
| palmatum | divided like the hand |
| papyrus | paper |
| panduraeforme | fiddle-shaped |
| paradisi | of paradise |
| peltatum | shield-shaped |
| pendula | hanging |
| persicum | of Persia |
| picta | painted, colored |
| pinnata | leaflets on sides of main leaf axis (from feather) |
| plumosa, plumosus | feathery |
| podophyllum | footlike leaf |
| pseudo-narcissus | false narcissus |
| pudica | shy |
| pulcherrima | very beautiful |
| pumila | dwarf |
| pusilla | very small |
| pyramidalis | pyramidal |

| Species Name | English Equivalent |
|---|---|
| radicanus | roots |
| recurvata | recurved |
| reflexa | bent back |
| regina | queen |
| retusa | rounded, shallowly notched end |
| rhombifolia | rhombus-leaved |
| rivieri | of Rivier |
| robusta | robust, stout |
| roebelanii | of Roebelan |
| romanzoffianun | of Romanzoff |
| rosa | rose |
| rubra | red |
| rubrotinctum | red, dyed, red-stained |
| sanderiana | of Sander |
| sandersii | of Sanders |
| saramentosa | bearing runners |
| schiedei | of Schied |
| schizopetalus | deeply divided petals |
| selloum | saddle |
| senilis | old, white-haired |
| sinensis | Chinese |
| soleirolii | of Soleirol |
| somaliensis | from Somalia |
| spathacea | with a spathe |
| speciosa | showy, good-looking |
| splendens | shining, brilliant |
| sprengeri | of Springer |
| squamiferum | scale carrying |
| tazetta | cup |
| tectorum | of roofs |
| terminalis | at the end |
| tigrina | tiger-striped |
| tirucalli | of Tirucall |
| tormentosa | matted, hairy |
| trifasciata | three-banded |
| truncatus | cut off square |
| uncinata | hooked at the point |
| undatus | waved |
| variegata, variegatus | variegated |
| veitchii | of Veitch |
| vera | true |
| verrucosa | warty |
| verschaffeltii | of Verschaffelt |
| victoriae-reginae | Queen Victoria |
| viviparum | live young |
| wendlandii | of Wendland |
| wildenovii | of Wildenov |
| woodii | of Wood |
| zonatus | zoned, banded |

# Fun with Plants

**P**lants aren't just functional, decorative items to be put in a spot, fed, and told to keep quiet. Plants can become almost part of the family — fun to play with and fun to watch grow. And plants aren't just cultivated things that come from a greenhouse. You have the sources of great-looking plants right in your refrigerator.

### How to Grow a Citrus Tree

Save the fattest seeds from the next orange, grapefruit, or kumquat that you eat. If you want a lemon tree, you can try lemon seeds too. Wash the seeds well and soak them overnight. Then plant them about ½ inch deep and 1 inch apart in a pot of either potting soil or vermiculite. Put the container in a sunny spot and keep the soil slightly moist at all times. When the seeds sprout, you'll have a nice, shiny, green clump growing together. If you want to raise fruit, transplant the seedlings into separate containers, keep them moist in bright sunlight, and give them loving care for about 8 or 9 years.

### How to Grow a Sweet Potato Vine

Get a good plump sweet potato that looks cheerful (no bad scars) and about ready to sprout. Ask your produce seller if it's been treated to prevent growth. If it has, you'll grow nothing but frustrated. So put it back and shop elsewhere until you find one that hasn't been treated. Put the whole sweet potato (pointy side down) in a container of water so only the bottom half stays wet. Put the container in a bright, sunny spot, and if you have used a glass or clear plastic container, you can watch the roots grow and grow. When the vines start forming, you can train them to grow up around your window or let them just hang down. Be sure to remember to keep the water covering the roots.

## How to Grow a Pineapple

Buy a ripe pineapple with a nice full-looking top (crown). Cut off the crown with about a half-inch of the pineapple attached. Wash the crown. Peel the rest of the pineapple and enjoy it. Next day, remove the bottom two rows of leaves from the crown and any fruit that is attached to it. Put the crown in water, and when the roots form in a week or two, you can plant it in a sandy potting soil. Pineapple likes to have water sitting in its crown, so pour water right over the top of the plant when watering. Enjoy the plant's beauty, but don't wait for the fruit. Even if it ever comes, it's not worth eating.

## How to Grow an Avocado

Start with a ripe avocado. Cut through the outer skin carefully and separate the avocado into two parts. Remove the large brown seed (the pit) from the center. Give the pit a bath and set it aside. Enjoy the fruit. Later, place the pit rounded side down in water (only half covered by water) or soil like a citrus plant. Place the container in filtered sunlight. Keep the water halfway up the pit, or keep the soil evenly moist. Be patient, and with luck, it may eventually sprout. Avocado pits are picky, and they'll work or not work equally well in soil or in water. It's the nature of the plant to grow tall with long skinny stems. But if you want a bushier plant, you'll have to be strong-hearted and cut it back to about 6 inches when it is 12 inches high.

## Sprouts, or Instant Vegetable Gardening Inside

Mung beans are probably the easiest to sprout, although lentils also take just four or five days. Rye and wheat will sprout in two days, and alfalfa in six or seven. Buy your beans or grains from a supermarket, Oriental food store, health food store, or mail order house. Don't buy any that are intended for planting outdoors since they may have been treated.

One-half cup of dry beans will produce about four cups of sprouts. Wash beans or grains in water and soak overnight or for twelve hours. Then place them in a container that will hold the moisture without becoming soggy; an 8 to 10-inch clay pot is good. Cover the drain hole with a broken piece of pot or nylon net, put in the beans, cover them with a clean, damp dishtowel, and put the pot in a dark place. Sprouts grown entirely in the dark will be pale yellow. For green sprouts, give them plenty of light. Rinse twice a day, drain, and replace the re-dampened towel. When the sprouts are long enough you can use them in salads or with Oriental dishes. They will keep in a plastic bag in the refrigerator for two or three days.

If you don't have clay pots available you can use a wide-mouth canning jar or even a dark brown applesauce jar. If a dark jar is available, you won't have to bother hunting up or clearing out a dark place.

### Beet Baskets, Potato Heads and Hairy Hearts

Root vegetables such as beets, carrots and turnips can resprout their tops if they are cut off and set in water. In a short time the leaves start growing, producing a fresh green grove. It is even more fun if you turn the root vegetable upside down and carefully carve out most of the inside to form a "basket." Add hangers and fill the "basket" with water. When the leaves start growing on the hanging vegetable baskets they turn upward like full green moustaches.

Potato heads can be carved out of potatoes and the bald pate covered with grass or curley cress seed. Kept moist, the head soon sprouts green hair. Potato heads make a great activity for St. Patrick's day.

You can sprout a hairy heart out of a sponge. Cut hearts, shamrocks, or any other shape that you want out of a cellulose sponge. Thoroughly wet the sponge, squeeze it out, and sprinkle it with grass or curley cress seed. In a few days you will have a novel plant creation to admire or give away.

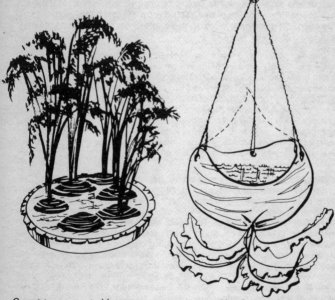

*Carrot tops sprouted in water.*     *Hanging turnip basket.*

### Herbs in the Kitchen

You can grow a few herbs in the kitchen if you have a good bright windowsill or you can supplement natural light with a fluorescent fixture. Two four-foot fluorescent tubes can produce enough of your favorite herbs for flavor and garnish all year long, providing you are not too heavy handed in your harvesting.

Although in the beginning it may be easier to start with plants from the grocery, plant shop or friend, you can start many of them from seed. Keep the fluorescent lights 6 to 10 inches above the pots until the herbs start to grow. You can raise the lights a little as the plants get larger. They should be kept on for 14 to 16 hours a day and the light intensity can be increased by using mirrors or aluminum foil on cardboard, underneath or around the sides, to bounce the light back on the plants.

**Basil** *(OCIMUM basilicum)* is an annual herb belonging to the mint family. It is a small, bushy plant that grows to be about two feet high. You can cut the leaves and dry them, but harvest the leaves before the basil flowers. In order to have a longer harvesting time keep cutting or pinching off the flower stalks. Fresh leaves can be used for flavoring salads and the dried leaves are often used instead of oregano in pizza, stews, sauces and sausages. Seeds should be covered with soil an eighth inch to a quarter inch and the plants should grow at least 6 to 8 inches apart. The seed will germinate in two to three weeks depending on conditions.

**Chives** *(ALLIUM schoenoprasum)* along with onions and garlic, belong to the lily family. Chives are small, grasslike perennials that normally grow 6 to 12 inches high. The bright green leaves may be used in salads or chopped and sprinkled in vegetables and potatoes, or in any recipe calling for a mild, delicate onion flavor. You can start harvesting them about 6 weeks after planting, but don't snip the leaves down too far or you will kill the plant. If possible, it is a good idea to have three or four pots going at one time and snip the tops off each in turn. If you are not interested in eating chives, you can admire the lovely lavendar blooms that grow in small pom-poms at the end of long stems.

**Dill** *(ANETHUM graveolens)* is an annual of the parsley family. Its name is derived from an old Norse word, *Dilla,* meaning to lull. Dill was suppose to have a soothing effect on crying babies. It was also used as a weapon against witchcraft and was an important ingredient in love potions. Dill leaves, known as dill weed, can be finely chopped and used fresh or dried in soups or salads or with seafood. Dill seed is used either whole or ground as a flavoring in pickling cucumbers and sprinkling on potatoes and other vegetables. Dill vinegar is made by soaking the dill seeds in vinegar for several days. Grow the plants four inches apart. You can start snipping the leaves off as soon as the plant looks large enough. Grown indoors, dill stems become very long and don't have leaves. If you want seeds, grow the plant outdoors.

**Parsley** *(PETROSELINUM crispum)* is a hardy biennial (grows for two years only) that belongs to the same family as dill. The Greeks used it to crown the victors of the Isthmia games and scattered it over the tombs of the dead. The Romans put bunches of parsley on their banquet tables to purify the wine fumes and cut down on intoxication and hangovers. Fresh leaves can be used to flavor salads, soups and stews as well as decoratively filling an empty space on a plate. Parsley seed is slow to germinate and it can be speeded up by soaking the seed in warm water overnight. When harvesting, cut off the outside leaves. This will encourage new growth to sprout from the center of the plant.

**Thyme** *(THYMUS vulgaris)* is another perennial herb belonging to the mint family. Although there are over 100 different species of thyme, the common garden thyme *(THYMUS vulgaris)* is the one more generally grown. It is often used for flavoring grains, fish chowders, meats and poultry. If recipes call for a sprig of thyme, use 1/2 teaspoon of ground thyme. Roman soldiers used to bathe in water in which thyme had been soaked to gain vigor and strength. Later, in the days of chivalry it was the custom for fair ladies to give their knights scarves on which a sprig of thyme had been embroidered. Grow the plants about 12 inches apart which will give them a lot of room to spread. Begin harvesting when the first flower clusters appears.

## Windowsill Gardening

Windowsill gardening can be a fun way to start plants. The supplies you need are:

> A one-gallon size zip-lock plastic bag (a regular
> plastic bag may be used)
> Peat moss and perlite in equal amounts
> A label with date
> Stem cuttings

To make your cutting, choose a stem that has new growth at the tip. Count down three sets of leaves, and then cut sharply across the stem ¼ inch below the third set of leaves. Cut the last set of leaves off your cutting, and trim down the other leaves if they're too large for the bag, but be careful not to injure the growing tip.

When you've made your cuttings, you're ready to put together your windowsill garden. The first stage of windowsill gardening is the planting stage.

1. Add water to the peat moss and perlite mixture — just enough so when a handful of mixture is squeezed, a few drops of water will come out.

2. Place enough mixture in the bag so it's 2½ inches deep.

3. Firm the mixture by pressing a hand down on the outside of the bag until the surface is firm.

4. Turn the top of the bag down.

5. Poke a hole in the mixture for each cutting, spacing so that four cuttings will fit.

6. Place the cuttings into the hole. and using your thumb and forefinger. press around it to firm the soil.

7. Sprinkle the cuttings with water (about five squirts from a water bottle). Don't overwater!

8. Place the label in the bag so that the date can be read from the outside.

9. Zip up the bag. If a regular bag is used. fasten it tightly closed with a rubber band or wire twist.

10. Pick up the bag from the top only.

In the second stage of windowsill gardening. the cuttings grow their roots and become whole new plants.

1. Place the sealed bag in a north window for two weeks. Don't place it in the sunshine or the plants will bake. If the weather turns very cold. be sure the plants are protected from sudden chills.

2. In two weeks. open the bag so the plants will get used to the normal room conditions of dryness and less warmth.

3. If the soil dries out. water it lightly.

4. After three days of conditioning. the cuttings should be ready to transplant.

5. Check the root growth by tugging gently. If the plants give resistance. then the roots have formed.

6. Carefully lift the plant out of the moss and perlite by digging around it with your fingers.

7. Transplant the cutting into a container that has good drainage. such as a flower pot. milk carton. or styrofoam or plastic cup with holes punched near the bottom.

8. Fertilize the new plant lightly.

Now you have a complete new plant that's ready to love you and grow for you.

1. Place the plants. after transplanting. into a sunny window.

2. Water them when the soil shows any dryness. but be sure there's good drainage.

3. Pinch the plant back as it gets bigger to promote bushy growth.

4. ENJOY!

### Seedlings

You can also grow plants from seeds. Seeds can be grown in trays, dishpans or those pot pie pans that you have been hoarding in the cupboard. For starting seeds, the soil mix should drain well and hold moisture evenly. You can use peat moss and perlite in equal amounts, or expanded vermiculite. Vermiculite is disease-free and since the roots do not cling to it there is less transplanting shock. Whatever you use, be sure that it is evenly moist before planting the seeds. If you don't have too many seeds you can sprinkle them on the surface. If you have a lot of seeds, or different kinds of seeds, plant them sparsely in rows. (The rows can be marked by pressing a ruler or a pencil in the soil mix which has been pressed flat.) Whether you cover seeds or not depends on the size of the seed. A rule of thumb is to cover them with a layer of mix equal to the thickness of the seed. Some very small seeds are never covered. If your mix was premoistened you won't have to water. If the mix was dry (horror!) carefully punch holes in the bottom of the container (if it didn't have any) and set the whole container in a pan of water so it can soak the moisture up from the bottom. When it is moist the mix looks darker.

Place the container in a plastic bag, closing the bag tightly. Place the bag in a north window, out of direct sunlight. There is no need to water until the seeds germinate and you release the tray from its "hothouse" — usually in about two weeks. The seedlings are ready to be transplanted into individual containers when you see the third set of leaves. (The very first leaves to poke through the soil are usually unidentifiable, rounded leaves.) If you let the seedlings grow too long their roots will become hopelessly entangled.

Styrofoam cups, plastic pots or peat pots make good individual containers for seedlings. Fill the pots with the same light soilless mixture of peat and vermiculite or peat and perlite; carefully transplant the seedlings and put the little pots on a tray and place them in a plastic bag for a few days. Wire coat hangers arched over the tray are excellent props to keep the plastic from collapsing.

A one-step way of starting plants is to sow seeds directly into blocks or cubes of prepared, compound potting mix (available from garden centers, plant stores and nurseries) — or into an egg carton or small styrofoam cups filled with the peat and vermiculite mix. Be sure the container is thoroughly damp before planting the seeds. Plant three or four seeds in a block and put the block pots in a plastic tent. If more than one seed comes up, cut off the weaker ones, leaving the largest, healthiest looking plant. Whether you start the seedlings in individual pots, or transplant them to single containers, they should be taken out of the plastic tent once they are established. Although transplanting windowsill seedlings takes time and sometimes is a lot of work, often it is the only way to get plants you've read about but never have been able to buy.

*Windowsill seedings grow under a plastic tent.*

## Hanging Gardens

When you have no windowsill, have aggressive pets, or when the large number of your plants has you climbing the wall, consider the hanging garden. Hanging baskets have been used for ages in conservatories to fill unused space decoratively, and plant people today are finding that a hanging garden can work at home to add beauty, promote privacy and storehouse more plants.

There are many kinds of containers available on the market today. Plastic containers with attached or detachable drainage saucers are the most widely used. The old-fashioned baskets made of sphagnum moss, lined wire or redwood are great outside but drip indoors. Watch out for disease problems on plants below. Clay and metal containers are also used and if there is no drainage hole then it is a good idea to double pot (put the pot with the plants inside the decorative container). When creating hanging gardens consider the following: how will water drain, where will it go, how long will the container last, have you used sturdy material for supports (wire and monofilament last a lot longer than leather and hemp). Remember, after filling and watering the garden might be too heavy for its hanger or the support.

Is the container easy to hang and water? A pulley can help bring it down to working level. In potting the hanging garden there should be enough room for watering as well as for roots and plants. When all is finished what is the effect — do you see plant or pot? One plant or several of the same kind will look fine, but combinations of compatible plants can be even more fun. Depending on the location of the basket, there are many plants that can be used for your hanging gardens.

## Terrariums

The word *terrarium* started coming into use in around 1890 as the land equivalent of aquarium. It was generally a place where you kept lizards and other small animals. Today, the term refers to almost any collection of plants growing together, usually in a decorative manner. Basic terrarium containers are a bottle, or a completely enclosed space; a box, a container with a lid that can be either closed, partially open, or open; and a dish.

**Bottle.** If you're planting materials in a bottle, you should choose plants that are tolerant of high humidity and preferably are slow-growing since they are rather difficult to remove. Suitable plants are ferns, strawberry begonias, dwarf gesneriads, baby tears, small peperomias, and pileas.

**Box.** With a box, a great variety of plants is possible since humidity can range from moderate to high, and the plant material (because of the ease of removal) is almost unlimited. Almost any house plant does well in a box — begonias, coleus, small palms, African violets, moss . . . — provided the sizes and humidity requirements of the different plants are compatible.

**Dish.** In dish gardens, the humidity is the same as the surrounding environment, so plants that have low humidity requirements are usually most effective. The succulents are most satisfactory; and cactus, euphorbia and geraniums provide interesting shapes and textures.

## Terrarium Construction

**Potting Mix.** If you're making your own potting mix, a good formula is

⅓ peat moss, ⅓ perlite, and ⅓ vermiculite. If you start out with dry ingredients, add one cup of water to every four cups of mix. If you use a mix about this consistency to start out with, you won't run into the problem of too much water in your terrarium.

**Drainage.** One to two inches of washed sand or gravel at the bottom of the container will keep the plants' feet from sitting in water.

**Plants.** You can buy your plants, beg them, or grow your own. The possibilities and availability are constantly changing, which is what makes terrarium construction the challenging hobby it is.

**Planting.** The number of plants you use depends on the size of your container. The plants should be compatible with each other — that is, they should be tolerant of the same conditions of temperature, humidity, light, and water. Extremes of temperature are hard on plants, and although many plants require a lot of light, they are often "cooked" if they are put in direct sunlight on a windowsill.

**Have fun:** Feel the power that comes from creating an entire environment.

## Bottle Gardens

The first thing to do when embarking on bottle gardening is to wash the bottle and dry it until it's sparkly clean. Remember, once the bottle is planted, you'll never be able to really get in there to wash it again. So make this last washing a good one.

When you're satisfied that the jar is clean — and dry — pour the sand or gravel into the bottle until it is one or two inches deep, depending on the size of the bottle. Since most bottles don't have drain holes in the bottom, the sand or gravel is important for drainage. On top of the sand or gravel, pour the soil — about two inches worth.

The plants for your bottle garden should be tolerant of high humidity and preferably should be slow growing since they are rather difficult to remove if they get too big. Of course, you can always attach a razor blade to the end of a bamboo stake and use it like a machete to trim them back, but it always seems such a shame to be cutting plants back all the time. If you do use the razor-blade trick, bend the end of a coat hanger to make a hook for pulling the cut pieces out. Popular plants for bottle gardens are dwarf African violet, aluminum plant, artillery plant, asparagus fern, baby's tears, begonias, ferns, piggy-back plants, peperomias, palms, selaginella, strawberry begonia, and wandering Jew. The wandering Jew grows fast, but makes you feel like a great bottle gardener.

For planting, use a piece of bamboo that has a spoon taped to the end to dig a hole in the soil for the plant. Carefully remove enough soil from the plant's root ball and roll it tight so it will fit through the neck of the bottle. Place the plant in the hole you dug for it, and, again using the bamboo with the spoon, cover the roots with soil. Continue doing this until the bottle is planted just to your liking. If the inside of the bottle gets dirty while you're planting, the easiest way to wipe it out is with a cotton ball attached to the end of a piece of wire coat hanger. Your bottle garden won't need much watering, but when it does be sure to add the moisture little by little. Remember, there's no hole in the bottom of the bottle for extra water to drain out. You can use a spray mister for watering or a drinking straw filled with water.

A razor blade on a bamboo stake makes a machete.

Dig a hole with a spoon taped to a bamboo stick.

Use a newspaper funnel to add sand and soil.

## Bonsai and Saikei

Bonsai is a method of dwarfing trees and growing them in containers. Saikei is the creation of miniature landscapes. The main goal of bonsai and saikei is to create the impression of a graceful landscape by the development of trees that appear aged and have unique and striking characters. This is achieved by a fairly exacting process of pruning, shaping (usually with the aid of wire), cutting back roots, and frequent careful watering.

Traditionally, either deciduous or evergreen trees are used. Maple, flowering apricot, holly, pine, spruce, and juniper are favorites. Flowers and fruits will be in normal size, but the trunks, branches and leaves will be dwarfed.

Although some bonsai connoisseurs feel that the only true bonsai are those grown from seed, many select a plant that has some character already. Keeping in mind the tree's final shape, bonsai "artists" select the branches they intend to train and prune away all the unwanted branches. They leave only one branch at each level. This accents the trunk and creates a feeling of openness and age (see figure). Then they pinch back the rest to encourage end growth, and prepare the branches for attaining the proper shapes. Bonsai "artists" train their trees very slowly; they never force branches into unnatural shapes.

The training of the branches is usually done by wiring. Soft copper wire (sizes 10 to 26, depending on the thickness of the branches) is wrapped around the branches in careful and regular spirals. The il-

*Study the tree and prune it down to the essentials.*

lustrations give basic techniques for training bonsai.

The container should be an integral part of the whole landscape. Since the tree or trees is the focal point for the viewer, the design and color of the container should blend in quietly. Proportions are vital in both bonsai and saikei; a basic rule is that the height of the container should be 1/5 or less than the height of the tree.

The container should have several drain holes widely spaced. Small pieces of wire screening should be laid over these holes and fixed in place before the soil, rocks, and trees are put in the container. These will prevent the soil from running out. The soil itself is basically a 1/3 loam, 1/3 sand, and 1/3 humus mixture. This will vary according to the type of tree, with evergreens requiring more sand and flowering and fruiting trees requiring more loam.

Bonsai generally spend much of their time out of doors. They must, however, be protected from extreme weather conditions in both winter and summer. Landscapes can be composed of a single tree or a group of trees, with a stark landscape or with one carefully and imaginatively designed to suggest the seashore, a vast area, or a rocky location. The striking appearances that can be created thoroughly justify the demanding preparation and care.

Indoor plant materials can be pruned and trained along the lines of various bonsai and saikei styles for an instant effect. This fast effect has to be balanced with the fact that they grow out of shape very quickly. You have complete control over the appearances of bonsai and saikei. This means you can create a plant to suit a particular corner of your home.

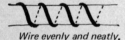

*Wire evenly and neatly.*

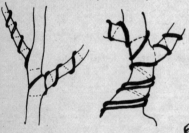

*Twist the wire clockwise to train the branch to the right counter-clockwise to train the branch to the left.*

*The bonsai's final shape.*

Some References on Bonsai and Saikei

Brooklyn Botanic Garden. *Handbook on Bonsai: Special Techniques*. Brooklyn, Brooklyn Botanic Garden, 1966. *(Plants & Gardens* Vol. 22, no. 2, Summer, 1966).

Hull, George F. *Bonsai for Americans*. New York, Doubleday, 1964.

Kawamoto, Toshio. *Saikei: Living Landscapes in Miniature*. Palo Alto, Calif., Kodansha, 1967.

Murata, Kyuzo. *Bonsai Miniature Potted Trees*. Tokyo, International Publications Service, 1964.

Perry, Lynn R. Bonsai: *Trees and Shrubs*. New York, Ronald, 1964.

Stowell, Jerald P. Bonsai: *Indoors and Out*. New York, Van Nostrand - Reinholt, 1966.

Yashiroda, Kan. Bonsai: *Japanese Miniature Trees*. Newton Centre, Mass., Branford, 1960.

Yoshimura, Yuji, and Halford, Giovanna M. *Japanese Art of Miniature Trees and Landscapes*. Rutland, Vt., Tuttle, 1957.

The best way is to learn by doing, either at workshops or under the guidance of someone who knows.

American Bonsai Society, 953 South Shore Drive, Lake Waukomis, Parkville, Missouri 64151.

Bonsai Clubs International, 445 Blake Street, Menlo Park, Calif. 94925.

Bonsai Society of Greater New York, Inc., Box E, Bronx Park, Bronx, New York 10466.

Bonsai Society of Texas, Box 11054, Knoxville, Texas 75235

Midwest Bonsai Society, 800 West Buena Avenue, Chicago Ill. 60613.

**Forcing Bulbs**

The first rule to follow when buying bulbs for forcing, is to pick out the best grade of bulbs you can find. Buy exhibition or top-size bulbs because these will give you the best results.

The second rule, if this is your first try at forcing bulbs, is to stick with tulips, daffodils, crocuses, grape hyacinths, and scillas. You'll have a wide variety and will be sure of success.

The bulbs are planted in pots in the fall, at about the same time as outdoor planting takes place. It's possible to continue planting until

December, but earlier planting is more satisfactory because of the time it takes for good roots to form.

Almost any container can be used to plant the bulbs in as long as it has a hole for drainage. A good soil mix is equal parts sand, peat moss, and loam.

Now with the pots clean and the soil mixed, you are ready to plant. Place pieces of broken pots over the holes in the bottom of the container. This will keep the soil from sifting out. Then partially fill the pots with soil. Allow enough room above the soil for the tips of the bulbs to be even with the rim of the container. Place the bulbs close together, almost touching and press them gently into the soil. Now add more soil, and firm it around the bulbs. Leave about a half-inch of space between the soil and the top of the pot for watering. Label the pots so that you know what they are and give them a good drink of water. Now they're ready for their winter rest and rooting.

They need a cold dark spot with a temperature between 40° and 50°F. You need to be able to check the rooting process and water the bulbs as they need it. An outdoor trench or cold frame can be used or a cold cellar if you have one. You might also try a dark corner of your garage — provided it's not a heated garage.

The pots of bulbs should be left in the cold for 10 to 12 weeks, but make sure the soil doesn't dry out. At the end of this time, check and see if there's a good root system and that the tops are about an inch long.

When the bulbs are well rooted, bring them into the place where they are to grow and bloom. Place the pots next to a window where it's cool and gets good light. Keep the soil moist but not wet and turn the pots a quarter turn each day. If you don't, you'll have leaning lovelies (but maybe you like them that way).

For more fun, don't bring all of the pots in at one time. Bring them in at intervals so you have continuous flowering.

Remember:
- Buy top quality bulbs.
- Don't let the pots dry out.
- Be sure there's a good root system before bringing them into the place where they're to bloom.
- Once inside give them moisture, sunlight, and keep them cool.
- If they're all really beautiful, share them with a friend.

An even easier way to force bulbs is to buy ones that have already been started by someone else and are ready to bloom. You get all of the beauty and none of the pain.


**Forcing Hyacinths Or Fooling Them
So They'll Bloom Inside**

A hyacinth can be forced either in soil or in water. If you're forcing it in soil, plant the bulb in soil in a pot with good drainage. If you're forcing it in water, use a hyacinth jar or a quart food jar with clean rocks in tne bottom to keep it from falling over. Set the bulb just over the water. If the bulb is smaller than the neck of the jar, use toothpicks to hold the bulb above the water.

Whether you use soil or water, put the bulb in a cool place (40 to 50°F), and cover it with a newspaper cone to keep the bulb in the dark. Check it every week to make sure that the soil never dries out or that the water level stays at the bottom of the bulb. If the water gets cloudy, change it.

In about 8 to 15 weeks, the bud will begin to push out of the bulb and the roots will have gone to the bottom of the jar. Move the plant to a warmer spot (55 to 60°F if possible) for 3 to 5 days, keeping the cone on. Then remove the cone and put the hyacinth in the window. Give the container a quarter turn each day to keep the flower growing evenly.

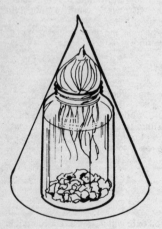

*Cover the bulb with a newspaper cone.*

# Glossary

**Aphids:** small insects that suck the juices of plants.

**Air Layering:** a form of plant reproduction where roots are encouraged to form on a stem before it is cut off.

**Annual:** a plant that grows from seed to maturity in one season.

**Binomial System:** the two-name system for formal (scientific) identification of plants.

**Bog Plant:** a plant found in nature growing in wet, spongy, poorly drained ground.

**Bonsai:** the art of growing a dwarfed potted plant by special methods of culture such as trimming the roots and branches.

**Bract:** a small leaf usually directly attached to a flower-stalk.

**Bud:** an incompletely opened flower or a small bump, on the stem or root of a plant, that can develop a branch or flower.

**Bulb:** a scaly bud (usually grown underground) which develops leaves and roots and bears flowers.

**Cladodes:** the green things (looking like leaves or needles) that grow on asparagus.

**Cultivars:** (culti-var) fancy word for cultivated varieties of plants.

**Cutting:** a piece of a plant (stem, leaf, or root) capable of developing into a new plant.

**Division:** the separation of one large plant into two or more small ones.

**Dormancy:** when active growth is temporarily halted in a plant, or when it dries up and just rests for a while.

**Double Potting:** placing a smaller pot (that is porous or has a drainage hole) inside a larger pot (that is non-porous and has no drainage hole) for better balance, more attractive appearance, or for better drainage.

**Epiphyte:** a plant that needs no soil and grows in the air.

**Exotics:** plants not native to that area; often applied to plants that are striking or unusual.

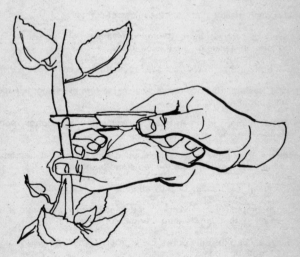

*Stem Cutting*

*Boston Fern*

**Fern:** flowerless, seedless plants that have fronds with divided leaflets.

**Forcing:** the process of making plants leaf or bloom out of their normal season.

**Fronds:** the ''leaves'' of a fern.

**Genus:** a category of biological classification; a class, kind, or group of plants marked by common characteristics.

**Germinate:** when the seed starts to grow; to sprout.

**Glochides:** barbed hairs or spines such as cactus have.

**Hybrid:** the offspring resulting from parent plants of two different kinds.

**Hydroponics:** growing plants in nutrient-rich water.

**Humus:** soil made of decayed plant or animal matter.

**Layering:** producing plants by laying the stem flat on the soil and pinning it down so that roots can grow at the leaf joints.

**Loam:** a soil mixture of clay, silt, and sand.

**Mealybugs:** cottony insects that suck the juices of plants.

**Mulch:** a protective covering that holds moisture and keeps down weeds.

**Off-shoots** (Offsets): new plants that grow out from the base of a plant or bulb.

**Over-potted:** a plant that has been placed in a pot that is much too big for it.

*Mealybugs*

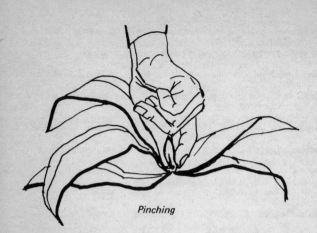

*Pinching*

**Pinch:** to remove the growing end of a stem to make it branch out.

**Pit:** the stone or seed of a fruit.

**Plantlets:** small plants attached to the parent plant by runners.

**Pollen:** the white or yellow dust in flowers that works as the male element in seed making.

**Pot bound:** a plant in too small a pot for its needs.

**Propagation:** the growing of plants by seeds or division.

**Prune:** to trim for better shape or fuller growth.

**Pups:** small plants (offsets) growing at the base of bromeliads.

**Quarantine:** keeping one plant separate from the rest until you are sure it doesn't have insects or a disease.

**Rhizomes:** underground stems.

**Runners:** trailing stems that root.

**Rosettes:** a cluster of leaves in a crowded circle.

**Root ball:** roots and the soil they hold together.

**Root bound:** a plant whose roots occupy practically all of the pot.

**Root cutting:** piece of root used for producing a new plant.

**Scale:** a hard, shiny-shelled insect that sucks the juices of plants.

**Sheath:** thin often overlapping parts of a plant that serve to protect flowers or buds.

**Spathe:** a leaflike organ that envelopes a flower-bearing clublike spike.

**Species:** a group of like plants forming a subdivision of a genus.

**Spider Mite:** small spiders that suck and scrape plants.

**Spore:** a small reproductive element of non-flowering plants like ferns.

**Stem cutting:** piece of stem used for producing a new plant.

**Succulents:** juicy plants with fleshy tissues designed to hold water so they can survive for long periods of dryness.

**Tendrils:** twisting extensions of stems by which plants cling for support.

**Tuber:** a swollen underground stem with eyes or buds.

**Variety:** a subdivision of a species; also used to designate a cultivar, or cultivated variety.

**White Fly:** a small sucking insect that flies about when the plant is shaken.

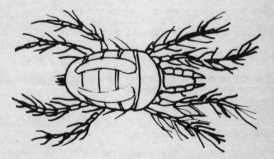

*Spider Mite*

# Index

The first boldface number refers to the "Plant Descriptions" and the second boldface number refers to "Plants at a Glance."

tomentosa